Table of Contents

Part I: The Dimensions of Communication

> *Successful Intercultural Communication, 4; The Nature of Culture, 4; The Meaning of Culture, 5; Culture is Learned, 5; Cultural Universals, 7; Cultural Variability, 7; The Nature of Communication, 8; Persuasion: The Primary Purpose of Communication, 9; Understanding: The Key to Persuasion, 10; Information: The Basis of Understanding, 10; Barriers and Gateways to Intercultural Communication, 11; Differences in Verbal Communication, 11; Differences in Nonverbal Communication, 16; Ethnocentrism, 18; Lack of Empathy, 20; Differences in Perception, 22; Summary, 25*

> *The Problem of Identification, 29; What an Arab Is Not, 30; Evolution of the Term "Arab", 31; The Pre-Islamic Era, 31; The Islamic Expansion Era, 32; The Modern Era, 32; Summary, 33*

> *Arabia: The Birthplace of Islam, 35; Muhammad the Prophet, 36; Muhammad the General and Statesman, 37; Muhammad the Social Reformer, 38; Muhammad the Man, 39; Muhammad the Empire Founder, 39; The Meaning and Pillars of Islam, 39; Profession of the Faith, 40; Prayer, 40; Almsgiving, 40; Fasting, 40; Pilgrimage, 41; Holy War, 41; Sources of Authority in Islam, 41; The Quran, 41; The Hadith, 42; The Ijtihad, 43; Islam as a Cultural Force, 43; Muslims, Christians, and Jews, 43; The Islamic Civilization, 45; Decline of the Islamic Empire, 46; Islam in the Twentieth Century, 47; Revivial of Islam, 48; Causes of the Islamic Revival, 51; Prospects of the Islamic Revival, 52; Summary, 53*

Communicating with the Arabs
A Handbook for the Business Executive

A.J. Almaney
A.J. Alwan
DePaul University

Waveland Press, Inc.
Prospect Heights, Illinois

For information about this book, write or call:

Waveland Press, Inc.
P.O. Box 400
Prospect Heights, Illinois 60070
(312) 634-0081

093719

Part IV: Conversational Arabic

About the Authors

A.J. Almaney is a professor of management at DePaul University. He holds an M.A. in political science and a Ph.D. in communications from Indiana University. He has also done post-doctoral work in management at the University of Chicago. His articles have appeared in a number of journals including the *Management International Review,* the *Columbia Journal of World Business,* the *University of Michigan Business Review,* and the *Journal of Communication.*

A.J. Alwan is a professor of management at DePaul University. He holds an M.B.A. in statistics and finance from the University of California, Los Angeles, and a Ph.D. in statistics and economics from the University of Chicago. Dr. Alwan has published several articles and a textbook entitled *Quantitative Methods for Decision Making.* His work experience includes employment with the International Monetary Fund and the Central Bank of Iraq.

Preface

Recently, an Iraqi official boastfully remarked to a Western reporter: "You in the West have always called us the land of the thousand and one nights. But now, we are the land of the thousand and one economic projects." It is true. The 1973 oil price increases, with their attendant phenomenal development programs, have transformed the Arab oil-producing countries into one of the fastest-growing markets in the world. The area is being coveted by European, Asian, and American firms, with each vying to capture a larger slice of this highly sought-after market.

Within the past few years, scores of American businessmen have flocked to the Arab world in quest of lucrative business deals. Many of them returned home empty handed. Their failure, for the most part, could not have been blamed on their inability to furnish the Arabs with quality goods and services at competitive prices. Nor could It have been ascribed to their lack of managerial expertise or financial backing. Rather, their failure was basically due to poor communication. It was the businessman's lack of sufficient knowledge of the Arabs that rendered him unable to understand and to deal appropriately with the Arabs' patterns of thinking and behaving.

However, a growing number of businessmen are becoming cognizant of the central importance of communication to their success in dealing with the Arabs. They are earnestly seeking information that could enhance their communication skills. But their pursuit of this goal is hampered by the lack of a single source of information. Typically, information on the religious, political, linguistic, and socio-psychological forces at work on the Arabs, with which the businessman ought to be familiar, is dispersed throughout literature on the Middle East, thus making the learning process tedious and time-consuming. And since it is intended chiefly for specialists in the area, such material tends to be so detailed and complicated as to limit its usefulness to the businessman.

Our book is an effort to enable the businessman to develop a better understanding of the Arabs. Specifically, we have attempted to achieve two objectives: (1) to piece together, in one book, material on those fundamental forces which play a determining role in influencing the Arabs'

vii

thoughts and actions, and (2) to present the material in a concise and coherent manner so that the businessman will not have to plough through
voluminous details for which he has little or no use.

Although the book is primarily intended for the businessman, it can be
used profitably by other non-specialist readers. Students interested in the
Arab world, but who have little or no previous academic study of the area,
will find the book helpful in acquiring a general grounding in the various
influences at play in that vital part of the world.

The book falls into four parts. Part I focuses on those forces that exert
compelling influences on the manner in which the Arabs think and behave.
Part II is designed to provide the reader with basic information on 12 Arab
countries judged to be of particular interest to the businessman. Part III
contains valuable tips on the fundamentals of negotiating contracts with
various Arab countries. The information in this part has been excerpted from
*An Introduction to Contract Procedures in the Near East & North Africa,
2/E,* a publication of the International Trade Administration, United States
Department of Commerce. In Part IV, we have attempted to provide the
reader with a carefully selected list of Arabic words and expressions which
can be used throughout the Arab world.

We would like to express our thanks to Brother Leo Ryan, Dean of the
College of Commerce and to Dr. F. James Staszak, Chairman of the
Department of Management at DePaul University for their encouragement
and backing for the project. Our thanks are also due to Mrs. Dianne
Cichanski, Secretary of the Department of Management and to Mrs. Peach
Henry, Manuscript Secretary, at DePaul University for their assistance in
typing parts of the manuscript. Our special thanks, of course, go to our
wives, Kathy and Joan, for their editorial assistance and unfailing support
and patience.

Almaney and Alwan

Part I

The Dimensions of Communication

Chapter 1

Introduction:
Intercultural Communication

In a social gathering involving a group of American and Arab business-men, an Arab, in a totally friendly manner, accused an American executive of attempting to put something over on him. The American, smilingly, told the Arab that was not his intention, and that the Arab had misunderstood him. When the Arab, still in a friendly frame of mind, repeated the accusa-tion, the American said: "Now, you are getting very silly." At hearing this, the Arab's demeanor suddenly changed. His face turned red, and he was visibly upset and embarrassed. Just as suddenly, the Arab rose and with an angry and shaky voice demanded an immediate apology. "Nobody calls me silly," said the Arab. Completely bewildered and confused at this sudden turn of events, the American hurriedly offered his apology.

The American could not understand why a harmless word like "silly" would evoke such a hostile reaction from the Arab. To the American, the word meant nothing more than acting in a lighthearted manner. What the American did not know was that, to the Arab, the word "silly" had a much stronger connotation. It meant stupid, imbecile, and crazy.

The word "silly," like all other words, does not have a meaning of its own. It is the user of the word who imposes certain meanings on it, and the type of meaning he attaches to the word is a product of the cultural environment in which he happens to be reared. In the above incident, the American used the term "silly" within the cultural context of his society, not realizing that the same word has a different meaning to a person raised in an entirely different cultural setting. The result was a serious misunder-standing.

Dealing with the Arabs represents a special case of the general process of intercultural communication. This latter process is quite complex and can be fraught with numerous potential pitfalls. The complexity and potential pitfalls involved in intercultural communication stem primarily from the fact that the process occurs among individuals whose values, customs, and expectations generally tend to be divergent, if not contradictory. Conse-quently, the more knowledge an individual has of another cultural group with whom he comes into contact, the greater his chances of success in

3

communicating with that group. Conversely, lack of knowledge constitutes one of the most serious impediments to effective communication.

Successful Intercultural Communication

The business executive's success in communicating with a culturally divergent group is largely contingent upon his ability to satisfy two requirements:

1. An adequate appreciation of the complexities involved in the general process of intercultural communication.
2. A deeper understanding of the specific forces which shape the thoughts, feelings, and behaviors of the particular cultural group with which he wishes to communicate.

In this chapter, we will deal solely with the first requirement. Our purpose is to provide the reader with a good grasp of the intricacies involved in the process of communicating across cultural boundaries. Toward that end, we will briefly explore the nature of culture, the nature of communication, and the barriers most commonly encountered in intercultural communication.

In Chapters 2-7, we will focus on the second requirement. We will seek to explore those specific forces—the understanding of which can be the key to success in communicating with the Arabs.

The Nature of Culture

Irrespective of the particular group with which he needs to interact, the business executive will do well to gain some knowledge first about the nature of culture in general.

Knowledge of the nature of culture serves two purposes. The first is that it enables the executive to be more tolerant of cultural differences. By understanding the workings of culture, the executive comes to develop a better grasp of the assumptions underlying many of what appear at the surface to be inexplicable behaviors of foreign people. Consequently, he is more apt to exhibit a greater degree of sensitivity to the customs, beliefs, feelings, and expectations of members of a foreign culture.

The second purpose for understanding the nature of culture is that it helps the executive gain new insights into the peculiarities of his own culture. Normally, people tend to take their cultural behaviors for granted. They rarely question the logic of their cultural behaviors or doubt the propriety of many of their values. Their own culture is the only mold within which their minds operate; it is the only culture they know. As a result, people accept their culture as they accept the surrounding atmosphere they breathe.

By studying culture, the executive is compelled, consciously or subconsciously, to take an inquisitive look at his own customs, habits, and beliefs for comparison purposes. To his surprise, he often discovers that many of his cherished values and long-held traditions are as difficult to explain or defend as those of foreign cultures. In this manner, knowledge of culture can contribute to the executive's greater understanding of the characteristics of his own cultural patterns. Conversely, ignorance of other cultures often translates into ignorance of one's own culture, for as the saying goes: "He knows not England who only England knows."

With the above two purposes in mind, we will now seek to examine certain aspects of culture. Specifically, we will deal with the meaning of culture, how culture is learned, cultural universals, and cultural variability.

The Meaning of Culture

Culture can be defined as "that complex whole which includes knowledge, belief, art, morals, law, customs, and any other capabilities and habits acquired by man as a member of society."[1]

Culture may be classified by three large categories of elements: artifacts (which include items ranging from arrowheads to hydrogen bombs, magic charms to antibiotics, torches to electric lights, and chariots to jet planes); concepts (which include such beliefs or value systems as right or wrong, God and man, ethics, and the general meaning of life); and behaviors (which refer to the actual practice of concepts or beliefs). For example, whereas money is considered an artifact, the value placed upon it is a concept, but the actual spending and saving of money is behavior.

Culture is Learned

The type of artifacts we use, the concepts we uphold, and the behaviors we engage in are all learned. Learning a culture takes place through a process of transmission whereby the older generation passes down its cultural patterns to its offspring. The formal aspect of this process is what we call education, and it takes place through such social agencies as schools, churches, and homes, as well as play groups, cliques, and gangs. All these agencies play, in varying degrees, a role in conveying the beliefs, mores, and folkways of society to the newcomers.

The fact that a person speaks English and not Arabic, or that he is a Christian and not a Muslim, is the result of where he is born or raised. The same is true with the fact that he eats with a fork and not with his hands, wears a hat and not a turban, and uses an automobile and not a camel. Actually, "the mass of what any person receives from his culture is so great as to make it look at first glance as if he were nothing but an individual exemplor of his culture, a reduction of it abbreviated to the scope of what one personality can attain."[2]

All that remains of the individual which is not culturally induced consists of his individual peculiarities as a unique human being and his innate general capacities. The individual features comprise such traits as speaking with a lisp or a drawl, having a bass or a tenor voice, or being interesting or dull. The general human capacities, which are generic, ensure that the normal person has the faculty of learning to speak, to read, to use tools, and to practice a religion. But the kind of speech, tools, and religion the individual will ultimately use or adopt will absolutely depend on the culture in which he is born.

All these choices in life represent adjustment on the part of the individual to his cultural environment. The individual's biological organism brings only the capacity to adapt in a number of ways. Since the young child is living with a group that has already made certain compromises and choices, he is bound to learn the adjustments and choices of his group.

To illustrate, let us consider the adaptation a child makes to one of his innate biological impulses, namely hunger. Unlike animals which inherit behavioral patterns that dictate their selection of food from the environment, the human child must learn what to eat and what not to eat. Very early in the child's life, the parents begin to teach the child what to eat, when to eat, where to eat, the order in which to eat different foods, and the values prescribed to each type of food. The what, when, where, and how will be determined by the cultural behavior of the group in which the child is growing up. If the child grows up in the American society, he will learn that pork, beef, milk, fresh eggs, certain fowl, vegetables, cereals, and cake are proper foods to eat. If he is reared in China, he will eat things such as birds' nest soup and well-aged eggs, and rice. If he is reared in some other societies, he will eat snakes, worms, grasshoppers, or lizards.

But the process of socialization does not end here. The child is also taught an attitude toward adjustment. He grows up with the notion that it is human, natural, good, intelligent, and healthy to eat his group's types of food; and it is inhuman, unnatural, barbaric, nauseating, and even immoral to eat foods his group does not eat. Often, reference to the types of food others eat is used as a proof of their inferiority.

Thus, contrary to popular belief, our likes and dislikes of certain foods are not determined by an inheritied biological response to taste. Rather, they are largely culturally acquired behavioral patterns. In fact, many foods which are taboo in our culture are almost indistinguishable in taste from some which we consider delicacies. On the other hand, certain delicacies in our culture are distasteful to some groups that are unfamiliar with them. One anthropologist tells the story of giving chocolate bars to Malagsie children in the interior of Madagascar. After tasting them, the children threw them away and ran to the stream to wash the nasty taste from their mouths.[3]

By being born into a society, every individual is also born into a culture which deeply molds and colors his thinking and ways of doing things. If the culture gives life supernatural settings and certain religious rituals, children's personalities develop a mystical, religious nature. If religious practices are taboo or unknown, children grow up with atheistic beliefs. If martial music is common, if the marching of soldiers is frequently honored, and if warlike patterns are constantly glorified, then personalities, as a rule, develop correlative traits.

Cultural Universals

Human beings everywhere share the same physiological thrusts which furnish a kind of biological basis for culture. The general form in which many of these drives are satisfied is the same in all cultures. For example, the hunger impulse is satisfied through the intake of food, thirst through the absorption of liquid, and sex through conjugation. Also, members of divergent cultural groups tend to deal with fatigue through rest, restlessness through activity, somnolence through sleep, fright through escape from danger, pain through avoidance by effective acts.[4]

In addition to having universal physiological impulses, all cultures have in common certain social problems as well. These include rearing of children, maintaining social order, regulating relations with outsiders, regulating relations with the supernatural, and providing meaning and motivation for life. All those denominators which are common to mankind are referred to as cultural universals. Cultural universals manifest themselves in such behaviors as family, courtship, marriage, sexual restrictions, ethics, division of labor, language, cooperative behavior, cooking, dancing, decorative art, faith healing, funeral rites, games, greetings, magic, music, mythology, religious rituals, soul concepts, tool making, and trading.

Cultural Variability

Although all societies have the same basic impulses and wants, they differ in the specific forms in which such impulses and wants are satisfied. Whereas all people get hungry and all have a desire for social order, the methods they choose in satisfying these needs tend to differ widely.

Food-producing and food-preserving techniques, though a universal cultural pattern, vary greatly from one cultural group to another. Some societies follow the grazing of herds; others grow farm crops. People who work in urban centers exchange their labor for money, which they in turn exchange for food. Food taboos, another universal pattern, is also characterized by great variations. Some societies are vegetarians, while others prohibit pork but allow poultry, fish, and beef. Some groups enforce their food taboos throughout the year, whereas others enforce them only on special days of the week or the year.

Differences in the manner in which various cultures satisfy their needs and solve their problems are called cultural variations. Recognizing such variations in the cultural systems of the Orient and the Occident, Rudyard Kipling wrote: "East is East, and West is West," although his contention that "never the twain shall meet" may prove to be a short-lived prophecy.

Causes of Cultural Variability

What causes cultural variations? Or what factors would determine the manner in which one group selects a certain means of satisfying its needs and another group a different means?

This is not an easy question to answer, for no complete and satisfactory explanation has yet been furnished for variations in cultural patterns. There are, however, some highly probable and plausible causes for the variations, three of which are geographic conditions, long physical isolation, and historical accidents.

1. Geographic Conditions

Whether a group of people lives in deserts, forests, or mountainous areas will determine to a considerable measure what cultural patterns it will develop. Such geographic factors as temperatures, rainfall, soil, topography, and wind currents influence both animal and plant life with corresponding effects on human life. Specifically, geographic conditions influence many phases of food-gathering devices, clothes, shelter, sports, and technologies associated with the material culture. The Eskimos, for example, do not build frame houses or hunt tigers. Nor do the Malagans put up igloos or know anything about hunting seals.

2. Long Physical Isolation

Societies that have been physically isolated for a long period of time, due to lack of communication and/or transportation difficulties, develop their own unique cultural patterns. They tend to be free of any external forces that might lead to the creation of some type of cultural uniformities. Physical isolation results in the growth of myraids of local cultural elements, a notable case of which is the evolvement of different language systems.

3. Historical Accidents

Cataclysms of nature (such as earthquake, flood, or fire), loss of war, attainment of victory, and a number of other humanly unpredictable events all influence the evolution of cultural patterns in one way or another. Whereas some of these events might give rise to new cultural patterns, others might lead to the alteration or modification of the prevailing ones.[5]

The Nature of Communication

Thus far in our discussion, we have dealt with only one of the major components comprising the process of intercultural communication, namely, culture. We will now turn our attention to another major component which is communication.

For practical purposes, we will limit our discussion of the nature of communication to three topics: (1) persuasion as the primary purpose of communication, (2) understanding as the key to persuasion, and (3) information as the basis of understanding.

Persuasion: The Primary Purpose of Communication

Generally, people engage in communication with a view to achieving one or a combination of the following purposes: to inform, to amuse, or to persuade.

There are occasions where people initiate communication with the purpose of imparting some factual information or general "truths." Here, the communicator makes an honest effort to avoid manipulating the message to further his private interests. He will not tell only one side of the story, nor will he overplay certain conclusions to the neglect of others that might be equally valid. Instead, his primary purpose is to provide facts and to tell all sides of a story. When the impartation of the general "truth" becomes the main purpose of the message, the communication is said to be informative in nature.

In some situations, the purpose of communication is not to inform but to amuse others. In this case, the communicator attempts to provide entertainment, fun, or pleasure to other people. He might want them to laugh, have a good time, or just relax. If the message receivers exhibit such behaviors, the communicator is said to have achieved his purpose, and the communication is considered successful.

When the purpose of communication is to persuade, the communicator makes an intentional effort to manipulate the message in certain ways. He would overplay one side of the story and stress certain conclusions. He might even go so far as to explicitly tell the receiver what conclusions he ought to accept or reject.

A consensus exists among authorities in communication that the primary purpose of communication is persuasive, regardless of the form that it might take. According to this view, people engage in communication with the primary purpose of influencing others. One of the earliest thinkers to uphold this position is Aristotle who defines rhetoric, a term he uses synonymously with communication, as "the faculty of observing in any given case the available means of persuasion."[6] Contemporary writers tend to agree with Aristotle's viewpoint. Berlo, for instance, states: "Our basic purpose in communication is...to influence—to affect with intent."[7] Campbell and Hepler express a similar notion by saying that although the importance of persuasion may vary among communication situations, persuasion is always present to some degree.[8]

To persuade someone is to get him to accept an idea, to assume an attitude, to have a certain feeling, or to take a specific action. If the primary purpose of communication is to persuade, successful communication can then be defined as the ability of the communicator to persuade the receivers to do what he wants them to do.

The above discussion clearly suggests that intercultural communicators, such as multinational executives, are by definition persuaders. Undoubtedly, the informative purpose is crucial to the executive's success, but their ultimate goal remains persuasion. For example, a business executive who travles to the Arab world must equip himself with a great deal of factual information about the products or services he wishes to sell. But, in so doing, his purpose is obviously not merely to inform the Arabs of the availability of his products or services but to use the factual information as a tool to persuade the Arabs to accept and buy what he has to offer.

Understanding: The Key to Persuasion

If persuasion is the principal purpose of communication, no communicator can expect to achieve this without first developing a thorough understanding of those he seeks to influence.

To understand someone is to know him as fully as possible, to clearly perceive his needs, feelings, characteristics, and expectations as an individual. Understanding also involves comprehension of the cultural forces which determine the manner in which he thinks and behaves. In practical terms, understanding implies avoidance of saying and doing things that are likely to offend others or contradict their beliefs and traditions. It also implies designing our messages in such a manner as to take into consideration the needs and expectations of others as a prelude to getting them to respond favorably to our messages. Without understanding, persuasion is difficult to accomplish.

Information: The Basis of Understanding

Understanding does not take place in a vacuum; rather, it depends on and must be preceded by information or knowledge. As Francis Bacon, back in the Elizabethan Age, explained: "The human understanding is no dry light. It does not burn by itself. It requires fuel.''[9] The keenest of minds cannot operate effectively unless provided with the relevant facts. Cleverness, insight, imagination, ingenuity, originality, and intuition are essential for understanding, but they are not sufficient. The judgment of one who possesses relevant knowledge is usually preferable to the hunch of one who thinks or feels he is right.

Knowledge as a requisite for the development of genuine understanding is, then, neither a new nor an unfamiliar concept. It is practiced daily by salesmen, advertisers, politicians, authors, doctors, business managers, husbands, wives, and parents. Professional communicators, in particular, realize full well that before they can influence members of their audience, they must gather pertinent information about them. They want to have some knowledge about their age, sex, income, education, religion, ethnic background, geographical location, socioeconomic status, beliefs, and many other characteristics. It is only in light of such information that the communicator can design his message in such a way as to enhance its chances of influencing the audience in the desired manner. Other things being equal, the more knowledge the communicator has of the receiver, the more effective his message can be and the more likely it is to accomplish its purpose.

The type of knowledge the communicator requires takes on an added significance as he begins to interact with individuals or groups belonging to an entirely different cultural system. When communication occurs within the boundaries of one cultural setting, the communicator is already equipped with an information base. By growing up in the same environment as those he intends to communicate with, he has already accumulated a vast reservoir of information that he can draw upon. On the basis of this information, he can make decisions about their beliefs, values, attitudes, and likes and dislikes.

But when the same person crosses cultural frontiers to communicate with another group, he has no information base to speak of. What information he might have is either inadequate or fictional. When such is the case, the communicator will not only fail to achieve his purpose but also will run the risk of evoking the anger, hostility, resentment, and rejection of those he set out to influence.

Barriers and Gateways to Intercultural Communication

Barriers to successful intercultural communication are numerous and can vary markedly from one situation to the next, depending on which particular cultural group we are talking about. Clearly, making a complete inventory of such barriers can be a formidable task. It is possible, however, to isolate certain universal barriers which, if present, could cause serious misunderstandings and conflicts among divergent cultural groups, irrespective of their particular characteristics. Such universal barriers include: differences in the verbal and nonverbal communication systems, ethnocentrism, lack of empathy, and differences in perception.

Differences in Verbal Communication

A great deal of communication is carried out verbally, that is, through a system of oral and written symbols commonly known as language.

There are two ways in which language affects the way we communicate: (1) It affects our ability to encode or express our thoughts clearly, and (2) it affects our ability to formulate these thoughts systematically.

Language as Thought Encoder

Whenever we engage in any type of communication, we have a purpose. But to be achieved, this purpose must first be encoded or made public. It must, in other words, be converted into some tangible behavior, one common form of which is the linguistic expression or the word.

This implies that if we are to encode our purpose successfully, we must be equipped with some basic linguistic skills. We must have at our command an adequate number of words to express our meanings accurately. We need to know how to pronounce or spell these words correctly. And we need to have a working knowledge of grammar. These skills enable us to make public our thoughts, feelings, and attitudes and to share them with others. And through these skills, we are able to influence the thoughts, feelings, and attitudes of those with whom we want to communicate. The acquisition of such skills is, therefore, indispensable to effective communication. Without them, communication is not likely to occur, and any deficiency in the encoding skills will lead to deficiency in communication.

Language as Instrument of Thought

To most people, the encoding function of language is the only way in which language relates to communication. They consider language as merely a vehicle of thought; it is something independent of thought and reality. This notion is based on the assumption that reality is present in much the same way to all normal people, and that different people basically deal with the same environmental components. Consequently, various languages are regarded as different sets of sound, expressing basically similar thoughts about a "universal" reality. In other words, language and thought are viewed as independent processes. Thinking, or the formulation of ideas, depends on the laws of reason, whereas language is but a tool of expressing what has already been formulated nonlinquistically.

Although popularly accepted, this assumption is challenged by many anthropologists, linguists, and psychologists who believe that language serves not only as an encoder but also as a shaper of thought. Perhaps no one is more responsible for advocating the compelling impact of language on thought than Benjamin L. Whorf who states:

> Language is not merely a reproducing instrument for voicing ideas but rather is itself the shaper of ideas, the program and guide for the individual's mental activity, for his analysis of impressions, for his synthesis of his mental stock in trade. We cut up and organize the spread and flow of events as we do largely because, through our mother tongue, we are parties to an agreement to do so, not because nature itself is segmented in exactly that way for all of us to see. Our language, then, may affect even our perception of language.[10]

Whorf's theory is the product of his comparative analyses of various languages. In comparing the English and the Eskimo languages, for example, Whorf noted that the English speakers have one word for the white stuff that falls on the ground in the wintertime. The Eskimos, however, have several words, denoting falling snow, wind-driven snow, snow on the ground, slushy snow, and snow packed hard like ice.

Thus, whereas the English speaker can think of snow in one or two ways, the Eskimo, who considers all these types of snow as sensuously and operationally different, can think of the same thing in several ways. Such a difference in the way a certain physical phenomenon is thought about is, according to Whorf, due to a structural difference between the English and the Eskimo languages.

Although Whorf's theory has not been conclusively proven, it has not been flatly refuted either. Most linguists today agree on one thing: the causal relationship between language and thought runs in either direction. In thinking about the environment, we have occasion to formulate certain ideas which must be expressed in certain linquistic terms. Once the terms are incorporated into the language, they begin to determine the thought processes. It may be safely concluded, then, that although language may not be the sole determinant of thought, it is an important one, and its influence should not be misunderstood.

The implications of the Whorfian theory for the multinational executive are obvious. The thoery suggests that people who speak different languages think and consequently communicate differently. People who acquire their first language learn more than a set of vocal skills; they take on the world view of their language community. Different peoples, therefore, differ not only on the use of words, but also on what these words have to say.

The theory also suggests that peoples are not guided by the same physical evidence to the same conclusion unless they share a common language. Those who speak Arabic or Chinese may perceive and interpret the physical and social stimuli differently from those who speak English, with profound effects on their beliefs and approaches to problem solving.

The mere presence of language differences should provide the multinational executive with his first clue to the presence of a built-in communication barrier. One important way of overcoming this barrier or minimizing its effect is for the executive to become fairly adept at the language of the people he has to communicate with. In so doing, he acquires more than a vehicle of communication. He will learn new modes of thought and patterns of communication. He will also have access to the window through which others see the world and will be better able to understand why they think and behave the way they do. If learning a foreign language is not possible, the executive should at a mimimum be aware of the presence and significance of the language barrier. In this way, he will be able to anticipate communication breakdowns, stemming purely from language differences, and make allowances for them in terms of time, energy, and patience. In other words, mere recognition of the implications of language differences should enhance the executive's understanding, and his consequent acceptance or tolerance, of cultural differences.

Unfortunately, not all executives have an adequate appreciation of how vital learning a foreign language can be to their communication success. Some merely lack awareness of the damaging effects language differences can have on their ability to communicate at an optimal level. Others seem to have a condescending view of certain foreign languages. Such a view stems largely from a sense of superiority which leads them to believe that their own language is the "best," the "most logical," and the "most natural."

Thus, while many executives may be tolerant of the peculiarities of French, German, Spanish, and other Indo-European tongues, a language family to which English belongs, they are puzzled at what appears to them to be "inferior," "illogical," and "unnatural" tongues when they encounter entirely unrelated languages such as Arabic, Chinese, or Japanese. Such an attitudes is often manifested in the statement: "If they want to do business with me, they will have to speak English." Executives with this attitude might spend years in a foreign country without being willing or able to say "good morning" in the language of that country.

Some executives rationalize their reluctance to learn foreign languages by arguing that it is foolish to expend so much effort learning the language of a people who can speak English. As one American executive put it: "To hell with the local language. They can understand me in English if I talk loud enough."[11] Such an attitude is hardly conducive to effective communication. For one thing, not all foreigners speak and understand English. This point became amply clear to the Illinois Congressman, Paul Simon, who was in Cairo in 1977 to confer with Egyptian officials about that nation's finances. After his finance meeting, Simon planned to pay a visit to President Sadat at his country home. Simon joined four staffers from the U.S. embassy and was about to get into a car and begin the trip to Sadat's home. A language barrier suddenly appeared. The four officers from the embassy could not speak Arabic, and the Egyptian driver could not speak English. Obviously, the driver had not been instructed as to where the Americans were going. The Americans kept saying, "Sadat, Sadat," and the Egyptian driver, who did not know what the Americans wanted, kept smiling in utter confusion.

Undoutedly, there are many natives who can speak English. But many of these "are likely to be from the more U.S.-oriented part of the population so there is a danger that communicating through them will result in a slanted and restricted contact with the country. They may themselves be in touch with only a limited section of the population and they may be inclined to tell the U.S. businessman what they think he wants to hear."[12]

Furthermore, it should be acknowledged that in many parts of the world, the American businessman today needs foreign nations more than they need him. In the past, when the U.S. enjoyed virtually an unchallenged dominance of the world market, the American could get by with the statement: "If they want to do business with me, they will have to speak English." In today's highly competitive world market, the responsibility of selling, of creating a favorable communication climate lies with the American. The American must compete with the Germans, the French, the British, the Japanese, the South Koreans, and the Taiwanese in courting the same customer.

To be competitive, the American businessman must offer the customer more than high-quality goods at competitive prices. He needs to show the customer that he is interested in him, that he respects him and that he is willing to please him. One way of achieving this is for the American to attempt to speak the customer's language, or at least to be familiar with some basic expressions that could leave a positive impression on the customer.

Unfortunately, ignorance of foreign languages among American businessmen is so widespread it has become an affliction, with serious repercussions on their ability to compete effectively in the world market. As one writer put it:

> One of our national shames is the illiteracy of most Americans in foreign languages. It is a long-standing affliction, but as long as we Americans dominated the world, the problem had no more impact on our conscience than a falling feather.

> But the time is passing when Americans could get along on English alone. The United States must now get in line after Europeans, Japanese, Koreans, Taiwanese, and even Russians to win the world's business and affections. Businessmen...from these nations usually are multilingual; our people are not. So we sometimes lose because of our affliction.[13]

The American businessman's attitude toward learning foreign languages appears to be part of a national declining trend. Ten years ago, there probably was not a single institution of higher learning in the U.S. which did not teach foreign languages. Even many high schools required one foreign language for students planning to attend college. In 1965 some 31 percent of high school students studied foreign languages. In 1970, the figure was 28 percent; in 1977, it dropped to 20 percent, and is still going down.

In 1977, only 9 percent of degree-credit college students were enrolled in foreign language courses. In the same year, it was found that only 14.3 percent of college freshmen could speak a second language, no matter how many courses they had absorbed.[14] To make matters even worse, only 10 percent of college-level institutions now require applicants to have taken a foreign language. Fewer colleges make it a must to pass a foreign language course for graduation. And the percentage of M.A.'s and Ph.D.'s proficient in a foreign language keeps dwindling. In contrast, the rest of the world goes the other way, teaching its young people a second and third language as basic requirements. For example, there are more teachers of English in the Soviet Union than there are students of Russian in the U.S.

The policy of American multinational firms regarding their executives' need for foreign languages is not uniform. Some firms require perfect knowledge of at least one foreign language and offer language training as well as financial incentives to their executives. Other firms tend to minimize the value of foreign languages, again on the faulty premise that the fluency with which foreign nationals speak English obviates the need for the American to learn theirs.

Recently, the number of firms recognizing the necessity for foreign languages is on the rise, however. This growing interest may be attributed to two major factors: The first is that, as a professional communicator, the executive should recognize the needs to master the language of the people whose attitudes and actions he plans to influence. Without language facility, his persuasive ability will be considerably limited. As one top executive said: "As is the case with missionaries, one just cannot sell religion unless he is able to talk the language of the local people."[15]

The second factor is the growing recognition that by learning a foreign language, the executive could create a good impression among the natives who will more likely respect him and appreciate his interest in their language. "There is no greater compliment to a foreigner," said one executive, "than to try to learn his language — even if you don't fully succeed."[16]

Differences in Nonverbal Communication

Language is not the only code through which communication is carried out. There is another code, the nonverbal, through which people receive and send out messages. Nonverbal messages, estimated to make up 65 percent of human communications, consist of such clues as facial expression, gestures, postures, glances, smiles, emblems, clothes, colors, spacial distances, and customs.

Each culture has its own distinct nonverbal communication system. Children learn this system long before they master verbal skills and rely on it as their major vehicle of communication. As they grow up, nonverbal behavior becomes so deeply rooted in their psyche that they engage in it rather unconsciously.

When a member of one cultural group attempts to communicate with a member of another cultural group, he will discover that the system which he has always taken for granted is no longer workable. Sometimes, it is downright inefficient, since the other cultural group might have an entirely different system. This means that the "outsider," if he is ever to succeed in his communication, must go through another socialization process to learn or at least to understand the nuances of the new system.

Communication difficulties stemming from differing nonverbal systems have been brought into focus by Edward Hall in his now class work, *The Silent Language.* Hall points out how people's concepts of such things as time and space vary among cultures, and how the variations can influence the communication behavior of cultural groups. For instance, how late a person can show up for an appointment without communicating disrespect, or how far apart he must stand to communicate friendship, intimacy, or acquaintanceship are all conditioned by the person's cultural background.

Societies differ in their nonverbal communication patterns in countless ways. The literature on cross-cultural communication is replete with illustrations showing how various cultures differ with regard to such things as gestures, greetings, punctuality, competition, honesty, loyalty, and concepts of time and space. To make the point, a few examples here should suffice. In his account of how certain cultures differ markedly in their manner of greeting, Hiller says:

> Among the Wanyiak, people meet by grasping hands and pressing their thumbs together; dwellers in the region of the Niger join their right hands and separate them with a pull so that a snapping noise is made by the thumb and fingers. The handshake of the Arab seems to be a scuffle in which each tries to raise to his lips the hand of the other. The Ainus draw their hands from the shoulders and down the arms to the fingertips of the person greeted, or they rub their hands together....Among the Polynesians, Malays, Burmese, Lapps,...a usual salute is that of smelling each other's cheeks.[17]

Smelling another person's cheeks as a form of greeting is also used by the Arabs. To the Arab, to be able to smell a friend is reassuring. Smelling is a way of being involved with another, and to deny a friend his breath would be to act ashamed. In some rural Middle Eastern areas, when Arab intermediaries call to inspect a prospective bride for a relative, they sometimes ask to smell her. Their purpose is not to make sure that she is freshly scrubbed; apparently what they look for is any lingering odor of anger or discontent. The Burmese show their affection during greeting by pressing mouths and noses upon the cheek and inhaling the breath strongly. The Samoans show affection by juxtaposing noses and smelling heartily. In contrast, the Americans seem to maintain their distance and suppress their sense of smell.

Difficulties in intercultural communication become quite common and often serious when the communicator is simply unfamiliar with the nonverbal codes of a certain culture. For instance, in the United States it is customarily the host who fixes a specific time for a dinner invitation. In the Middle East, it is the guest who must specify the time. Thus, when an American hears an Arab saying, "Won't you have dinner with us?" or "Come anytime," the American will not take the invitation seriously. Yet, to the Arab, the words are meant literally. It is the essence of politeness to leave it to the guest to set a time at his convenience. If the guest fails to set a time, the Arab assumes that he does not want to come.

Another example of the confusion resulting from unfamiliarity with the nonverbal codes of communication comes from Tunisia. In 1976, Vice-President Nelson Rockefeller headed a United States delegation to participate in ceremonies observing the 20th anniversary of Tunisia's independence. The Tunisians greeted Rockefeller with gun shots in the air. This unexpected welcome caused considerable worry to the U.S. Secret Service agents. Unfamiliar with the traditional Arab greeting, one of the agents pulled out his pistol, rushing to Rockefeller's side. It took a few minutes for the agent to realize that the gun shots were not a hostile act but a part of Tunisia's welcome to Rockefeller.

Sometimes, communication difficulties occur not because the "outsider" is unfamiliar with the nonverbal codes of the foreign culture, but because he considers certain cultural differences to be insignificant and not worth complying with. For example, refusing a cup of coffee is a trivial matter to Americans and will seldom result in misunderstandings. In Saudi Arabia, though, it amounts to a slap in the face. One American executive, who turned down a cup of coffee from a Saudi businessman, was baffled when a colleague suddenly turned cold and distant. The American did not realize that to the Saudi a cup of coffee is more than a gesture of friendliness; it is an expression of hospitality which is a highly valued pattern in the Arabic culture. To deprive an Arab of the chance to be hospitable is to deprive him of the occasion to be honorable. Likewise, an American will not offend his colleagues in the United States by leaning back in his chair and placing his feet on the desk while talking to them. If he were talking to an Arab, his posture would be demeaning. The Arab feels insulted when someone points the sole of his shoes at him—an act usually reserved for communicating contempt.

There are situations in which the outsider consciously violates the accepted codes of conduct in a foreign culture. The dire consequences of such an action became painfully clear to two engineers associated with a British firm that was enlarging an airport near Medina in Saudi Arabia. Found guilty of moonshining, the British engineers were publicly flogged in the town square and were sentenced to six-month jail terms for breaking the Muslim ban on alcohol. It is worth noting that this punishment caused a considerable furor in the British Parliament. One member, while introducing a motion urging the Foreign Secretary to recall the British Ambassador from Saudi Arabia, declared: "This is an appalling and outrageous piece of barbarism." Showing equal insensitivity to the Saudi customs, another deputy said: "It's time Saudi Arabia's laws were brought into harmony with those of the civilized world."[18]

We stated earlier that knowledge of the verbal communication system of a foreign culture can be of considerable value to the multinational executive. But such knowledge alone will not ensure communication success. The executive must, in addition, familiarize himself with the nonverbal system of the country where he operates. In fact, cultural anthropologists consider nonverbal skills as far more important than verbal skills in determining communication success abroad.

It is important to note that in his quest to understand the nonverbal system of another culture, the executive's purpose should not be to look for those elements that will reinforce his prejudices or preconceived notions of the inferiority of that culture. Rather, his purpose ought to be to gain insights into the culture so as to be able to function in it effectively. The executive should never lose sight of the fact that his success will depend greatly on his willingness to accept the cultural patterns of another society as they are, not as they should be.

Ethnocentrism

The third barrier that could impair the effectiveness of intercultural communication is ethnocentrism. Ethnocentrism refers to the sense of cultural superiority which members of a particular society feel toward other societies; it is a tendency to elevate one's own value system and to denigrate the value system of other groups. When members of a given cultural group exhibit a high level of ethnocentrism, they tend to perceive their own values as the only "logical," the only "natural," and the only "correct" values.

Like many aspects of human behavior, ethnocentrism is learned. From the earliest years of childhood, we begin to absorb our group's cultural patterns, conforming to those behaviors for which we are rewarded and avoiding those for which we are punished. Over the course of many years of socialization, the learned cultural patterns begin to determine our perception of what is "good" or "bad," "beautiful" or "ugly," and "right" or "wrong."

One study on how the aesthetic judgment of school children can be conditioned by their cultural environment illustrates this point quite well. A group of American school children from the first through the tenth grades were shown pictures of a dozen different national flags and were asked to choose the "best looking" flag. The most popular choice among the first graders was the Siamese flag, with a white elephant on a red background. The tenth graders, however, unanimously chose the American flag. The study also showed a similar pattern of preferences for houses, clothes, and street signs.[19]

Practically all cultural groups exhibit some measure of ethnocentrism. Cross-cultural studies indicate that many of the values considered "right" in one society may be considered "wrong" in another society. It has been reported, for example, that the Greenland Eskimos thought that the Europeans who arrived on their shores had come to learn virtue and good manners from the natives. This underscores the notion that when peoples with strong ethnocentric attitudes come into contact, neither conforms to the expectations of the other, and each tends to reject the behavior of the other as "inferior," "savage," "barbarian," or simply "naive."

Ethnocentrism is human and can serve a useful purpose, as it maintains a sense of common identity within a particular culture, which is necessary for an orderly society. But when the ethnocentric attitude is carried to an extreme, it will have detrimental effects on communication among culturally divergent individuals who might have to work together to achieve a common goal. An American executive, for example, who considers English to be the "best" or the "most logical" language will not apply himself to learn a foreign language which he considers "inferior" or "illogical." Likewise, if he considers his nonverbal communication system to be the "most civilized" system, he will tend to reject other systems as "primitive." In this sense, ethnocentrism may lead not only to a complete communication breakdown but also to antagonism and conflict.

How can the negative effects of ethnocentrism be minimized? First, and as we indicated earlier, we must form some idea of what culture is and how it functions. We must also develop some knowledge of the variety of ways in which different human groups have gone about solving universal problems. Second, we should examine each of the foreign values in the context of its total cultural setting. Many of the foreign customs and beliefs, which to the American might appear peculiar, could be properly understood when seen within the larger cultural context of which they are a part. The more we know of other cultures, the more evident it becomes that no society could hold together unless its patterns of thinking, feeling, and acting are reasonably systematic and coherent. However different other peoples may seem, their ways are not as peculiar, unnatural, or incomprehensible as they appear to the culturally uninformed observer.

In many cases, beliefs, which at first glance appear incoherent, often have some logical basis; they make sense, especially to those who subscribe to them. For instance, the Trobriand Islanders (of North-Eastern New Guinea) do not believe that there is any connection between sexual intercourse and the birth of a child. Instead, they believe that when a woman passes near a sacred spot in their tribal area, a spirit enters her womb, and it is from this that the child grows. To an outsider, this belief appears utterly peculiar and completely mythical. Upon a closer examination of other cultural aspects, however, it is possible to find the rationale behind it. The belief is simply based on the fact that the Trobriands begin intercourse at a very early age, before the female is biologically able to conceive. Thus, a very young girl who does not get pregnant immediately following intercourse may not associate pregnancy with intercourse.[20]

Of course, not all beliefs have a logical basis or can be easily explained. Often people do not know why they act the way they do except that they have always done so. When an American is asked why he calls the brothers of his parents and the husbands of his parents' sisters by the same kinship term, he will be hard pressed for a logical explanation. He might say: "Because they are all uncles," or "What else could you call them?" And when asked why he does not eat ice cream for breakfast, he might say, "It wouldn't taste good," or "Nobody does it." Such habitual behaviors and beliefs are socially conditioned. People come to accept them not out of reasoning but out of conformity. They simply follow the example set by their fellows and yield to the pressure of their opinion.

Lack of Empathy

The fourth barrier to intercultural communication is lack of empathy. Empathy is the process through which we make predictions about the psychological states of other people; it is the ability to project ourselves into their personalities with the purpose of understanding them or seeing things "through their eyes." Empathic ability is crucial to any type of communication. Without it, we will be unable to make predictions about other people's emotions, attitudes, and values; and without such predictions, our ability to understand others and to influence them will be severely impaired.

Empathy involves mental images that we carry in our heads about other people. It is these images that enable us to understand why others might be happy or sad, hostile or friendly, introverted or extroverted, and conservative or liberal. To some degree, our mental images are a reflection of the make-up of our own unique personality. What makes us happy, we reason, should make others happy also. To a larger measure, though, mental images are a cultural product; they are shaped by the value system of the society in which we grow up. It is our culture that generally dictates the conditions under which people would be pleasant, affectionate, angry, hurt, or distant.

Mental images can be a valuable predictive and interpretive tool of behavior as long as they are employed within the cultural setting in which they have been developed. Once they are transferred to another cultural environment, they are not likely to have much validity or usefulness. Since other societies have a value system that is different from ours, the meanings they attach to certain behaviors tend to be different. Consequently, continued reliance on our culturally inspired approaches to empathy could very well lead to false expectations and false interpretation of behavior.

An example of how false expectations and interpretations could lead to communication difficulties comes from the following incident involving an American executive stationed in the Middle East. On their weekly meeting day, the unit heads of an American organization walked into the conference room in the field of operations in a Middle Eastern town. As the men took their seats around a long table, John Smith, the American executive, was already in the room, engaging those present in a friendly premeeting conversation. Omar Muhammad, who had just arrived, sat in a chair not too far from the executive. John Smith turned to Omar Muhammad and asked: "How's the wife, Omar?" Omar flushed, blushed deep red, mumbled some incomprehensible sounds. John Smith, smiling, nodded contentedly. At the time the staff knew that Omar Muhammad's wife had been hospitalized for the previous six weeks.

To Omar and the Middle Easterners present, the friendliness and concern implied in the remark of the American executive were offensive and in poor taste. John Smith had violated the cultural code of the situation. The subject of women and their relationship to their men is a very intricate question, involving the concepts of honor and shame in the Middle Eastern society. John Smith's well-meant question was offensive because, to the Middle Easterner, that was a private matter not to be asked about in public. Had John Smith asked the question in private, it would have created the desired effect.[21]

Whenever we cross cultural boundaries with the purpose of communicating with members of another society, it is imperative that we go through a process of acquiring new mental images about how people would feel in certain situations, what their behavior signifies, and how to respond to their behavior in the most appropriate manner. Such a process could be facilitated if we constantly asked the questions: "Why do the natives behave the way they do?" "What does their behavior mean?" And "How would I behave and feel if I were a member of their society, given its traditions, customs, and mores?"

Such questions have the value of prompting us to go beyond the superficial interpretation of behavior to unravelling the historical, political, religious, and economic forces that have given the society its distinguishing cultural features. Knowledge of these forces should enable us to construct new mental images and to develop new empathic skills that are more appropriate for the unique requirements of the foreign cultural setting. Individuals who carry out this process successfully are said to be well adjusted and adaptable individuals.

Unfortunately, business executives who achieve a high level of empathy are sometimes accused of "going native," a label with obvius negative connotations. There are occasions when these executives are transferred by their firms from the country with which they are thoroughly familiar to another with which they are totally unfamiliar. This practice is based on the erroneous premise that executives who become too knowledgeable of the culture of a foreign nation run the risk of abandoning their own culture, of becoming too sympathetic to the place they are posted in, and of being unable to carry out decisions made at their company's home office.

From a communication standpoint, "going native" is not only a desirable, but an ideal state for which every business executive must strive.

Differences in Perception

The fith barrier to intercultural communication stems from differences in perception. The term "perception" refers to "the ways in which organisms respond to the stimuli picked up by their sense organs."[22] It involves a complex process by which people select, organize, and interpret sensory stimulation.

We do not normally perceive all the physical and social stimuli in our environment. We perceive only what we are looking for, and we ignore what we are not looking for. This shows that our mental apparatus is not an indifferent receptacle mechanism; rather, it tends to be highly selective in the type of stimuli it perceives. When certain stimuli and not others are noticed, the process is called selective perception. It is selective perception that accounts for many of the differences in the manner in which we observe the same environmental stimuli.

Determinants of Perception

What causes selective perception? Why does one person perceive one thing and another perceive another thing in the same environment? And why do two individuals perceiving the same stimulus come out with two different impressions or conclusions?

Reality does not consist of "impartial" facts that everyone sees in the same way. What exists "out there" is what we think exists. More specifically, what we perceive is a consequence of at least three factors: nature of the stimulus, our personal interests and needs, and our cultural background.

Nature of the Stimulus. The quality of stimuli determines which stimulus will be selected out for perception. A single white person in a crowd of black people is much more likely to be noticed than if that individual were seen among many other white people. Also, the slogan most frequently and most loudly repeated is more likely to come to the attention of people than the infrequently and softly mentioned ones. Contrast, then, is one of the most attention-getting attributes of a stimulus.

Personal Interests and Needs. Suppose that 20 persons chosen at random were to scatter through the streets of a big city such as Chicago, London, Paris, or Cairo for a day and meet in the evening to compare their observations. Would they have perceived the same things? Most likely not. Most of the women would have noticed the attractive tailors and haberdashers. Some would have noticed the restaurants; others the art galleries and bookshops. Personal interests will dictate what each person sees.

The effect of personal needs on perception can be illustrated in the following experiment. Two groups of children (one a poor group from a settlement house in one of Boston's slum areas; the other a rich group from a school, catering to a more affluent section of Boston) were asked to judge the size of various coins. The study showed that the poor group overestimated the size of the coins considerably more than did the rich group.[23] The two groups' differing needs for money dictated their perception of the size of the coins.

Cultural Background. What people perceive can be influenced to a great measure by their culture. As Walter Lippmann once noted, "...we do not first see, and then define, we define first and then see. In the great...outer world we pick out what our culture has already defined for us, and we tend to perceive that which we have picked out in the form stereotyped for us by our culture."[24] In other words, we see things not as they actually are but as we, a product of a given culture, are.

In the Southern states, for example, people customarily make a very fine distinction between who is "white" and who is "colored." Hence, most Southerners of either race are very conscious of skin color. Yet, in other parts of the world, such as the Arab countries, where there is a great variety of skin color, people seem to be less observant with regard to color differences. The Arab, no doubt, knows such differences exist, but as these do not have the cultural significance for him that they have for the American, he fails to observe them or to see them as closely as certain Americans do.

One by-product of culture which influences perception is the frame of reference. The frame of reference denotes those factors which determine the particular qualities of people or events. Such statements as: "All Jews are shrewd;" "all Blacks are lazy;" "all Russians are inscrutable;" and "all Arabs are untrustworthy" represent different frames of reference. The frame of reference, then, provides stereotyped images by which we judge a particular individual on the basis of the presumed characteristics of the cultural group of which he is a member.

Whenever we perceive a stimulus, our frame of reference compels us to assimilate the stimulus in such a manner so as to fit our existing store of knowledge. Suppose that an American who firmly believes that all Arabs are untrustworthy and are unkempt meets an Arab who is honest and neat. Will this particular experience change the American's perception of the Arabs in general? Probably not. Most likely, the American will ascribe some "ulterior motive" to the honest Arab who will then be seen as a "make-believe" honest Arab. The American will also regard the neat Arab as an "exception."

Perceptual differences, then, constitute a formidable barrier to intercultural communication, and coping with them can be quite a frustrating and arduous task. There is nothing we can do to eliminate completely differences in the way people respond to their environment. There are, however, certain steps which can help the business executive minimize the damaging effect of perceptual differences on his communication.

The first step consists of the executive's recognition that differences in people's perception are natural and inevitable. As long as human societies are conditioned differently, there will always be differences in the manner in which they respond to their environment. Furthermore, as long as societies continue to have their own distinct cultural patterns, they are bound to have their own unique ways of observing the world around them.

The second step involves the executive's willingness to accept the differing ways in which another cultural group perceives its environment. Since there is nothing that we can do to compel others to restructure their perception, we should be ready to accept their ways of organizing their perception even though those ways are at variance with ours.

Finally, the executive's acceptance of another cultural group's observation of its environment should be coupled with acceptance of that group's perception of itself. As we pointed out in our discussion of ethnocentrism, each culture tends to upgrade its values and downgrade the values of other peoples. Consequently, the executive should strive to avoid criticism of another cultural group's values and see the group as it perceives itself or as it likes to be perceived.

To illustrate, there is an enormous difference between what the Arabs actually are and how they perceive themselves. The Arab societies are generally illiterate, economically backward, militarily weak, and politically divided and unstable. Some of them are, in fact, still struggling to extricate themselves from the throes of the 19th century. Yet, the Arabs display a tremendous sense of pride. They are proud of their culture, of their history, and of their past accomplishments. Many Arabs even consider themselves as superior to advanced societies.

Faced with this apparent contradiction between the Arabs' reality and their self-image, the executive would be wise to look at the Arabs not as they really are but as they perceive themselves.

The golden rule that should guide the executive in his dealings with any cultural group is: *Perceive other cultural groups as they like to be perceived.*

Summary

The purpose of this chapter is to introduce the business executive to the process of intercultural communication. It is pointed out that if the executive is to succeed in communicating with members of another cultural group, he must be able to satisfy two conditions. First, he needs to develop an adequate appreciation of the intricacies of the general process of intercultural communication. Second, he must gain a deeper understanding of the specific forces which shape the thoughts, feelings, and behaviors of the praticular cultural group with which he wishes to communicate.

The chapter focuses on the first condition; it deals with some of the major aspects of intercultural communication with which the executive should be familiar. These aspects include culture, communication, and barriers and gateways to intercultural communication.

A summary of the major points covered under each of these topics follows:

Culture

1. Culture refers to all the nonphysiological products of human personalities.
2. Culture is learned.
3. All human beings share similar social needs. These are called cultural universals.
4. The different forms in which different societies go about satisfying their basic needs are culled cultural variability.

Communication

1. The primary purpose of communication is persuasion or influencing others.
2. Persuasion cannot be achieved without first developing a thorough understanding of those we seek to influence.
3. At the heart of understanding is knowledge or the collection of information about those we seek to understand.

Barriers and Gateways to Intercultural Communication

1. Intercultural communication is usually hampered by five barriers: verbal systems, nonverbal systems, ethnocentrism, lack of empathy, and differences in perception.
2. Differences in the verbal systems obstruct communication in two ways:
   a. Individuals who speak different languages cannot possibly exchange meaningful messages.
   b. People who speak different languages tend to think differently.
      To ease the undesirable results of language differences, the executive should develop at least some working knowledge of the language of those with whom he wishes to interact.
3. Differences in the nonverbal systems can lead to a host of difficulties.

The executive who is unfamiliar with the nonverbal codes of a foreign society will most likely encounter resentment, hostility, and rejection by members of that society.

4. Ethnocentrism is the sense of cultural superiority which members of a particular society feel toward other societies. When carried to an extreme, ethnocentrism can lead to disharmony and confict.

   To minimize the detrimental effect of ethnocentrism, the executive should:

   a. Engage in self-analysis with a view to identifying any extreme ethnocentric tendencies and attempt to eliminate or reduce the biases they might give rise to.

   b. Refrain from passing judgment on isolated cultural elements or values. The executive should examine each element in the context of its total cultural setting.

5. Empathy consists of mental images that serve as predictive tools of other people's behaviors and feelings. Mental images that are indiscriminately transferred from one cultural setting to a different one could lead to communication breakdowns.

   The executive must, therefore, endeavor to develop new mental images that fit more neatly into the setting of the foreign culture if he is to communicate with it successfully.

6. Perception is the process by which people select, organize, and interpret messages.

   To minimize the adverse impact of perceptual differences on communication, the executive should:

   a. Recognize that differences in perception are natural and inevitable.

   b. Be willing to accept the differing ways in which another cultural group perceives the world.

   c. Be willing to accept the manner in which another cultural group perceives itself.

Footnotes

[1] E.B. Taylor, *Primitive Culture* (London: John Murray, 1871), p. 1.

[2] A.L. Kroeber, *Anthropology: Culture Patterns and Process* (New York: Harcourt, Brace and World, Inc., 1963), p. 97.

[3] Earl H. Bell and John Sirjamaki, *Social Foundations of Human Behavior* (New York: Harper and Row, Publishers, 1965), pp. 30-31.

[4] Branislow Malinowski, *A Scientific Theory of Culture and Other Essays* (Chapel Hill, North Carolina: The University of North Carolina Press, 1944), p. 77.

[5] Kimball Young, *Sociology: A Study of Society and Culture* (New York: American Book Company, 1949), p. 41.

[6] Richard McKeon, ed., *The Basic Works of Aristotle* (New York: Random House, 1941), p. 25.

[7] David K. Berlo, *The Process of Communication* (New York: Holt, Rinehart and Winston, 1960), pp. 11-12.

[8] James H. Campbell and Hal H. Hepler, eds., *Dimensions in Communication*

(Belmont, California: Wadsworth Publishing Company, 1970).

[9]Ina Cornine Brown, *Understanding Other Cultures* (Englewood Cliffs, New Jersey: Prentice-Hall, 1963), p. 1.

[10]Benjamin L. Whorf, "Language and Stereotypes," *Technology Review,* Vol. 42, 1940, pp. 229-231.

[11]Dimitris N. Chorafas, *The Communication Barrier in International Management* (New York: The American Management Association, 1969), Research Study 100, p. 22.

[12]John Fayerweather, *Management of International Operations* (New York: McGraw-Hill Book Company, 1960), p. 17.

[13]Nick Thimmesch, "Americans Illiteracy in Language Costs Us Beaucoup," *The Chicago Tribune,* June 25, 1975.

[14]J. William Fullbright, "We're Tongue-Tied," *Newsweek,* July 30, 1979, p. 15.

[15]Dimitris Chorafas, 1969, *op cit.,* p. 29

[16]*Nations Business,* March 1965, p. 62.

[17]A.R. Lindesmith and A.L. Strauss, *Social Psychology* (New York: Holt, Rinehart and Winston, 1956), p. 45.

[18]*The Chicago Sun Times,* June 15, 1978, p. 28.

[19]E.L. Horowitz, "Some Aspects of the Development of Patriotism in Children," *Sociology,* Vol. 3, 1940, pp. 329-341.

[20]Branislow Malinowski, *Sex and Repression in Savage Society* (London: Rougledge and Kegan, 1953), pp. 9-10.

[21]F.S. Yousef, "Cross Cultural Communications: Aspects of Contrastive Social Values Between North Americans and Middle Easterners," *Human Organization,* Vol. 33, Winter 1974, p. 384.

[22]Alfred Lindesmith, et al., eds., *Social Psychology* (Hinsdale, Il: The Dryden Press, 1975), p. 172.

[23]J.S. Bruner and C.C. Goodman, "Value and Need as Organizing Factors in Perception," *Journal of Abnormal and Social Psychology,* Vol. 42, 1947, pp. 33-44.

[24]Walter Lippmann, "Stereotypes," in Bernard Berelson and Morris Janowitz, eds., *Reader in Public Opinion and Communication* (New York: The Free Press of Glencoe, 1953), p. 32.

Chapter 2

What Is an Arab?

In the previous chapter, we pointed out that persuasion is the primary purpose of communication, and that understanding is the key to persuasion. We also mentioned that understanding does not take place in a vacuum. Rather, it must be based on knowledge of the individual or group with whom we seek to communicate.

Since the central theme of this book revolves around the subject of communicating with the Arabs, the question that needs to be posed at this point is: What types of knowledge or information should the business executive gain about the Arabs if he is to enhance his ability to communicate with them effectively?

As is the case with any cultural group, the Arab's behavioral patterns are the product of interplay among a staggering number of forces. It would be pretentious on our part to attempt to make a complete inventory of every single force that contributes to the shaping of the Arabs' manner of thinking and behaving. It is possible, nevertheless, to reduce the major forces to five broad categories, the fifth of which should be of particular interest to the Western business executive. The categories are: Islam, Arab nationalism, the Arabic language, the Arabs' cultural patterns, and the Arabs' perception of the West.

Each of the above forces will be discussed in considerable detail in the forthcoming chapters. But for the moment, it is essential that we establish a clear idea as to who the Arabs are, or, more specifically, what the term "Arab" means. This type of knowledge is necessary if the executive is to develop a more complete picture of the Arabs as a cultural group.

The Problem of Identification

You cannot tell an Arab when you see one. You cannot recognize him by the color and features of his face, or his dress, or his religion. He may look like a Greek, Italian, Frenchman, Swede, Nigerian, Indian, or Indonesian. He may be dressed in white draperies in Abu Dhabi, tarbooshed in

Alexandria, burnoosed in Tangier, or resplendently mod on the boulevards
of Cairo or Baghdad. His wife may be utterly emancipated or veiled from
head to foot in the black draperies or *purdeh*. He may be a Muslim or a
Christian, and he may live anywhere from Iraq to Morocco.

The northern countries of Syria and Lebanon are a fine mixture of
Phoenicians, Turks, Venetians, Romans, Jews, and Western Crusaders.
Iraq's population is a mixture of Turks, Persians, and aboriginal, and so is
Jordan's. The Egyptians are a mixture of Abyssinians, Turks, Phoenicians,
Levantines, and Romans. To the West, Libya, Tunisia, Algeria, and
Morocco have as a substratum the Spanish, French, Romans, and
Phoenicians.

Despite the wide variations in their colors, physical features, traditional
costumes, and religions, the people of the Middle East (with the exception
of Israel, Iran, Afghanistan, and Pakistan) and North Africa are grouped
together as Arabs. But what is an Arab? Despite its familiarity, the term
"Arab" becomes strange and baffling when you dig into just what it means.
If you turn to the Arabs themselves for an answer, you will be amazed at
how vague, indefinite, and frequently unsatisfactory their answer is.

What An Arab Is Not

As is the case with many ethnic terms, it is easier to indicate what an Arab
is not than what he is. To start with, the term "Arab" does not indicate race
in the modern, anthropological sense. Along the eastern coast of the
Mediterranean, there are whole towns full of blond, blue-eyed, light-
skinned Arabs. Many leaders of the Arab world, in a gathering of diplomats, would be indistinguishable from Germans or Swedes.

But in the streets of almost any metropolis in the Arab world, the traveler
would still pass some Arabs whose black skin, kinky hair, and Negroid
features would not seem out of place in Ghana or Nigeria. Africa's contribution through slave trade and migration to the racial types of the Arab
world is quite evident. "So great is the variety in hues of skin color, head
shape, facial features, type of hair, and body build throughout the Arab
world that the term 'Arab' cannot be understood to indicate race."[1]

Neither does the term indicate the religion of those who classify themselves as Arabs. Contrary to popular belief, the two terms "Arab" and
"Muslim" are not synonymous. Although the majority of Arabs are
Muslim, many are not. For example, Egypt has a large Christian population, and Lebanon has a Christian majority. On the other hand, not all
Muslims are Arab. Turkey, Pakistan, Iran, and Indonesia, for example, are
all largely Muslim countries; but their people are not Arabs. Although all
Arab countries, except Lebanon, are predominantly Muslim, Islam is the
official religion in only a few. Most of these countries are Muslim only in
the sense that the U.S. is Christian.

Frequently, in discussion of the Middle East problems, we hear mention of "Jews and Arabs" in the area. This confusion usually results from erroneously interchanging the terms "Arab" and "Muslim," and "Jew" and "Zionist." In the early United Nations debates on the Palestine question, the United States Representative, Warren Austin, called upon "Jews and Arabs" to settle their differences in a "Christian" manner. Apparently, Mr. Austin, like so many non-Middle Easterners, failed to realize that not all Arabs are Muslims. This confused usage of the terms "Arab" and "Muslim" is still common today. In the minds of most Westerners, an Arab and a Muslim are one and the same.

Finally, the term "Arab" does not designate a nationality. Although the Arabs, as a collectivity, may be a nation, they are not as yet a nationality in the legal sense. There is still no single Arab state, even though many Arab nationalists aspire to one. An individual who calls himself an Arab may be described in his passport as of Iraqi, Lebanese, Jordanian, Saudi Arabian, Libyan, or Kuwaiti nationality. He will not be simply described as an Arab. There are Arab states and a League of Arab States, but as yet there is no single Arab state of which all Arabs are nationals.

Evolution of the Term "Arab"

Historically, the meaning of the term "Arab" has gone through three stages. It meant one thing prior to the advent of Islam, another during the Islamic expansion, and it means something else at the present time.

The Pre-Islamic Era

One of the dictionary definitions of an Arab is that he is a native of Arabia. This definition is true only in the sense that the Arabs' original homeland was Arabia or the Arabian peninsula. Covering an area of some one-and-a-quarter million square miles, the Arabian peninsula is bordered in the north by Iraq, Syria, and Jordan; in the east and south by the Persian (or Arabian) Gulf* and the Indian Ocean; and in the west by the Red Sea.

Mostly desert land, the Arabian peninsula was inhabited by two types of people. One type, mainly nomadic, had its roaming-ground country lying between the Euphrates and the center of the peninsula, down to the southern confines of the Hejaz and the Najd. The other type, largely sedentary, had established itself in the uplands of the south, roughly corresponding to Yemen and Hathramout.

Among the inhabitants of the Arabian peninsula, the term "Arab" denoted only the first group. So, in those days an Arab was any member of the nomadic tribes who wandered the vast desert in search of pasture. This usage was common even though Arabic was the common language of both the sedentary and the nomadic desert dwellers.

*For nationalistic reasons, the Arabs invariably use "Arabian Gulf" instead of "Persian Gulf."

Outside the Arabian peninsula, the term "Arab" was first encountered in the 9th century B.C., describing Bedouins of the north Arabian steppe. It continued to be used in this fashion for several centuries among the settled people of neighboring countries. Later, it was used by the Romans and the Greeks to denote the inhabitants of the entire peninsula.

The Islamic Expansion Era

When Islam was born in the 7th century, the term "Arab" continued for a while to maintain its old meaning. Thus, to the Prophet Muhammad and his followers, an Arab was a Bedouin of the desert. Even in the Quran, the Muslims' holy book, the term is used exclusively in this sense and never in reference to the townsfolk of Mecca, Medina, and other cities.

During the Islamic expansion, Muslims of the Arabian peninsula carried their religion as well as their language and culture to the conquered provinces of Iraq, Syria, Persian, and North Africa. At first, the term "Arab" referred to the invaders who came from Arabia. But when the Syrians, Egyptians, Berbers, and the other conquered peoples flocked within the fold of Islam and intermarried with the Arabs, the original high wall raised between Arab and non-Arabs tumbled down.

The nationality of the Muslim receded into the background. No matter what his nationality might originally have been, the follower of Muhammad now passed for an Arab as long as he spoke Arabic. An Arab henceforth became "one who professed Islam and spoke and wrote the Arabic tongue, regardless of his racial affiliation."[2] By the 11th century, Arabic had become not only the chief medium of everyday use from Persia to the Pyrenees, but also the primary instrument of culture superceding the old culture languages like Aramaic, Coptic, Greek, and Latin.

The Modern Era

Within the past fifty years or so, Arab intellectuals have been locked in what sometimes appear to be endless deliberations as to what constitutes an Arab. These deliberations have resulted in a somewhat modified meaning for the term "Arab." Today, Arab intellectuals seem to be almost unanimous in the view that the term "Arab" stands for a political and cultural concept with no ethnic significance.[3] According to this view, the Arabs constitute a single nation by virtue of their possession of a common language, a common culture, and a common territory that stretches from Morocco to the Persian Gulf.

The political-cultural approach to defining an Arab is a reflection of the resurgence of modern Arab nationalism. Initially aimed at driving out European domination, nationalism came to signify an important political force designed to unite all Arabs in one great nation, able to deal with European powers, and more recently the Israelis, on equal footing. In stressing this concept, many Arab intellectuals as well as political leaders make a point of consistently referring to the Arabic-speaking peoples as one nation or a group of sister nations. In fact, some Arabs feel offended when a foreigner uses the plural "Arab nations" instead of the singular "Arab nation."

In line with this approach, a gathering of Arab leaders once defined an Arab as follows: "Whoever lives in our country, speaks our language, is brought up in our culture, and takes pride in our glory is one of us."[4] It is worth noting that, in this definition, the words "and takes pride in our glory" have a special significance in distinguishing an Arab from a non-Arab. These words are meant to exclude those, notably Jews, who live in the Arab world and whose mother tongue and culture are Arabic but do not consider themselves Arab.

In short, the term "Arab" as used by contemporary Arab intellectuals connotes a state of mind. You are an Arab if you feel or believe that you are an Arab. And you will most likely feel or believe that you are an Arab if your native tongue and culture are Arabic, and if you identify with the problems and aspirations of the Arabs.

Summary

As a starting point to improving his understanding of the Arabs, the business executive should develop a clearer picture of who the Arab is. In this chapter, which focuses on that subject, the following points are made:

1. The term "Arab" does not indicate race, for there can be light-skinned Arabs and dark-skinned Arabs; blond Arabs and Arabs with kinky hair.
2. The term "Arab" does not indicate religion. Thus:
   a. Not all Arabs are Muslims; many are Christians.
   b. Not all Muslims are Arab: A Pakistani Muslim, an Indonesian Muslim, a Persian Muslim, or a Turkish Muslim is not an Arab.
3. The term "Arab" does not designate a nationality. Although the Arabs may be viewed as a nation, they do not constitute a nationality. There is a Jordanian nationality, an Egyptian nationality, an Algerian nationality, a Kuwaiti nationality, a Saudi Arabian nationality, and so on. But there is not an Arab nationality.
4. Today, the most widely accepted meaning for the term "Arab" is that an Arab is any person who resides in the area stretching from Morocco to the Persian Gulf, who speaks Arabic, and who takes pride in the Arabic culture and the Arabs' historical accomplishments.
5. To avoid offending many Arabs, the business executive would be prudent to use the singular "Arab nation" instead of the plural "Arab nations" in his conversations with the Arabs.

Footnotes

[1]Don Peretz, *The Middle East Today* (New York: Holt, Rinehart and Winston, 1963), p. 10.

[2]Philip K. Hitti, *History of the Arabs* (London: MacMillian and Company, Ltd., 1963), p. 240.

[3]Hazem Zaki Nusaiba, *The Ideas of Arab Nationalism* (Ithaca: Cornell University Press, 1956), p. 56.

[4]Bernard Lewis, *The Arabs in History* (New York: Harper and Row, Publishers, 1960), pp. 9-10.

Chapter 3

The Nature of Islam

In chapter 2, we suggested that if the business executive is to enhance his communication effectiveness with the Arabs, he will do well to gain insights into certain forces which condition the Arabs' attitude in general and their attitude toward the West in particular. These forces include Islam, Arab nationalism, the Arabic language, the Arabs' general cultural patterns, and the Arabs' perception of the West. In this chapter, we will focus solely on Islam.

If there is one factor which often throws a Westerner's vision of the Arabs out of focus, it is neither the geographic remoteness of the Arab world, nor the complexity of Arab politics. Rather, it is Islam. The blurred and frequently confused image most Westerners have of Islam makes it extremely difficult for them to communicate with the Arabs in a constructive fashion.

Islam plays a central role in the life of the Arabs. The Muslim milieu is a reservoir formed through thirteen centuries of rich and varied development from which the Muslim Arabs continue to draw attitudes, feelings, and assumptions about themselves and about other peoples. It is primarily Islam that determines the Arabs' conscious and unconscious reaction to their world.

Therefore, if we are to understand anything at all about the Arabs, a good knowledge of Islam becomes indispensable. For a business executive interested in improving his communication with the Arabs, his best route is through a short study of Islam.

Arabia: The Birthplace of Islam

As we pointed out in the previous chapter, Arabia (or the Arabian peninsula) occupies an area of some one-and-a-quarter million square miles. It is bordered in the north by Iraq, Syria, and Jordan; in the east and south by the Persian Gulf and the Indian Ocean; and in the west by the Red Sea.

Prior to the birth of Islam, Arabia was inhabited mostly by nomadic tribes whose livelihood depended on the rearing of camels and small cattle. Political power was fragmented among many tribes whose social patterns consisted of raiding one another for plunder, prestige, and the pursuit of traditional feuds. The social structure of the society was primarily based on tribal bonds.

The Arabs refer to the pre-Islamic era in Arabia as *Al-Jahiliya* which literally means the "age of ignorance." But since the pre-Islamic Arabs were cultured and lettered people, the term *Al-Jahiliya* is actually used in reference to that period in which the Arabs had no inspired prophet and no revealed book. The Bedouins of *Al-Jahiliya* age were pagans who developed no mythology and no involved theology of their own. Some of them worshipped the sun; others worshipped the moon; and still others worshipped stone idols which served as media through which worshippers could come into contact with the deity.

As the pastoral society of Arabia later gave way to a merchant economy centering on the city of Mecca, located on the north-south trade route, tribal institutions began to break down, and with them, religion and public morality. It was in this type of environment that the Prophet Muhammad began preaching his new religion of Islam.

Muhammad the Prophet

Muhammad was born into the *Quraysh* tribe in Mecca about 570 A.D. His father had died a few months before his birth, and his upbringing was taken over by his uncle Abu Talib. Abu Talib let the young Muhammad accompany him on his frequent caravans to Syria. Through his business connections, Muhammad met a wealthy widow, Khadija, who asked him to lead one of her caravans to Syria. Shortly thereafter, Muhammad, 25 years of age, married Khadija who was then 40 years old.

After his marriage, Muhammad turned to a contemplative life. He would often withdraw from his community to a cave in Mount *Hira* where he spent hours in contemplation. It was during one of his stays in Mount *Hira* that Muhammad, then 40 years old, experienced supernatural visitations. He became aware of a voice and a figure (that of angel Gabriel) which remained always in front of him whichever way he turned. "Gabriel," says the Quran, "stood on the uppermost horizon, then drawing near, he came down with two bows' lengths or even closer," telling Muhammad to:

> Recite in the name of thy Lord who created,
> Created man from a clot.
> Recite! For thy Lord is most gracious,
> Who taught with the pen,
> Taught man what he knows not.

During his subsequent visits, the angel ordered Muhammad to begin spreading God's word and to devote his life to it. At first, Muhammad preached the revealed word within a small circle of family and friends.

Khadija, his wife, was the first to respond to his call, to be followed by Ali, Muhammad's cousin.

The first prominent Meccan to convert to Islam, outside Muhammad's immediate family, was Abu Bakr, a wealthy and influential merchant. Soon, there were 39 other converts, all of whom prayed at home, keeping the faith a secret. Later, the news began to spread quickly that Muhammad had founded a new religion, and that he claimed to be God's prophet. At first, most Meccans looked at Muhammad with amused tolerance. But this turned to hostility when Muhammad went back to Mecca and told the worshippers to abandon their paganism in favor of the one God.

Before long, the Meccans realized that Muhammad was not a harmless crank but a dangerous revolutionary. He was calling their religion a fraud, their priests charlatans, their gods false, and their time-honored traditions worthless. As new converts, drawn mainly from slaves and lower-class people, began to swell the ranks of the believers, the ridicule and sarcasm, which had been used unsparingly by the Meccans, were no longer effective in stemming the spread of the new faith. It now became necessary to resort to active persecution. The Meccans began to attack Muhammad's weakest followers in an effort to force them to renounce their faith.

When persecution mounted, some of Muhammad's followers were forced to emigrate to Abyssinia. Muhammad, however, decided to remain in Mecca, thinking that he would be safe as long as his uncle, Abu Talib, protected him. But in 619, Abu Talib died, and so did Muhammad's wife, Khadija. Resistance to Muhammad became more open and violent. But despite the Meccans' harassment, Muhammad continued to live in Mecca, having found another protector in Moutim, a powerful member of Muhammad's own tribe.

At this time, an important event that proved to be a turning point in the history of Muhammad's mission took place. A group of Arab religious pilgrims came to Mecca to visit its idols and its famous Black Stone. (The Black Stone is a large chunk from a meteorite on which Abraham presumably sacrificed his son.) Some of these pilgrims were from Medina, a small town about 270 miles northeast of Mecca. When the Medina pilgrims heard Muhammad preaching, they believed that he was the prophet the Jews had been waiting for. The pilgrims immediately converted to Islam.

In 622, after his unceasing efforts to convert the Meccans to his religion had failed, Muhammad emigrated from the hostile Mecca to the safe abode of Medina. His departure is known as the *Hijra*, or flight; it marked the dividing line between the failure and success of Islam. Because of its significance to the Muslims, the *Hijra* has been made the starting point of the Muslim epoch. Thus, in the Muslim calendar, the year 622 is the Year One.

Muhammad the General and Statesman

Feeling rather secure in his new friendly base at Medina, Muhammad laid the foundations of the first Islamic government; Muhammad the prophet also became Muhammad the general and statesman.

To secure needed revenues for his government, Muhammad began sending raiding parties against Meccan caravans, engaging them in a series of skirmishes. His real battle against the Meccans took place in 624 at *Badr*. Word had reached the Meccans that Muhammad was amassing his men at the *Badr* well, just outside Medina, and a small army was sent to crush him. With his 300 men, Muhammad stood fast and defeated the 1000-man Meccan force. His victory was considered as a proof that Allah (the Arabic word for God) was on his side. Stories of the Prophet's triumph quickly spread, bringing more converts to the fold of Islam.

The Meccans soon returned to Medina, this time with a 3000-man army. Muhammad's men rashly left their citadels to confront the enemy at a place called *Uhud,* about a mile from Medina. The Muslims were routed. Muhammad explained the defeat as a test for the believers, telling his soldiers that they had been beaten because they had fought for wordly gain rather than for Allah.

In 627, a force of 10,000 men, a coalition of Meccans and Jews, prepared to attack Medina. Muhammad conscripted the entire population to dig a broad ditch around the city. The Meccan army pitched its tents for a siege, but after two weeks the siege was lifted.

Medina was a sound territorial base, but to make it more secure, the Prophet had to conquer Mecca. Instead of waging a frontal attack on Mecca, Muhammad chose to conclude a non-aggression treaty with his enemies. He succeeded in negotiating a treaty in which the Meccans for the first time recognized him as a legitimate religious and political leader. The Meccans also granted him the right to proselytize among the Bedouin tribes of Mecca and gave him permission to make pilgrimages to the city. The following year, Muhammad vistied Mecca where he was able to enlist the secret allegiance of several prominent Meccan figures.

Muhammad never relinquished his hope of conquering Mecca. His opportunity came when one Meccan tribe violated the non-aggression treaty by attacking a tribe under Muhammad's protection. Muhammad raised an army of 10,000 men and marched on Mecca. The Meccans capitulated with almost no resistance. Thus, in 630 Muhammad entered his birthplace as a conqueror.

Muhammad the Social Reformer

Once in Mecca, Muhammad ordered all idols destroyed, but left the old forms of worship almost unchanged. The Black Stone remained the focal point of pilgrimages, and the ritual of walking around the shrine seven times continued.

In his new role as the head of an Islamic state that included Mecca and Medina, he was given to dictating social as well as religious behavior. He instructed his followers to avoid eating pork. He banned gambling and drinking alcohol. Adultery was condemned, although the Prophet, aware of the seriousness of an ill-founded charge of adultery to an Arab's honor, ruled that four eye-witnesses were necessary to prove it. Also condemned was the killing of another man, except in a just cause. Stealing became punishable by cutting off the thief's hand.

As in other reforms, Muhammad was guided more by the social context of the time than by the need to express eternally valid dogmas.[1] For example, when he had to solve the problem of a society in which there were more women than men, due to the earlier wars with the Meccans, he proposed polygamy.

Muhammad the Man

Muhammad had much the same character as other religious teachers. He lived simply and humbly; he taught justice tempered by love and kindness. The fact that he was illiterate gave greater credence to his pronouncements and deeds.

From his own standpoint, Muhammad considered himself human, not divine. He was not like Christ, the Son of God. He could not perform miracles, and he did not rise from his tomb. His qualities were human, and so were his failings. From a Westerner's standpoint, one of Muhammad's remarkable qualities is that he was a self-made man.

Muhammad the Empire Founder

Muhammad laid the foundation of an empire which, within less than a century, became larger than the Roman empire at its greatest. Perhaps one of Muhammad's most outstanding accomplishments lay in his ability to unify the warring tribesmen of Arabia. Politically fragmented prior to the birth of Islam, these Arabs, now fired with the zeal of Islam, became a powerful force.

Breaking out of their homeland, the Arabs streamed with an incredible speed across the neighboring lands, spreading their faith, their language, and their culture. They swept eastward to India. They conquered Persia, Cyprus, and Crete; overran North Africa; dominated most of Spain; and crossed the Pyrenees into France, occupying Bordeaux. The Arabs' thrust into Europe was not halted until 732 when an Arab force was beaten at Tours, a city in west central France.

Muhammad did not live long enough to see the great empire which he had started to build. As he was planning a military expedition to Syria, he fell ill and died in 632.

The Meaning and Pillars of Islam

Islam means the act of giving one's self to God (or Allah). Hence, Islam is generally defined as submission to the will of God.

As a religious system, Islam requires its followers to adhere to five basic duties known as the "pillars of Islam." The pillars are: profession of the faith, prayer, almsgiving, fasting, and pilgrimage. To these, some Muslims add a sixth pillar, holy war.

Profession of the Faith (Al-Shihadah)

The first duty of a Muslim is open profession of the belief that "there is no god but Allah and Muhammad is the messenger of God" (*La Illaha Illal Lah Wa Muhammadun Rasulul Lah*). This profession is obligatory for all Muslims, and the genuine proclamation of this belief is sufficient to insure acceptance into the faith. Say *La Illaha Illal Lah Wa Muhhamadun Rasulul Lah* and you are nominally a Muslim. Conversion is as easy as that. Every day of his life, the Mulsim hears these words chanted five times from the mosque minarets.

Prayer (Al-Salah)

Performance of worship or ritual prayer is the second duty, prescribed five times daily between daybreak and nightfall. Although group prayer in unison, if possible in a mosque, is preferable, the Muslim can pray wherever he may be. At the prescribed hours throughout the Muslim world, it is common to see men bowed toward Mecca, in their fields, in their factories, on the decks of ships, or on building roofs.

Before he prays, a Muslim must be pure—the hands, feet, and face newly washed. Thus, perforce, a pious Muslim who does not neglect his prayers is never dirty.

Almsgiving (Al-Zakat)

Almsgiving is a manifestation of piety and love. Muhammad initiated the practice with a 2.5 percent levy on the Muslims' gross earnings. The proceeds were distributed to the poor and used to defray government expenditures. When the Muslim state, at a later stage, was not strong enough to collect this tax, almsgiving became an act of piety recorded in the Muslim's heavenly book of deed.

Fasting (Al-Sawm)

During the thirty-day lunar month of Ramadan, a Muslim cannot eat, drink, smoke, or indulge in any other bodily gratification such as sexual intercourse between dawn and sunset. Although all Muslims acknowledge the fast, strictness of observance varies. In Saudi Arabia, the obligation is legally enforced. In Tunisia, on the other hand, President Bourgaiba created a great controversy a few years ago when he advised his government employees not to fast lest observance interfere with the task of building up the nation.

Pilgrimage (Al-Haj)

The fifth pillar of Islam, pilgrimage, is enjoined upon all able-bodied Muslims who can afford it, at least once in a lifetime. This practice had existed in ancient Arabian rites, and Muhammad decided to continue it.

During the month of *Haj,* Muslims from all corners of the world converge on the *Kaaba* at Mecca. At the *Kaaba,* which houses the ancient meteoric Black Stone upon which Abraham was to have sacrificed his son, Isaac, the pilgrims go through a number of exercises and rituals similar to those in pre-Islamic times. These include the seven turns around the Black Stone and a seven-fold run between two mounds to commemorate Hager's running back and forth between these two mounds in search of a spring for Ishmael, her thirsty son, after Abraham had cast them out. The Muslims believe as firmly as the Jews that they are descended from Abraham, but through Ishmael.

The pilgrimage serves as a unifying force in Islam. At Mecca, Arabs, Iranians, Turks, Africans, Pakistanis, Indians, Chinese, Indonesians, Filipinos, Russians, and Americans are bound together in a common ritual of brotherhood that transcends their national and racial differences. Since Muhammad's death, non-Muslims have been banned from Mecca, although a few have gained entry in disguise during the time of pilgrimage to write of their observations.

Holy War (Al-Jihad)

Some Muslims consider holy war to be the sixth pillar of Islam. *Al-Jihad* is demanded of all believers by the Quran and offers a reward of salvation. Although it has come to mean increasingly the holy war of Muslims against non-Muslims, *Al-Jihad* literally means exertion and effort of a Muslim to promote the Islamic doctrine, which does not have to be through war.

Sources of Authority in Islam

The sources of the above pillars and other rules in Islam are the Quran, the *hadith* or the sayings of Muhammad, and the *ijtihad* or the right to free interpretation.

The Quran

The Quran is the definitive, sacred Book of Muslims. Meaning the "recital" or "discourse," the Quran is regarded by Muslims as the word of God, revealed to Muhammad through the angel Gabriel.

As each religion has its own miracle, Islam's miracle is the Quran. Its transmission from God through the passive instrument of the illiterate Muhammad is a self-evident miracle. To the Muslims, no human being could have written with such ravishing felicity; the language of the Quran is the best Arabic that one could possibly imagine. Memorized by thousands of millions of people over fifty generations, the Quran is the most read, memorized, quoted, and broadcast book in the world. Because it is accepted by Muslims as the word of God miraculously dictated to Muhammad, the Quran is considered infallible in all its prescriptions and prohibitions.

The Quran consists of 114 *suras* or chapters, compiled after Muhammad's death in 632 as he had left no written record of them. Initially, the *suras* had been transcribed on parchment, carved on camels' shoulders, or memorized by Muhammad's followers. Abu Bakr, the first caliph (successor), ordered the collection of the *suras*. But it was not until the 10th century that the present text of the Quran was adopted from a number of different versions.

The content of the Quran reflects Muhammad's changing needs. At first, he had to convince the pagans of Mecca to abandon their stone gods for the one God. Thus, the early *suras*, revealed when Muhammad had a few followers, contain a clear statement of the new faith and a series of what might be called incentives for conversion. For example, the faithful are promised a garden of earthly delights after death. Later, and as Muhammad turned into a political and military leader in addition to being the religious head of the state, the revelations became more practicable. They began to deal with such matters as social reforms, military operations, and the Prophet's own private life.

Actually, the Quran "supplies guidance, not only on God and prayer, but on the most intimate details and interrelationships. It contains the basis of Islamic social system and a regimen for conduct from the cradle to the grave."[2] The Quran, for instance, deals with such matters as war, peace, politics, economics, inheritance, marriage, divorce, clothing, sports, sexual intercourse. the suckling of children, and countless other worldly things.

The Hadith

After Muhammad's death, religious questions arose that were not specifically answered in the Quran and further guidance was, therefore, needed. The Muslims turned to the *hadith* as their second most authoritative religious source. The *hadith* or the sayings of Muhammad consists of incidents in the life of the Prophet as described by his companions and helpers. Accounts of such incidents were passed orally from one person to another and from one generation to the next.

In the 9th century, and after they had been "purified" of forgeries and fabrications, Muhammad's sayings were compiled and codified in six collections. These have come to form the common law of Islam, now accepted by the Sunni (orthodox) wing of Islam that comprises 90 percent of all Muslims in the world.*

---

*The Sunni Muslims are so called because of their adherence to the *Sunna* or traditions.

The Ijtihad

When Muslims expanded to other societies with differing social systems, it became evident that the traditions and even the Quran were not specific enough to deal with the growing legal needs of the new environment. Consequently, the Muslims developed the concept of the *ijtihad* which means the right to free interpretation. The *ijtihad* was designed to encourage local Muslim jurists to devise their own rules to deal with the unique problems in their environment and to act according to their own concept of what was right or wrong.

Because of the proliferation of various schools of Islamic thought in the 10th century, Muslim leaders, fearing possible division in the Islamic society, decided to close the door to *ijtihad*. Thereafter, all jurists were obligated to accept the opinion of their predecessors and were deprived of exercising their own private judgment.

At the turn of the century, a number of Muslim reformists attempted to revive the concept of the *ijtihad* as a way of rejuvenating Islam and enabling it to deal more effectively with the requirements of the 20th century. The reformists' efforts, however, failed in convincing the Muslim leaders to reopen the door to the *ijtihad*.

Islam as a Cultural Force

Islam is more than a religion; it is the totality of culture in both its social and individual aspects. It is a way of life. In this sense, one cannot speak of various theories of government, or law, or art as distinct from the theological tenets of Islam. All are encompassed in it, and one must speak of Islamic government, Islamic society, Islamic law, Islamic art, and so on.

When Muhammad emigrated from Mecca to Medina, he became more than a religious leader. He assumed the roles of a statesman, a judge, a military commander, and a social planner. In these capacities, he was able to introduce changes in his society so fundamental that their effects still govern the minds and behaviors of millions of Muslims throughout the world.

Thus, from its inception, the Islamic community had no separate secular loyalty. That is, the system that Muhammad established did not recognize separate spheres for "church" and "state." Rather, the two are so meshed together in classical Islam that it is impossible to talk about one in isolation from the other. The Islamic community created by Muhammad was at once a religious brotherhood, a political association, and a social order.

Muslims, Christians, and Jews

When Muhammad underwent his religious experience about 610, he could have had no adequate first-hand knowledge of the Christian and

Jewish scriptures, since these had not been translated into Arabic. But he had opportunities for conversation with Christians and Jews both on his caravan journeys and in Mecca itself. It appears that these contacts had contributed to Muhammad's knowledge of these two developed religions.

After emigrating to Medina to escape the Meccans' persecution, Muhammad had hoped to receive a cordial support from the Jewish community in Medina. Muhammad considered himself a successor of the major Hebrew prophets, notably Abraham, and he even adopted some Jewish forms of worship. For example, he enjoined his followers to celebrate Yom Kippur and to face Jerusalem when saying their prayers. But it soon became apparent to him that the Jews of Medina had no use for this new revelation. To the Jews, Muhammad was a false prophet and a political menace; they saw him taking over the power which they had shared with the pagan Arabs. Muhammad's efforts to persuade the Christians of Medina to accept his prophethood met a similar failure.

Rebuffed by both the Christians and the Jews, Muhammad retaliated by denouncing them as falsifiers of the Old and the New Testaments and as corruptors of the true teachings of Moses and Christ. During this period, Muhammad chose to stress the divergencies rather than the commonalities between Islam and the two monotheistic religions. Both Islam and Christianity, for example, agree that one God created the universe, that Christ was miraculously born of a virgin, that he rose into heaven, and that God will grant men eternal life if they obey His divine will.

Many of the parables and stories of the Quran are similar to those in the Old and the New Testaments. There are stories of Adam, Noah, Abraham, Moses, Joseph, David, Solomon, Elijah, Job, Zachariya, John the Baptist, Mary, and Jesus. The Muslims, however, reject the idea of God as Father, since it implies that God had a wife; and of Christ as the Son of God, which implies physical generation on the part of a pure being. They also reject the Crucifixion. Although Judaism had less influence on Islam, Islam regards Judaism too as formally identical with itself but as having been corrupted by the Jews.

Islam's relationship with the other two relgions stabilized when Muhammad concluded peace treaties with the Christian and the Jewish tribes who were regarded as *dhimmis* or peoples of the Book. The *dhimmis* were extended Islam's protection in return for an annual tax payment. Being outside the bounds of Muslim law, they were also allowed jurisdiction of their own canon laws as administered by the respective heads of their religious communities. Whereas the pagan Arabs were given the limited choice of accepting Islam or facing the sword, the Christians and the Jews were permitted to practice their religions if they paid the annual tax.

If a *dhimmi* choose to convert to Islam, he was freed from all tributary obligations. Far from its being a method of forcing the *dhimmis* to convert to Islam, the tax provided the Muslims with needed revenues.

In their treatment of the Christians and the Jews, the Muslims proved to be comparatively tolerant rulers. At a time "when the West was forcibly converting or often putting to death non-Christians, the Muslims were under no obligation to convert or exterminate other peoples of the Book.''[3]

Commenting on Islam's comparative tolerance toward other religious groups, Bernard Lewis, a leading authority on Islam, states:

> Unlike his Western contemporaries, the medieval Muslim rarely felt the need to impose his faith by force on all who were subject to his rule. Like them, he knew well enough that in due time those who believed differently would burn in Hell. Unlike them, he saw no point in anticipating the divine judgment in this world. At most times he was content to be of the dominant faith in a society of many faiths. He imposed on the others certain social and legal disabilities in token of his primacy, and gave them an effective reminder if ever they seemed disposed to forget. Otherwise he left them their religions, economic and intellectual freedom, and the opportunity to make a notable contribution to his own civilization.[4]

The Islamic Civilization

Following their conquest of the Fertile Crescent, Persia, North Africa, and Spain, the Muslim Arabs became heir to ancient cultures with traditions going back to the Greco-Roman, Iranian, Pharoanic, Assyrian, and Babylonian times. In art, architecture, philosophy, medicine, science, and government, they had a great deal to learn. And the Muslims proved to have an insatiable appetite for learning. They quickly absorbed the scholarship and experience of the conquered civilizations. With the help of their subject peoples, the Muslims began to assimilate, adopt, and reproduce their subjects' intellectual and aesthetic heritage.

In this way, they became entrepreneurs of knowledge, bridging the gap between the vanished world of the classical cultures and the new world of the Renaissance that was to come. By transmitting Greek and Roman thought back to Europe, the Muslims played a pivotal role in restoring the continuity of Western civilization which had been broken during the collapse of the Greek and the Roman empires.

For a time when Christian Europe was hamstrung by dogma, the Muslims were generally free to make what intellectual explorations they could. With extraordinary speed, the Muslims familiarized themselves with the whole known world. They became great travellers and sailors. Arab merchants were to be found in China, in Russia, and in many parts of Western Europe. They produced a succession of celebrated mathematicians, astronomers, physicians, architects, and historians. In the centers of their learning—in Southern Spain, in Egypt, in Iraq, and in North Africa—they achieved a splendid synthesis of Eastern and Western cultures.

The Muslims were highly skillful in adapting classical cultures to their own requirements. Elements that might have endangered their religious foundations were eliminated or neutralized. From this synthesis of the older classical cultures emerged a distinctive Islamic civilization with its own contributions in philosophy, medicine, mathematics, astrology, geography, architecture, and, above all, in literature.

Decline of the Islamic Empire

After Muhammad's death, the Muslim community was left leaderless, for he had left no son and had not designated a successor. Dispute over the choice of a caliph (a successor or head of the Muslim community) to succeed Muhammad created considerable confusion and split the Muslims into two factions. One faction, the *Sunni*, maintained that the caliphate ought to be an elective office. The other faction, the *Shi'i*, considered the caliphate as a God-given office that should remain within Muhammad's family.

The danger of a break between the two factions was averted when the majority of the Muslims elected the respected Abu Bakr (the first convert to Islam outside the Prophet's family) to succeed Muhammad. But after a short reign, Abu Bakr died and was succeeded by Umar who, ten years later, was murdered. The caliphate passed, again by election among the Muslims, to Uthman. When Uthman was murdered, the caliphate passed by election to Ali who, though a cousin and son-in-law of the Prophet, had been passed over in the previous elections. Due to this fact, the *Shi'is* regarded the first three caliphs as usurpers of power and recognized only Ali as the legitimate heir to Muhammad.

Ali's statesmanship was tested when he tried to remove Mu'awiyah, Syria's governor who was appointed by the previous caliph, Uthman. When Mu'awiyah resisted and a military confrontation between the two seemed imminent, Ali agreed to submit the matter to arbitration. The arbitrators awarded the caliphate to Mu'awiyah. Ali was later murdered by a group of his supporters who insisted that Ali had no right to submit the caliphate to arbitration, since it had been conferred upon him by the whole body of the faithful.

Dispute over the caliphate continued. And as a result, many factions set out to establish autonomous states in various parts of the Muslim world, thus shattering the somewhat short-lived unity among the Muslims.

Externally, the Islamic world became an easy prey for foreign invaders. The Christian kingdoms of Northern Spain seized an opportunity to invade the disunited Muslims, and the first Crusade took place in 1099. Though the brilliant Kurdish general Saladin succeeded in uniting Syria and Egypt and in driving the Christian Crusaders from Jerusalem, he was unable to do more than temporarily arrest the downfall of the Islamic rule. Early in the 13th century, the Muslims had to face a far more deadly menace when their eastern lands were invaded by the Mongols who came out of the steppes of Eastern Asia. Under their leader Jingis Khan and later his grandson Hulago, the Mongols captured Baghdad in 1258.

The fall of the Muslim rule coincided with the rise of the Ottoman

Empire. Damscus and Cairo were both captured by the Turkish invaders in 1517, and with the conquest of Baghdad in 1639, virtually the entire Arabic-speaking world had been brought under the Ottoman domination.

Thus, while Europe was emerging from its Dark Age and entering its most exciting age of discovery and exploration, the Arab world began to sink ever deeper into an abyss of misrule, anarchy, and stagnation—a Dark Age of its own.[5] In the late 19th century and the early 20th century, when the Ottoman Empire gave way to the imperialism of Western Europe, the Arabs changed masters flaccidly; most of the Arab world came under the control of several Western powers.

Islam in the Twentieth Century

The role of Islam in the institutional as well as the personal life of the Arabs has undergone a considerable change. Within this century, secular nationalism, European ideologies, and modern technology have placed Islam at cross-purposes with the prevailing mood of the Arab world.

From its very inception under the Prophet Muhammad, Islam has claimed to provide a political organization for the community of the Faithful. Islam never made a distinction between church and state, and its concept of the state was based on a community of believers that had no physical boundaries. Because of the difficulty of reconciling and integrating Islam's pattern of secular and religious power with the demands of modern nation-states, almost all of the Arab countries have, since achieving their independence after World War I, shown a tendency toward some form of secularism or subordination of political Islam to the needs of the nation.

The educated elite who took power in the Arab countries between World War I and World War II sought to introduce political systems modeled at least in part on those of the West. The new leaders became convinced that the old order of political autocracy must be repudiated if their political, economic, and social ambitions were to be fulfilled. With the growing popularity of Western ideologies in the Arab world, Islam's formal influence on the Arab political institutions began to weaken.

The most obvious sign of the waning of political Islam was the Arabs' abandonment of pan-Islamism, a movement whose aim was the unification of all Muslim countries in one greater state. Many Arab as well as Muslim leaders came to the realization that pan-Islamism was simply too unrealistic and too difficult to achieve. Perhaps most significant is the fact that when the Arab states established their first regional organization in the 1940's, they chose the concept of ''Arab'' league rather than a ''Muslim'' league.

Although Islam as a political institution has become subservient to nationalism, it does not mean that it has ceased to operate as a powerful force in the life of the Arabs. Thirteen centuries after Muhammad's death, the Arabs' life continues to be shaped by the mental universe of the Prophet. Islamic heritage still sets the Arab world apart from other regions and endows it with characteristics peculiar to itself. Attitudes toward authority, family life, and relationships of the individual to his fellow citizens are still largely determined by the classical Muslim patterns.

In Egypt, the revolutionary regime of Nasser invariable exploited the Egyptians' attachment to Islam by providing government-prepared sermons to village prayer leaders on matters of concern to the state. In Baghdad, capital of the Iraqi socialist regime, minarets that tower above the city's mosque pour forth the *muezzin's* (crier's) call to prayer five times a day. In Jerusalem, Palestinian laborers building apartment houses for the Israelis take off their shoes, face Mecca, and prostrate themselves in worship everyday just after noon. And throughout the Arab world, considerable prestige is still conferred on those who have been to Mecca; they are rewarded with the prestigious title *Al-Hadji* (the pilgrim).

Perhaps the most striking example of the intensity of religious feeling could be found in the 1973 Egyptian offensive against the Israeli Bar-Lev line in the Sinai. As the red, white, and black flag of Egypt fluttered over Sinai for the first time since the 1967 war, a spontaneous and delirious cry of joy rose into the desert air: *"Allahu Akbar, Allahu Akbar"* (God is the greatest, God is the greatest). The sight of sweating soldiers bursting into a religious chant might seem peculiar to the Westerner, but in the Arab world, the scene is hardly surprising.

Irrespective of their political orientations, Arab leaders always consider the religious reactions of both the *ulema* (religious scholars) and the masses in any decision they make. When Egypt's President Nasser launched his birth-control program, he had to secure the tacit approval of the then Rector of Al-Azhar (the Islamic University). But when a new Rector took over and disapproved of the program, the government quietly relaxed its efforts until some form of religious backing could be obtained.

In Tunisia, President Habib Bourguiba proposed in 1960 the abolition of fasting during the month of Ramadan, suggesting that the month-long fast with the resultant loss of work and productivity was a luxury his poor and developing country could ill afford. Bourguiba justified the abolition in terms of an Islamic law which allows a Muslim to break the fast if he is engaged in a holy war, or *jihad.* Bourguiba argued that his country was in a state of *jihad,* and that the struggle to obtain economic independence was comparable with a defensive war for national independence. In pursuit of this argument, he proposed new rules whereby restaurants, cafes, and other public places would keep normal hours. When Bourguiba sought to obtain a ruling, or *fatwa,* from the Mufti (grand religious leader) of Tunis, he was denied the *fatwa.* The great mass of the people observed the fast despite the President's wishes.[6]

The Revival of Islam

In recent years, there have been strong signs of an Islamic revival. This movement aims at spreading Islam out of the home and the mosque into the mainstream of political, social, legal, and economic life. It is designed to reestablish Islam as the basis of the modern state.

Throughout the Muslim world, stretching from the west coast of Africa to the Philippines, a conservative and militant religious movement is pressing for a return to the *Shari'a*, an Islamic code based on the Quran and the teachings of the Prophet Muhammad. To the Islamic revivalists, the movement signifies a fulfillment of a Quranic prophecy which states that a reform movement arises in the Muslim community once every century to rekindle the torch of Islam. Many Islamic leaders believe that such a moment has again arrived.

In Pakistan, militant Muslims overthrew the Westernized Prime Minister, Zulfiqar Al Butto, and established an Islamic state. In announcing the imposition of the *Shari'a,* the new head of state, Ziaul Haq, spelled out a list of Quranic punishments. Adulterers would be stoned to death, thieves would have their hands cut off, and Muslims caught drinking alcohol would receive lashes. A *zakat* (wealth tax) and an *ushur* (agricultural tax) would be used to finance the government's social welfare programs.

In Iran, an even more radical Muslim group took power in February 1979, after toppling the Shah and ending the Pahlavi dynasty. Under the leadership of the exiled Ayatollah Khomeini, the Muslim revivalists proclaimed Iran as an Islamic republic with the *Shari'a* as its cornerstone.

In outlining the features of the new regime, Khomeini expressed his hope of creating a society "in the image of Muhammad." Accordingly, gambling, drinking, interest charges, and prostitution were abolished, and Western-style laws were replaced by divine laws. For Muslims, sexual and family matters were to be ruled by Islamic laws and administered by the *mullas* (religious leaders). One month after coming to power, the revolutionaries in Iran executed six men charged with murder and sex and drug offenses. One youth was sentenced to death for raping an eleven-year-old girl, and several men were flogged for engaging in gambling and promiscuity.

In neighboring Afghanistan, the authority of the Marxist regime has been seriously challenged by fiercely religious tribes who have been mounting a guerrilla war to bring it down. The trouble began when sympathetic urbanites joined villagers who had marched to protest anti-Islamic measures and mistreatment of religious leaders. One particularly insensitive step taken by the government was the replacement of Afghanistan's green, red, and black flag with a red one. In a country that is 90 percent Muslim, that was an affront to a religion which traditionally includes the Islamic green in its national flag. Not surprisingly, attempts of the Afghani religious leaders to overthrow the Marxist regime draw inspiration from the Iranian revolution which has demonstrated to them that Muslim revivalists can overthrow an anti-Islamic regime even though it is supported by a great power.*

---

*In December 1979, the Soviet Union sent about 85,000 troops into Afghanistan to shore up its shaky Marxist government with no discernible success.

Thus far, success of the Islamic resurgence movement has been largely confined to non-Arab Muslim countries. The only Arab states that have formally embraced the *Shari'a* are Saudi Arabia, Libya, as well as a few Persian Gulf states. Actually, Saudi Arabia, since its creation as a state, has been the most vigilant of all countries in applying the *Shari'a*. Public cinemas, alcohol, and gambling are prohibited, and even coin-operated amusements are banned. In squares outside the central mosques in Riyad and Jiddah, public beheadings, amputations, and whippings are performed regularly on the first Friday of every month. In 1978, two Britons, accused of selling liquor, were flogged in public. And more recently, a Saudi princess was shot dead in the Jidda bazaar for eloping with a commoner; her lover was publicly beheaded.

In discussing the effectiveness of such measures as a deterrent to crime, the Saudi interior minister said: "Islamic law is the best method of preventing crime and of dealing with it after it occurs."[7] Lending its support to this contention, the Pakistani government declared that the rate of crimes of all kinds has dropped significantly since the adoption of the Islamic law. "If one severed hand can bring us six months of peace," said Pakistan's President, "then it is worth it."[8]

Islamic revival has been a cause of concern to a number of Arab countries, notably Egypt. In Egypt, Muslim revivalists have become prominent within the past few years. This is due partly to causes similar to those which provoked the Islamic backlash against Westernization and foreign influence in Iran and Pakistan. As Western investment, courted by President Sadat, increased, so did consumer goods, inflation, and rapid changes in morals and urban life styles. Perplexed, many Egyptians, like the Iranians and the Pakistanis, returned to religion. But Egypt's changing morals and manners of living are not the only causes of the religious resurgence. Muslim militants are bitterly opposed to Sadat's peace policies toward Israel, which has left Jerusalem—the third holiest site in Islam—still under Israeli control.

Today, the Islamic right wing is the most significant power center in Egypt; it aims at overthrowing the Sadat regime and replacing it with an Islamic government based on the Quran.* The fundamentalist fervor has taken place not only among the large numbers of the country's devout peasants, but also among university students. On the campuses of Egypt's twelve universities with a total enrollment of about half a million students, the Islamic activists control eight of the twelve student unions, and they are strong in the others. Perhaps a third of all coeds now wear the Islamic dress, covering everything except the face and the hands.

President Sadat is well aware of the potential threat the fundamentalists pose to his regime. Despite his warning that "politics and religion cannot mix," Sadat appears to have decided to control Muslim resurgence in his country by joining it. His government began circulating pictures of Sadat praying in a mosque and reverently kissing a copy of the Quran. To satisfy some Islamic demands, Sadat ordered the construction of more religious

---

*On October 6, 1981 (as this book went to press) several gunmen connected with the Muslim Brotherhood movement assassinated President Sadat as he was reviewing a military parade.

schools and the training of more preachers. Attempts are also being made to introduce religion as an official subject in universities, and committees in the Egyptian parliament are completing legislation to enact some aspects of the *Shari'a* into public law.

Causes of the Islamic Revival

Although the conditions giving rise to Muslim militancy vary from country to country, two underlying causes appear to be common in all. The first is the Muslims' repudiation of Western social values, and the second is their rejection of any type of non-Islamic political institutions.

Westernization has come to the Muslim world by one of two routes: the material and the personal. Material influences have come with such things as Western consumer goods, fashions, equipment, newspapers, magazines, films, radio, and TV. Personal influences have come from contact with Westerners in both the Muslim world and in the West. Western diplomats and businessmen operating in Muslim countries have directly or indirectly left their imprint on the thinking of many Muslims who came into contact with them. In the meantime, Muslim students studying in the West returned home with many Western ideas and attitudes. The same forces that shaped Western social patterns began to invade Muslim societies, but the rate of change in Muslim societies has been vastly accelerated. Changes which took the West four centuries to adjust to, and with considerable difficulty that is evident even today, have been compressed in Muslim societies into less than a century, in some countries even into a few decades.

The impact of the Western cultural invasion on Muslim societies has been unsettling; it resulted in an "explosive dislocation of the old ways that augurs a 'parting' from traditional Islam far more radical than anything that has gone in the past."[9] Along with such obvious things as traffic congestion, Westernization has put tremendous strains on the entrenched Muslim conventions and mores. It has "weakened parental authority and family cohesion and caused a movement from village to city. Young Arabs who have been educated in Western nations return home with new technical skills but also with less of the religious conviction their countries value so highly."[10]

The Muslim world is now beginning to experience some of the same social ills—broken homes, divorces, neglect of children, sexual promiscuity—that have characterized Western society since industrialization. All these new social phenomena are abhorrent to Muslims who perceive them as anti-Islamic and as a grave threat to their time-honored mores and traditions. In one sense, the return to Islam is a form of defense mechanism which is a consequence of the Muslims' rejection of what they call "Western decadence" and "Western immorality."

Another reason for the Islamic resurgence is disillusionment with non-Islamic political institutions. Since World War I, Muslim countries have adopted a variety of political systems, including Western-style parliamentary institutions, monarchical autocracies, and military dictatorships of both the socialist and the capitalist variations. Despite their differences, all these political systems share one characteristic in common; they are non-Islamic in nature.

Muslim radicals have always stood in opposition to these secular systems. Not only do they regard the systems as a symbol of foreign influence but they also hold them responsible for the social, economic, and political ills afflicting Muslim societies. Perhaps no greater factor has embittered the Muslim conservatives and turned their opposition to the secular regimes into political activism than the loss of Jerusalem, one of Islam's holiest cities, to the Israelis during the 1967 war. If there ever existed any hopes among the Muslim radicals of the ability of secular political systems to restore the past glories of Islam, these hopes died with the disastrous defeat of the Arabs in the 1967 war.

The loss of Jerusalem wounds all Muslims in the deepest sense, irrespective of their native country or the official policy of their rulers. A good case in point is the dramatic turn of events in Iran, following the downfall of the Shah. For many years, the Shah had maintained friendly and cooperative relations with Israel. In so doing, he not only ignored the sentiments of his Muslim-Arab neighbors but also disregarded the popular will of his predominantly Muslim population who sympathized with the Arab cause.

The hostile feelings of the Iranian masses toward Israel burst to the surface immediately after the Muslim revivalists came to power. One of the first acts of the new Iranian regime was to sever its diplomatic ties with Israel and to cut off all oil supplies to that state. After turning over Israel's diplomatic headquarters to the Palestine Liberation Organization, the new Iranian leaders pledged their total support for the Palestinian struggle against Israel. This kind of identification with the Palestinian cause is common to Muslims throughout the world, and it is primarily aimed at the recovery of Jerusalem and the restoration of Islamic dignity. The revivalists now believe that Islam is the answer to their problems, and that it will succeed where secular ideologies have failed.

Prospects of the Islamic Revival

The Islamic revival has its detractors. Aside from the Marxists who fear the devastating impact of a religious renaissance on their movement, many liberal Muslims are strongly opposed to making the *Shari'a* the law of the land. They fear that resurgent conservatism could turn Islamic societies increasingly inward, and could widen the gulf between the Muslim world and the West by slowling the urgently needed modernization of their backward countries. Emancipated women, who long ago discarded the veil and entered universities and the work force, fear that their hard-earned rights will be swept away once the strict Islamic laws are faithfully enforced.

Muslim revivalists do not view such difficulties as insurmountable. They maintain that Islam's greatest strength has always been a certain degree of flexibility under pressure. Throughout history, they say, Islam has been in constant interplay with the processes of society, and the result has been a working compromise between the Islamic code and the needs of each era. There are some signs indicating the Muslim revivalists' readiness to bend the law to suit the changing social requirements. The Pakistani government, for example, has assured women that their existing freedoms will not be rescinded. Like Saudi Arabia, Pakistan has also replaced bank interest charges with "income payments" or "service charges," practices not specifically prohibited by the Quran.*

Despite the complex social ills it normally engenders, the process of modernization currently sweeping the Muslim world is irreversible. The conservatives may be able to slow it down, but they cannot turn it back.

The big question facing the Muslim radicals is whether they can revive old morality and at the same time produce goods and services. In other words, will the new Islamic movement be able to meet the challenges of a technological world with an institution based on thirteen-centuries-old traditions and values? One cannot say with any certainty if Islam will succeed where the secular regimes have failed. It will all depend on how willing the Muslim leaders are in bending the 7th century Islamic law to suit the special requirements of the last quarter of the 20th century.

Summary

This chapter is designed to introduce the business executive to Islam, one of the principal forces conditioning the attitudes of the Arabs. The following statements summarize the major points covered in the chapter.

1. Islam means submission to the will of Allah, the Arabic word for God. It was revealed to the Prophet Muhammad in 610 A.D.

2. Muhammad considered himself, and is considered by Muslims, to be human. Unlike Christ, the Son of God, Muhammad is not divine. Hence, Muslims resent being called Muhammadans, an erroneous appellation based on a faulty analogy between the relationship of Christians to Christ and Muslims to Muhammad.

    There are many similarities between Islam and Christianity. Both agree that one God created the universe, that Christ was miraculously born of a virgin, that he rose into heaven, and that God will grant men eternal life if they obey His divine will. But the analogy between Christ (the Son of God) and Muhammad (the Prophet), with the attendant appellation of Muslims as Muhammadans, is incorrect.

*Islam condemns the practice of *riba* which means usury or the charging of interest. The Islamic doctrine stipulates that one cannot earn something unless one has made an effort and taken a risk. Ever since the emergence of the banking industry in the Muslim world, the question of interest has been the subject of heated debate. The orthodox Muslims refuse to accept interest, whereas the liberals accept it. The moderates accept gifts, commissions, or service charges in lieu of interest for investing their funds.

3. Islam is more than a religion; it is the totality of culture. In Islam, there is no separation of "church" and "state." The Islamic community, at least in the classical sense, is at once a religious brotherhood, a political association, and a social order.

   Islam is a regulator of conduct concerning such diverse matters as war, peace, politics, economics, authority, family life, the individual's relationship to his fellow citizens, inheritance, sexual intercourse, marriage, divorce, clothing, sports, the suckling of children, and so on.

4. Islam requires its followers to adhere to the following six duties which are known as the "pillars of Islam":

   a. Profession of the Faith (*Al-Shihadah*). The first duty of a Muslim is open profession of the belief that "there is no god but Allah and Muhammad is the messenger of God."

   b. Prayer (*Sl-Salah*). Prayer is prescribed five times daily between daybreak and nightfall.

   c. Almsgiving (*Al-Zakat*). Muslims are required to distribute 2.5 percent of their gross earnings to the poor.

   d. Fasting *(Al-Sawm)*. During the lunar month of Ramadan, a Muslim is enjoined from eating, drinking, smoking, and indulging in any bodily gratification such as sexual intercourse.

   e. Pilgrimage *(Al-Haj)*. All able-bodied Muslims with the financial means are required to make their pilgrimage to Mecca at least once in a lifetime.

   f. Holy war *(Al-Jihad)*. *Al Jihad* literally means exertion of a Muslim to spread the Islamic faith, which does not necessarily have to be through war.

5. Authority in Islam derives from the Quran, the *Hadith,* and the *Ijtihad*:

   a. The Quran is regarded by Muslims as the word of God, revealed to Muhammad through the angel Gabriel. The Quran is Islam's miracle. To the Muslims, no human being could have written with such ravishing felicity; the language of the Quran is the best Arabic one could possibly imagine.

   b. The *hadith* consists of the sayings of Muhammad as described by his closest companions. The Muslims resort to the *hadith* in settling issues with which the Quran does not clearly and specifically deal.

   c. Meaning "the right to free interpretation," the *Ijtihad* was devised to enable local Muslim jurists to deal with problems arising out of the Islamic expansion into alien societies.

6. The early Muslims were able to spread their faith with a remarkable speed. Within less than a century, the Muslims established an empire that was larger than the Roman empire at its zenith.

7. The Muslims produced a great civilization as evidenced in their enormous contributions in medicine, mathematics, astronomy, history, architecture, and literature.

8. Dispute over the legitimacy of certain caliphs (successors to Muhammad)

eventually led to the fragmentation of the Islamic world into splinter states making the Muslims vulnerable to foreign invaders.

9. In the 16th century, the Muslims of the Middle East had been brought under the domination of the Ottoman Turks. In the late 19th century and early 20th century, they came under the control of the West.

10. In recent years, there emerged an Islamic revivalist movement aimed at reestablishing Islam as the basis of the modern state. The movement received official embodiment in Iran, Pakistan, and to some degree in Libya.

Footnotes

[1]Sanche de Gramont, "Muhammad: The Prophet Armed," *Horizon,* Vol. 13, Summer 1971, pp. 20-23.

[2]Don Peretz, *The Middle East Today* (New York: Holt, Rinehart and Winston, Inc., 1963), p. 29.

[3]*Ibid.,* p. 34.

[4]Bernard Lewis, *The Arabs in History* (New York: Harper and Row, Publishers, 1960), p. 140.

[5]James Morris, "What is an Arab?" *Horizon,* Vol. 13, Summer 1971, p. 12.

[6]Bernard Lewis, "The Return of Islam," *Commentary,* Vol. 61, January 1976, p. 47.

[7]*Newsweek,* December 5, 1977, p. 77.

[8]*Newsweek,* February 26, 1979, p. 14.

[9]John S. Badeau, "Islam and the Middle East," *Foreign Affairs,* Vol. 38, October 1959, p. 61.

[10]Nicholas C. Proffitt, "The Arabs and the West," *Newsweek,* October 28, 1974, p. 38.

Chapter 4

The Dimensions of
Arab Nationalism

Our discussion in the previous chapter centered on Islam, one of the major forces influencing the Arabs' attitude. Another force with which the business executive ought to acquaint himself, as a means of developing a better understanding of the Arabs, is Arab nationalism.

The late King Ibn Saud of Saudi Arabia is reported to have said: "Two things are more important to me than anything else in my life. First is my religion, and second is my Arabism."[1] This statement sums up the pivotal place which not only Islam but also Arabism or, more specifically, Arab nationalism occupies in the Arabs' life. Arab nationalism has shown itself to be a powerful political and social force since the 19th century. It is deeply rooted in the religious and psychological dimensions of the Arabs' modern history. In this chapter, we will seek to explore the historical development and current status of the concept of Arab nationalism.

In the previous chapter, we pointed out that the disintegration of the Islamic Empire coincided with the emergence of Ottoman Turkey as a world power. In 1517, the Turks captured Damascus and Cairo and then succeeded in extending their rule over the entire Arabic-speaking countries. The Ottoman domination of the Arab world lasted for four centuries.

During this period, the Arab world slipped into a "Dark Age" of its own. The Muslim civilization, once far more advanced than anything that Europe of the "Dark Ages" could show, was but a ruin, displaying all the marks of decay. The Arab society of the 18th century had very few virtues; "its economy was not only stagnant but actually retrogressing. Its politics were characterized by venality, rapacity, insecurity and oppression. Its intellectual and artistic life was barren. Worst of all, it lived in a smug, self-satisfied lethargy, completely isolated from the outside world."[2] Agriculture, the mainstay of the economy of the region, languished under a regime which taxed unmercifully, and periodic famine and epidemic were regarded as a normal visitation of God's wrath.

Under these circumstances, the concept of nationality was unknown to the Arabs. In general, the Arabs identified themselves either in terms of their religious affiliation or the town of their origin. Thus, there was the

Sunni Muslim, the *Shi'i* Muslim, the Christian, and the Jew. And there was the Baghdadi, the Halabi (Aleppine), the Shami (Damascene), and the Misri (Cairene). In those days, the Arabs did not perceive themselves as members of a Syrian or an Iraqi nation, let alone an Arab nation.

The Arab Awakening

The Arabs' political awakening was an outgrowth of an intellectual renaissance whose impetus had come from the West. Of the numerous novel ideas the Arabs imported from the West, nationalism and political democracy were the most important.

Seeds of the Arab intellectual awakening were first sown during the latter part of the 18th century. In 1798, a French expeditionary force under General Napoleon Bonaparte invaded Egypt, opening a new phase in the history of Western influence in the Middle East. Along with his other equipment, Napoleon brought to Egypt an Arabic press which was the first of its kind in the Middle East. Originally used by the French invaders a a propaganda tool, the press, known as *Matba'at Bulaq,* became the official printing institution of the Egyptian government.

This abrupt contact with the West kindled the Arabs' intellectual spark and gave them the first knock that helped to awaken them from their long slumber. Contemporary historians view the French invasion of Egypt as "a watershed in history—the first armed inroad of the modern West into the Middle East,...the first impulse to modernization and reform."[3]

When the French invaders were later expelled from Egypt, the Arab intellectual revival found its greatest impetus in the efforts of Muhammad Ali to modernize Egypt. Considered as the founder of modern Egypt, this remarkable man of Persian and Turkish ancestry was raised in Albania, where his father was an Ottoman official. After becoming an officer in the Turkish army, Muhammad Ali was sent to Egypt with an Ottoman force to drive out the French occupation force. In 1803, after the French had evacuated Egypt, Muhammad Ali was appointed as the Ottoman Sultan's viceroy with the title of Pasha of Egypt. In 1805, he became Egypt's undisputed military and political figure.

Realizing the potentiality of the new contacts with the West as a means of solidifying his power, Muhammad Ali engaged in a concerted effort to modernize Egypt. He started dispatching Egyptian students to be trained in Europe and launched a program designed to establish schools not only for military science but for medicine, pharmacy, engineering, and agriculture.

In Syria and Lebanon, the first real impetus to intellectual awakening was provided by Ibrahim Pasha, Muhammad Ali's son, and by Western Christian missionaries. Called by his admirers the founder of modern Arabism, Ibrahim Pasha occupied Syria from 1831 to 1841. During this period, he established a secular school system patterned after the educational system introduced into Egypt by his father. He also pursued a liberal policy which opened the door to Western influence and attracted Europeans to the Middle East in increasing numbers.

Among the various Western groups who descended on the Middle East and who proved to have a significant and lasting impact on Arab renaissance were the rival Christian missionaries. In the process of propagating their religious doctrines, Western missionaries had fostered an intellectual awareness that was instrumental in undermining the political and social structure of the Ottoman regime. Taking advantage of Ibrahim Pasha's liberal policies, Christian missionaries began opening their own religious schools. Thus, the American Presbyterian missionaries, who brought with them their own Arabic press as an aid to their educational activities, operated 33 schools by 1860. In 1866, they opened the Syrian Protestant College which was later renamed the American University of Beirut. The French Jesuits were also permitted to open a number of schools, one of which was the Universite de St. Joseph.

The impact of French culture on the Arabs was significant. Muslim and Christian Arabs were both profoundly influenced by the rich stream of French political and social philosophy. However, while the French Catholics made valuable contributions to the progress of Syrian education in general, the American Protestant missionaries played a greater part in the revival of Arabic as a literary language after four centuries of neglect under the Ottoman rule. The Americans "unconsciously inspired the first nationalist aspirations, in the propagation of which some of their students and locally recruited teachers played a leading part."[4]

Unlike the French Catholic missionaries, who worked principally among the native Arab Catholic population, the American Protestant missionaries had no clientele. To secure wider circulation of the Protestant Bible, the American missionaries used their Arabic press to print an Arabic Bible and Protestant missionary tracts. Of even more importance to the Arab renaissance, the American Protestants printed textbooks and other educational materials in Arabic for use in their schools. In this manner, the American Protestant missionaries contributed more than any other group to the revival of Arabic language and literature.

The Arab intellectual renaissance was reflected in the proliferation of Arabic newspapers. Egypt witnessed its first newspaper in 1828 when Muhammad Ali founded *Al-Waqa'i Al-Misriyah* (Egyptian Events), which is still the official organ of the government. Syria had its first newspaper, *Hadiqat Al-Akhbar* (Orchard of News) in 1858. Twelve years later, Butrus Al-Bustani started in Beirut a political, scientific, and literary publication called *Al-Jinan* (Gardens). In 1876, Al-Bustani began publication of an Arabic encyclopedia (*Da'irat Al-Ma'arif*) of which he completed the first six volumes. The writings of this Christian scholar, which also included a dictionary and several textbooks, prepared the way for arousing national consciousness and starting the Arab national movement.

The Arabs' rediscovery of the West and the consequent cultural transformation of the Arab society has had the revitalizing effect of a renaissance.

The fog of ignorance, which for four centuries had dimmed the Arabic culture, was gradually being lifted.

Arab Nationalism and Islam

Arab nationalism began as a purely intellectual movement, pioneered principally by Lebanese and Syrian Christians who were educated at the American University of Beirut. From the very start, the Christian Arabs played a leading role in the study of Arab history and the revival of the Arabic language and were among the key exponents of secular nationalism The Muslim Arabs, however, showed little interest in secular nationalism and were attracted more to the idea of a pan-Islamic movement to counter what they considered at the time as the encroachment of the Christian West on the Arab world as symbolized by the French and the British occupation of Egypt and Algeria in the 1880's when the Ottoman Empire was in a state of disintegration.

During the early stages of their involvement in the national movement, the Muslim Arabs looked to their past for an emotional propeller, and they found it in Islam. By dwelling on Islam's past glories and by pointing to the golden age of the Islamic Empire, the Muslim nationalists hoped to ignite a sense of nationalistic fervor among the masses. They stressed the notion that Arab nationalism truly came into being with the birth of Islam in the 7th century and the consequent expansion of the Arabs and the establishment of a great Islamic Empire marked by a brilliant cultural heritage. Known as pan-Islamism, this movement was based on the concept of a brotherhood of the believers, and it aimed at the creation of an independent Islamic state based on a broad religious identity without regard to language differences or historical traditions.

Pan-Islamism was counterbalanced by the force of a secular nationalistic movement based on pan-Arabism. Whereas the pan-Islamic movement was espoused solely by Muslim Arabs, pan-Arabism was led primarily by Christian Arabs. As was mentioned earlier, the idea of Arab nationalism had begun among Christian intellectuals before it did among Muslims. Educated in foreign schools and strongly influenced by Western culture, the Christian Arabs had read Arab history through the lenses of modern Western scholarship. Consequently, they were little concerned with the Islamic revival and were attracted more by a national rather than a religious identity.

The Christian Arabs were the first to give impetus to the Arab renaissance and the first to formulate an ideology of modern Arab nationalism. Through their intensive studies of Arabic history and culture, the Christians showed that the Arabs had developed a highly advanced civilization after as well as before the birth of Islam. More importantly, they showed that the Christians had contributed significantly to this civilization. Arabic civilization, therefore, had not been a purely religious venture from which the Christians could be excluded. On the contrary, it had many features completely unrelated to religion.[5] Thus, in place of the religious bond, the Christians chose common language and common culture as the binding cement of Arab nationalism.

The Christian Arabs, however, were cognizant of the fact that they could not realistically become leaders of an Arab revolutionary movement whose aim was to free the predominantly "Muslim" Arabs from the rule of a "Muslim" Turkish ruler. Convinced of the essentiality of Muslim support, the Christians endeavored to persuade the leading Muslim Arabs with the soundness of secular nationalism. To that end, the Christians utilized their newspapers and magazines as a platform for the propagation of their ideology. When the Muslim Arabs joined the Christians in the new secular movement, Arab nationalism came to be a truly significant political force.

Emergence of National Societies

At the start of their movement, the Arab nationalists' demands were modest. They did not advocate complete separation from the Ottoman Empire; they merely called for local autonomy within a multinational "Ottoman Commonwealth of Nations." At one point, their hopes appeared closer to reality when the Young Turks seized power in Turkey in 1908 in an effort to salvage the Ottoman Empire from complete collapse.

Prior to the Young Turks' takeover, signs of debilitation of the Ottoman Empire were evident everywhere. The European powers, awaiting an opportunity to replace the Turkish domination in the Middle East, quickly moved in when it became obvious that the Turkish hold on the Arabs was rapidly slipping. By the end of the 19th century, the French had conquered Algeria, Tunisia, and Morocco; and the British had occupied Egypt.

To ward off the European encroachment on the rest of their empire, and motivated by a desire to introduce internal reforms, a diverse group of political and military Turkish leaders joined forces to overthrow the despotic rule of the Ottoman Sultan. In 1908, a coup d'etat, engineered by the Young Turks under the guidance of the Committee of Union and Progress (CUP), ultimately succeeded in ending the despotism of Sultan Abdul Hamid.

The new regime in Turkey was a welcome development to the Arabs who believed in the Young Turks' promises of progress and equality among all the Ottoman subjects. The Arab nationalists expected the new regime to lead to a large measure of autonomy and local government.

It was under these circumstances that the first Arab nationalist society emerged. In 1909, a group of leading Arabs organized and Arab "Literary Club" in Constantinople. Thinking that it was a purely cultural center, the Committee of Union and Progress felt no need to interfere with the activities of the club. The Literary Club, however, developed into a center for Arab nationlists in the Turkish capital. Soon thereafter, an Egyptian officer in the Ottoman army, Aziz Ali, organized a secret nationalist society, known as *Al-Qahtaniyah,* aimed at achieving complete equality of the Arabs and the Turks.

By this time, at least ten other organizations opposed to Turkish domination sprang up among the Arabs in Istanbul, Damascus, Beirut, Aleppo, Baghdad, and other cities. The most significant and the most radical of these groups was the Young Arab Society *(Al-Fatat),* founded in 1911 by seven Arab students studying in Paris. The birth of *Al-Fatat* was the Arabs' answer to the Young Turks' failure to show any readiness to grant autonomy or equality to the Arabs. In fact, the Young Turks not only reneged on their earlier promises of equality but went beyond that by insisting that all Arabs become Turkified within a homogeneous Ottoman state. Some radical members of the Committee of Union and Progress even wanted to abolish the Arabic language and translate the Quran into Turkish. When the Muslim *ulema* (religious scholars) protested, Islam itself was attacked.

Realizing that the Young Turks had no intentions of granting any type of local rule to the Arabs within a decentralized Ottoman state, members of *Al-Fatat* abandoned all hope of cooperation with the Turks. Radicalized by the Turks' intransigence, the Arab leaders adopted as their rallying cry complete Arab independence and creation of a sovereign Arab state in the Middle East.

In 1913, on the initiative of *Al-Fatat,* an Arab congress was convened in Paris, in which representatives of all Arab national groups participated. The congress drafted a platform known as the Paris Agreement, spelling out the Arabs' demands for independence. When the Committee of Union and Progress refused to respond to the Arabs' demands, Aziz Ali, the Egyptian officer, founded a new secret revolutionary society in 1914. Called *Al-Ahd* (The Covenant), the new organization consisted mainly of Iraqi army officers who were the most numerous regional group of Arabs in the Ottoman army. Members of *Al-Ahd* vowed to devote their lives to becoming proficient officers so that they might be fully prepared to become military leaders of the Arab revolution. *Al-Ahd* became to the Arab army officers what *Al-Fatat* was to the civilian upper-class intellectuals.

Aziz Ali's role in the nationalist movement became known to the Turks. Consequently, he was arrested and brought to trial on charges of treason. In 1915, Jamal Pasha, the Turkish governor in Syria, held a series of treason trials which resulted in the execution of 34 nationalists and the deportation of hundreds of prominent Arabs and their families to remote parts of Anatolia. By now, the Arab nationalists, even those who were moderate in their views, became convinced that a complete break with the Ottoman Empire was inevitable.

The Arab Revolt

Instead of dampening the nationalistic fervor, the suffering and oppression endured by the Arabs under the Young Turks' rule produced a widespread sense of rebelliousness among the Arab masses. What used to be secret revolutionary societies now turned into openly defiant political parties, all of which struggled for the one goal of achieving Arab freedom and independence.

When Turkey entered World War I on the side of the Central Powers, it became evident to the Arabs that the defeat of Turkey and her allies would bring about the partition of the Ottoman Empire. Aware of the imperialistic schemes of the Allies, the politically literate Arabs became convinced that if they did not receive assurances of their independence from one or more of the Allies, their countries would be divided as spoils of war. Consequently, the Arabs decided that their aspirations for independence could best be achieved through some type of understanding with the superpower of the Allies, Great Britain.

With this in mind, the Arab nationalists drafted the Damascus Protocol, setting forth their demand for a recognition of the independence of the Arabs. Negotiations between the Arabs and the British were carried on through an exchange of letters between Sherif Husein, keeper of the holy places in Mecca, and Sir Henry McMahon, the British high commissioner in Egypt. The negotiations led to a form of military alliance known as the Husein-McMahon Agreement. On the basis of this agreement, Great Britain promised to lend its support to Arab independence; in return, the Arabs agreed to provide military support for the Allied forces operating in the Middle East.

When a Turkish force, dispatched to reinforce the Ottoman troops stationed in Yemen, arrived in Medina, Sherif Husein became alarmed. He feared that his correspondence with the British might have become known to the Turks, and that the force had been sent to deal with him. After receiving the news from Syria of the political executions, Sherif Husein and his sons decided that nothing was to be gained by further procrastination. On June 5, 1916, Sherif Husein fired a shot in the air, heralding the start of the Arab Revolt.

European Colonialism

As Great Britain was making commitments in support of the Arabs' national aspirations, secret political arrangements among the various Allies were being formulated to carve up the Ottoman Empire. In 1915 Great Britain, France, and Russia reached an accord concerning their interests in the Middle East. Known as the Sykes-Picot Agreement, the accord proved to be a vital key to the future of the Ottoman Arab lands.

When World War I ended with the destruction of the Ottoman Empire, all Arab provinces were placed under British and French control. Great Britain's share included Egypt, Iraq, Palestine, Transjordan, and the skeikdoms of the Arabian peninsula. France was awarded Syria and Lebanon. Russia's claims to the spoils of war had been renounced by the Bolshevik Government which later came to power in 1917.

During the post-war period, Great Britain and France intensified their efforts to solidify their control over the area. Great Britain attempted to make permanent her direct rule over Egypt, Iraq, Transjordan, and Palestine. France pursued a divide-and-rule policy aimed at encouraging the aspirations of minority groups living in small geographical areas.

In 1919 the American President, Woodrow Wilson, made an effort to persuade the British and the French to modify their colonial schemes and grant the inhabitants of the area the right to self-determination. To that end, Wilson set up a commission, known as the King-Crane Commission, which was dispatched to the Middle East with the purpose of feeling out the wishes of the people.

Encouraged by Wilson's initiative, the Arab nationalists convened a General Syrian Congress in Damascus. The Congress expressed its strong desire for the establishment of a United Syrian monarchy under Emir Faisal (one of Sherif Husein's sons) to include an area from the Taurus Mountains to the borders of Arabia and from the Mediterranean to Iraq. After visiting Syria and meeting with the Arab nationalists, the King-Crane Commission issued a report in which it expressed its opposition to the French design to divide the Levant (The area encompassing Syria, Lebanon, Transjordan, and Palestine) into smaller states. In its recommendations, the Commission stated:

> The territory concerned is too limited, the population too small, and the economic, geographic, racial and language unity too manifest to make the setting up of independent states within its boundaries desirable, if such a division can possibly be avoided. The country is very largely Arab in language, culture, traditions, and customs.[2]

The French as well as the British governments, who had previously boycotted the King-Crane Commission's activities, now ignored its recommendations.

Arab Independence

The Arabs' reaction to the new colonial rule of the European powers was swift. In some countries, agitation against foreign domination took the form of armed rebellion, in others, it was more constitutional in character.

In 1920, the Syrian General Congress transformed itself into a constituent assembly, declaring the independence of Syria (with Emir Faisal as its king) and demanding the evacuation of British and French troops from the entire area. Responding to the challenge, the French army ruthlessly crushed the nationalists and drove King Faisal out of the country. In Iraq, the British had to contend with a costly rebellion; and in Palestine, the British scheme to establish a Jewish homeland was met with protest and riots which in 1936 developed into a full-scale revolt.

After the French had succeeded in crushing the Syrian General Congress, the Arab nationalists sought to chart a new path for their movement. Instead of attempting to create an independent and unified state in the Middle East, they chose to work for the independence of each individual Arab country. Without publicly renouncing their aspirations for Arab unity, various Arab leaders focused on their own country's local problems, giving little thought to an over-all Arab policy.

Gradually, the Arabs were able to gain their freedom and independence by forcing the British and the French to relinquish their political and military control of the area. In the Arab East, Syria and Lebanon became independent republics in 1945. Transjordan was declared an independent monarchy in 1946. Sudan gained the right to self-determination in 1953. In Egypt, the 1954 Anglo-Egyptian agreement put an end to 70 years of British occupation. Iraq, which was first declared independent in 1932, with some restrictions, became a sovereign state in 1955. In 1961, the Sheikdom of Kuwait became independent; and in 1971, the United Arab Emirates (consisting of seven princedoms*) was proclaimed as an independent state. Of course, Saudi Arabia and Yemen had already been independent since they never fell to European domination. The only Arabs to be denied the right to self-determination have been the Palestinians who lost most of Palestine to the Israelis.

In the Arab West (*Al-Maghrib*, or the Arab states of North Africa), the Arab nationalist movement was slow in developing. Following a protracted struggle against European control, the North African Arab states finally achieved their independence. In 1951, Libya became an independent kingdom. In 1956, Tunisia was proclaimed an independent republic, and, in the same year, Morocco became a sovereign constitutional monarchy. In 1962, the Algerian revolution brought about Algeria's independence. Other members of the African Arab states, Somalia, Mauritania, and Djibouti, achieved their independence in 1960, 1970, and 1977 respectively.

Collapse of Parliamentary Systems

After coming into contact with the West, the Arabs were greatly impressed with the West's superior forms of government, military apparatus, and civil organizations. When Great Britain and France took the initiative in introducing in the Middle East political innovations closely modeled on their own institutions, they received the overwhelming support of the Arabs.

Parliamentary institutions proved to be a dismal failure in many Arab countries; they were soon to be swept away in a torrent of coups d'etat that characterized Middle Eastern politics between 1949-1958. The constitutional governments of Syria (1949), Egypt (1952), Iraq (1958), and Sudan (1958) were overthrown. In each of these countries, the coup d'etat replaced the

*The princedoms comprising the United Arab Emirates are: Abu Dhabit, Dubai, Sharjan, Ajman, Ummul Qaiwan, Ras Al-Khaimah, and Fujairan.

old parliamentary system with a centralized military government. Later, similar coups took place in Yemen (1962) and in Libya (1968), resulting in military dictatorships.

The demise of parliamentary systems cannot be attributed to one single factor. Rather, a host of forces have combined to replace the parliamentary institutions with military or one-party form of government. What follows constitutes a summary of the major forces.

Foreign Meddling in the Political Process

The continued presence of foreign influence during the delicate phase in which parliamentary institutions were being introduced seriously sabotaged the democratic process. French control of the Lebanese and Syrian political life made impossible the establishment of parliamentary habits and democratic processes. It made mockery of such practices as the peaceful and orderly competition among political parties, formation of political oppostion, and free election. In the Lebanese and Syrian general elections, held between 1927 and 1938, the French authorities manipulated the election in such a manner as to insure the election of the approved candidates only.

Britain's meddling in the internal political affairs of Egypt and Iraq, though more subtle than that of France, had similarly frustrating effects on the attitudes of those engaged in the political process. The British constantly used their influence to determine the character and composition of national governments.

Foreign-sponsored parliamentary systems gave the appearance but not the substance of democracy. The systems lacked those fundamentals (free election, political opposition, etc.) that infuse life and vitality into Western democracies. The colonial powers' constant meddling in the political process produced a deep sense of frustration and disillusionment, especially among the growing middle class of the interwar period. In one sense, then, the failure of the parliamentary system may be blamed not on any built-in defects in the system itself as much as on the manner in which the system was practiced.[7]

Superimposition of Parliamentary Systems

Western political institutions were clumsily grafted onto the Arab countries without adequate consideration as to whether these institutions were actually serviceable. It may be argued that a transplant of British and French forms of government in the Arab countries might have succeeded had it been accompanied by careful adaptation of Western constitutional law and administrative practices to the native milieu. This was not done. The high degree of illiteracy, poverty, ignorance, and feudalism which pervaded Arab societies, was not conducive to the cultivation of the sophisticated arts of democratic government.[8]

Instead of developing a well-thought-out plan to prepare the natives for democracy or to come up with an indigenous political institution, the Arab leaders merely chose the easy route of superimposing ready-made copies of Western systems on their countries. The Arab leaders operated on the naive assumption that what works in the West would also work with equal success in their countries. In some cases, parliamentary systems were transplanted merely because they were a symbol of modernity and progress.

Monopoly of Power by a Privileged Class

The Arab leaders who spearheaded the Arab national movement early in this century came from the upper strata of the society and represented only a small urban minority. They were primarily concerned with freeing their countries of foreign domination. Having attained this goal, they turned out to be more interested in sharing power among themselves than in facilitating the smooth working of the democratic process. Their politics consisted of a bloc-party system, primarily designed to safeguard the status and the influence of their social class. The young and progressive leaders of the 1920's became old and conservative power monopolizers in the 1940's.

Emergence of Doctrinal Parties

In the 1940's, a new generation of Arab nationalists grew to maturity; they were molded by influences radically different from those to which the older generation had been exposed in its formative years. Actually, the first doctrinal parties were formed within the growing groups of the educated class in the early 1930's. Among these were the People's Party in Iraq, the Syrian Nationalist Party in Lebanon, and the Arab Renaissance Party in Syria. Although the Communist Party was founded in the 1920's in a number of Arab countries, it did not possess real strength until the 1940's.

Although the various doctrinal parties differed in their goals, they all shared a common characteristic which set them apart from the political groupings of the old generation; each possessed a systematic ideology as a basis for its political and social action.[9] When some of these parties were denied membership in the exclusive parliamentary club controlled by the old guard, they went underground, using violent methods to bring down the parliamentary systems.

Desire for Rapid Change

Although the younger nationalists subscribed to the ideals of democracy, they found the constitutional process painfully slow in achieving the economic and social progress their countries sorely needed. What aggravated the situation was the fact that few members of the old guard were genuinely interested in mounting any serious programs to alleviate the blight of the countryside and the city slums. Whatever reforms the old guard introduced were centered at the top of the society. Throughout the Middle East, the peasants, constituting four out of five of the population, continued to live in poverty, unaffected by Westernization in the big cities.

Disillusioned with the ability of the constitutional order to fulfill their expectations for rapid reforms, the young nationalists argued that "what the Arab society needs is not a constitutional government that functions slowly and hesitantly, but a vigorous leadership that will revitalize, by force if need be, the dormant forces of the Arab peoples."[10] According to them, "the framework of the past is too outmoded, rigid, and shot through with privileges to be adopted as a basis for a modern state with a higher standard of living for the common man."[11] Before a truly progressive modern state could emerge, there had to be a total change in the social and political structure.

Denied participation in the political process, many of the younger nationalists looked to the army for leadership. The army was perceived as the best agent for bringing down the old order and for carrying out social and economic changes since it possessed power, discipline, and a sense of duty. Furthermore, it was thought that a military government would be more responsive to the needs of the masses. Since most Arab officers came from humble backgrounds, they would more likely identify with the masses and be more committed to their welfare than the old feudal rulers.

The Palestine Defeat

No single factor contributed to the collapse of parliamentary systems as much as the Arabs' defeat in the Palestine war of 1948. The shock of the defeat at the hands of a relatively small, foreign, Jewish force made the Arabs painfully aware of the ineptness and the widespread corruption of their regimes. The fact that the Jews were able to establish a state in their midst and keep their vastly superior numbers at bay had brought the Arab ego to a debasing low. The shattering effect of the war was so great it may be stated that "although the Arabs had started stumbling toward modernization at the end of the nineteenth century, they were not really aroused to a full awakening until after their defeat in Palestine in 1948."[12]

The overwhelming blow to the Arab national pride was particularly felt by army officers. Many junior officers, greatly angered by the Palestine debacle, decided that the only way to restore Arab honor was to remove the corrupt political regimes which were held responsible for the disaster. By now it became clear even to the skeptics that the pattern of progress the Arab world needed had to shift from creeping evolution to radical revolution.

Consequently, a series of military coups d'etat swept the Arab countries, beginning with Syria. But the most dramatic aftermath of the Palestine defeat was the Egyptian revolution of 1952. Led by Gamal Abdul Nasser and his group of young officers, Egypt's new revolutionary regime not only refused to collaborate with members of the old guard but completely destroyed their political, economic, and social bases. After abolishing the European-style monarchy, Nasser dissolved all political parties, discarded the Western-style constitution, and later proclaimed Egypt as a socialist state. Nasser's radical political, economic, and social ideas quickly spread to other Arab countries, serving as a source of inspiration to other revolutions soon to occur in Iraq, Sudan, Libya, and Yemen.

Nationalism and Arab Unity

Arab nationalism and the quest for Arab unity go hand in hand; Arab unity constitutes the premise as well as the goal of Arab nationalism. The basic premise underlying Arab nationalism is that the Arabs constitute one single nation, residing in a territory that stretches from the Atlantic Ocean to the Persian Gulf. Throughout this region, the Arabs possess certain common characteristics such as language, culture, historical heritage, and religion. To the Arab nationalists, achieving a unified Arab state in the region was not only logical but highly desirable. It would enable them to pool their resources in the face of the accelerating challenges of the 20th century and would help them to develop into a politically and economically respectable world power.

Attempts at creating a unified Arab state go back to the late 19th century when Muhammad Ali (founder of modern Egypt) and his son, Ibrahim, entertained such a scheme. After his son had conquered Syria, Muhammad Ali became the supreme ruler of an important portion of the Arab world which included such key centers as Mecca, Medina, Cairo, Jerusalem, and Damascus. However, Muhammad Ali failed to realize his dream. For one thing the concept of nationalism was still beyond the comprehension of the poverty-stricken villagers and townspeople. For another, Muhammad Ali and his son were not Arabs; they were of Albanian origin and had not even mastered the Arabic language "Their advocacy of an Arab national revival, wanting in the incentive of race and the eloquence of a rich language, lacked the force of spontaneity. Their driving motive was personal ambition, and their desire to revive the Arab Empire sprang primarily from their desire to acquire an empire."[13]

Plans for an Arab empire emerged once more early in the 20th century. This time they were pushed by Sherif Husein who engineered the 1916 Arab Revolt against the Turks in the hope of establishing an Arab kingdom encompassing the Arabian peninsula and the Fertile Crescent (Syria, Lebanon, Jordan, Palestine, and Iraq). These plans were thwarted by the British and the French governments who had a different scheme for the future of the Arab lands.

Instead of fulfilling their promise of helping Sherif Husein establish his envisioned kingdom, the British and the French divided the Middle East into smaller states under their direct control. The creation of such states proved to have a detrimental impact on the future of Arab unity; it resulted in the emergence of local loyalties, local political alignments, local economic systems, and, above all, local separatist tendencies. The West, the Arabs now argue, "had calculatedly thwarted the aims of Arab nationalism. It had left the Arabs disunited and weak so that, at the first opportunity, it could re-establish its domination.''[14]

The relentless effort of Arab nationalists to create some type of unity eventually culminated in the birth of the Arab League. In 1945, seven independent Arab countries established the League as a loose regional organization, designed to safeguard Arab independence and to promote political, economic, and cultural cooperation among member states as a prelude to achieving full Arab unity. By 1977, the number of member states rose to 22, including the Palestinian Liberation Organization as a full-voting member.

Since its inception, the Arab League's principal weakness has been its lack of power to enforce its resolutions except, of course, when such resolutions are agreed to unanimously by member states. The League is not a supernational organization, and its members have surrendered none of their sovereignty. Because of fundamental ideological differences among the Arab countries, particularly in regard to Arab unity, the League has all but abandoned its role as a promotor of political unity among the Arabs. Instead, the League's major efforts have been confined to promoting educational and cultural cooperation among member states.

Actually, the most aggressive moves toward Arab unity took place not within but outside the Arab League. For example, in 1958 Syria joined Egypt in forming the United Arab Republic under the leadership of Egypt's President Nasser who at that time had emerged as the most popular political figure and the principal advocate of Arab unity. In the early euphoria of this union, Yemen joined in what came to be known as the United Arab States. The Egyptian-Syrian union was short-lived, however; it broke up in 1961 when Syria pulled out after a military coup. Aside from the fact that the union was hastily executed for political considerations, the union was weakened by the Egyptian domination of the Syrian political process and by the physical separation of the two countries.

Even less successful was the Arab Federation formed by Iraq and Jordan, two weeks after the creation of the United Arab Republic. The Federation fell apart following the collapse of the Iraqi monarachy in a bloody revolution in 1958. In 1970, after Nasser's death, consultations among Sudan, Syria, Egypt, and Libya were undertaken to create a new federation. As a result, Syria, Egypt, Sudan, and Libya joined in the Union of Arab Republics. This move once again failed when Libya and Syria announced their opposition to President Sadat's entry into peace negotiations with Israel.

Although all Arabs agree on the desirability of unity, there is no consensus as to the mode of its achievement. Efforts in that direction have been frustrated by ideological differences, vested local interests, and intra-Arab distrust. Consequently, the road to Arab unity remains long and difficult; it is still a far-away dream.

Becoming increasingly aware of the enormous hurdles blocking their road to unity, the Arabs have within the recent past shifted their emphasis from achieving comprehensive unity to the establishment of a broader base of educational, cultural, and economic integration. Toward that end, they have been working at the promotion of economic cooperation, use of common textbooks, exchange of students and teachers, establishment of a network of communication and transportation, and the facilitation of the free movement of skilled and unskilled labor.

Arab Nationalism and Socialism

Socialism is viewed by Arab nationalists as an extension of Arab nationalism; it was born out of the failure of traditional regimes to carry out rapid industrialization, economic development, and social justice programs. Whereas Arab nationalism has as its primary goal the attainment of Arab sovereignty, socialism aims at achieving greater industrialization and social equality. The Arab socialist's emphasis on industrialization as a vehicle for achieving social justice has resulted in the transformation of government into a social agent, responsible for drawing up and implementing comprehensive plans for economic development. Acceptance of socialism as an official philosophy in some Arab countries has necessitated the take-over by government of all the principal means of production.

What is commonly known today as "Arab socialism" draws much of its substance from Western social ideology as well as Islam. Arab intellectuals, studying and traveling in Europe became acquainted with the various aspects of Western socialism after the turn of the century. While some intellectuals admired Western democracy and marvelled at its achievements, others saw in socialism the remedy for the backwardness of their societies and the solution to the immense social disparities between the haves and the have nots.

Socialism in the Arab world has also been influenced by Islam. Such Islamic ideas as charity, social justice, mutual assistance, and communal solidarity have been reinterpreted in light of contemporary social needs and have provided the emotional propeller for the new socialist doctrine. Rather than rejecting Islam, Arab socialists used its social ideas to provide their ideology with its moral strength and its unique features which distinguish it from other brands of socialist thought. The Islamic teachings gave socialism its non-Marxist character which may account for the appellation "Arab socialism" and also for some of the hostility many Arab socialists often exhibit toward Marxism.

Although socialism in the Arab world began to develop after World War I, it did not emerge as a meaningful political force until World War II. By the 1950's, socialism became a somewhat popular ideology in a number of Arab countries, just as it had in many other developing nations in Africa and Asia. Numerous socialist groups flourished in the Middle East, and many political organizations that were not really socialist adopted socialist slogans to compete for popular favor. Even the conservative members of the Muslim Brotherhood movement in Egypt used the teachings of Islam to develop their own brand of Islamic socialism.

The most prominent socialist party to emerge in the Arab world is the Arab Renaissance (*Baath*) Party. Organized in 1941 by Michel Aflaq (a Christian Syrian who studied in France), the party advocated the creation of a unified Arab world with socialism as its guiding doctrine. Aflaq's theory is to recreate in modern form the ancient glories of the Islamic-Arabic civilization. Present-day geographical divisions, according to the Baath's ideology, are only superficial and would disappear with a revival of national consciousness. The Baathist socialist doctrine advocates the nationalization of industry, distribution of government lands to sharecroppers, and creation of extensive social services.

The Baathists view socialism as a key to progress which in turn is viewed as a key to Arab unity. Without socialism, the citizens' well-being and the country's economic independence cannot be achieved. In the meantime, without social justice and economic independence, a unified Arab world would not be able to withstand the encroachment of the great powers. In the Baathist ideology, socialism and nationalism have, therefore, become synonymous.[15] In the 1950's, the Baathist ideology gained sufficient acceptance among the intellectual groups and army officers to enable it to come to power in Syria (1963) and Iraq (1968).

In their political structure, the Arab socialist governments constitute a one-party rule, backed by the military. Although fundamentally altered, the concept of democracy has not been theoretically dropped. To the Arab socialists, genuine democracy does not rest in such things as individual freedom and parliamentary structures. Rather, it stems from the true social and economic liberation of the individual and the consequent achievement of social justice and equality for the masses. A one-party regime, it is argued, is the only way to attain that goal with optimal speed and efficiency.

The Arab World in Transition

Since their 1916 revolt against the Ottoman domination, the Arabs have generally been endeavoring to attain three major objectives: sovereignty, economic progress, and political unity. Thus far, the Arabs, with the exception of the Palestinians, have become masters of their own lands. Their efforts at achieving economic progress have produced mixed results.

The only objective which has completely eluded the Arabs is political unity. Today, the political regimes run the gamut from theocracies to those based on socialist or even Marxist philosophies. Aside from the existence of monarchies and republics, there are conservative regimes and there are moderate and radical regimes. Not only do ideological schisms exist between the monarchies and the republics or the conservative and the radical regimes, but such schisms are also common among the conservatives themselves as well as among the radicals. Distrust, jealousy, and mere personality conflict are as much to blame for intra-Arab rivalries as genuine ideological differences. As a result of these conflicts, the ideal of Arab unity remains an elusive goal.

Since their rejection of the Western-style parliamentary systems, the Arabs have not been able to come up with a viable alternative. At one point, it was thought that "Arab socialism," which gained considerable popularity in the 1960's, might be the galvanizing force that could lead to a broader ideological consensus. Now, however, there are serious doubts that this will be the case. Although socialism has been adopted as the official philosophy of the regimes of Iraq, Syria, Libya, and South Yemen, it was dealt a serious setback in Egypt when President Sadat steered his country away from socialism in favor of economic liberalism and a limited form of parliamentary institution.

The Arabs are still in a process of transition. They have yet to settle on a political form of government that will enable them to achieve prosperity and unity and to regain their sense of national honor by arriving at some type of acceptable solution to the Palestinian problem. They are, in other words, still in quest of a future that is brighter than their present and their recent past. In the meantime, the Arab world continues to be in the throes of change, and it will undoubtedly be restless and unsettled for many years to come.

Summary

The purpose of this chapter is to enable the business executive to develop a better understanding of another force influencing the Arabs' attitude, namely, Arab nationalism. What follows is a summary of the major points covered in the chapter:

1. The concept of Arab nationalism first emerged as a result of the Arabs' contact with the West:
   a. In 1878, Egypt was invaded by Napoleon Bonaparte who introduced the first Arabic press in the Middle East.
   b. The French invasion of Egypt paved the way for further contacts. Western Christian missionaries descended on the Middle East, propagating their doctrines and, in the process, fostering an intellectual awareness among the Arab elites.
2. The Christian Arabs were the first to formulate an ideology of Arab nationalism based on common language, common culture, and shared territory. The Muslim Arabs espoused the idea of pan-Islamism, aimed at the creation of an independent Islamic state. Later, the Muslims joined ranks with the Christians in advocating a secular nationalistic movement primarily directed at freeing the Arabs from the Ottoman Turks who ruled the Arabs for nearly four centuries.
3. During World War I, the Arabs reached an accord (known as the Husein-McMahon Agreement) with Great Britain. Accordingly, Great Britain (the leader of the Allies) promised to back the Arab independence

movement in return for the Arabs' support for the Allied forces operating in the Middle East.

4. In 1916, the Arab Revolt against the Ottoman Turks, who sided with the
   Central Powers, began.

5. When World War I ended, the Allies reneged on their promises. Instead
   of granting independence to the Arabs, they divided the Middle East
   among themselves as spoils of war.

6. The period between World War I and World War II was marked by
   numerous Arab uprisings, aimed at freeing the Arabs from their new
   British and French masters.

7. After gaining full or partial independence, many Arab countries experi-
   mented with Western-style parliamentary systems. Most of these systems
   failed and were replaced by military dictatorships or one-party rules.
   The failure of parliamentary systems may be attributed to the following
   factors:
   a. The continued British and French meddling in the Arabs' political
      process.
   b. The clumsy superimposition of parliamentary systems on societies
      lacking in Western constitutional traditions.
   c. Monopoly of power by a privileged Arab class.
   d. Emergence of doctrinal parties.
   e. The Arabs' desire for rapid change.
   f. The Arabs' 1948 defeat in Palestine.

8. Since its inception, Arab nationalism has had three broad objectives.
   These are sovereignty, economic progress, and political unity:
   a. With the exception of the Palestinians, the Arabs have been able to
      attain full independence.
   b. The Arabs' efforts at achieving economic progress have produced
      mixed results.
   c. Arab unity has proved to be an elusive goal. Efforts in that direction
      have been hampered by local vested interests, ideological differences,
      and mere distrust.

   Disagreement among the Arabs on the particular form Arab unity
   ought to take may, at least in part, account for the instability and
   restlessness which characterize Arab politics at the present time.

Footnotes

[1]Osgood Caruthers, "Enigma That is the Arab," *The New York Times Magazine,*
October 20, 1957, p. 80.
[2]Charles Issawi, "The Arab World Heavy Legacy," in J.H. Thompson and R.D.
Reischawer (eds.), *Modernization in the Arab World* (Princeton, New Jersey:
D. Van Nostrand, Inc., 1966), pp. 13-14.
[3]Bernard Lewis, *The Middle East and the West* (Bloomington, Indiana: Indiana
University Press, 1964), p. 34.

⁴George E. Kirk, *A Short History of the Middle East* (New York: Frederick A. Praeger, 1959), p. 103.

⁵Hazem Z. Nuseibeh, "The Religious Factor in Arab Nationalism," in Benjamin Rivlin and Joseph S. Szyliowicz (eds.) *The Contemporary Middle East: Tradition and Innovation* (New York: Random House, 1965), p. 242.

⁶J.C. Hurewitz, *Diplomacy in the Near and Middle East* (Princeton, New Jersey: D. Van Nostrand Company, Inc., 1956), p. 67.

⁷Hisham Sharabi, *Nationalism and Revolution in the Arab World* (Princeton, New Jersey: D. Van Nostrand Company, Inc., 1966), p. 57.

⁸Maurice Harari, *Government and Politics of the Middle East* (Englewood Cliffs, New Jersey: Prentice-Hall, 1962), p. 162.

⁹Hisham Sharabi, 1966, *op. cit.*, p. 59.

¹⁰Benjamin Rivlin and Joseph S. Szyliowicz (eds.), *The Contemporary Middle East: Tradition and Innovation* (New York: Random House, 1965), p. 442.

¹¹John S. Badeau, "The Arab World in Quest of a Future," in J.H. Thompson and R.D. Reischawer (eds.), *Modernization in the Arab World* (Princeton, New Jersey: D. Van Nostrand Company, Inc., 1966), p. 6.

¹²Osgood Caruthers, 1957, *op. cit.*, p. 80.

¹³George Antonious, *The Arab Awakening: The Story of the Arab National Movement* (New York: Capricorn Books, 1965), p. 27.

¹⁴Kemel H. Karpat (ed.), *Political and Social Thought in the Contemporary Middle East* (New York: Frederick A. Praeger Publishers, 1968), p. 29.

¹⁵Fauzi M. Najjar, "Nationalism and Socialism," in Abdeen Jabara and Janice Terry (eds.), *The Arab World: From Nationalism to Revolution* (Wilmette, Illinois: The Medina University Press International, 1971), p. 11.

Chapter 5

The Significance and Effects of the Arabic Language

There are few societies in which language plays as important a role as it does in the Arab society. It is, therefore, important for the business executive to develop a good understanding of the place Arabic occupies in the life of its speakers. In this chapter, we will seek to explore the significance of the Arabic language and the effects it has on its users.

The Arabic language is the vehicle of one of the world's great literatures, extending from the pre-Islamic poetry of nearly 1500 years ago to the current production of works of all kinds. Since medieval times, Arabic has enjoyed a universalism that can favorably be compared with Greek, Latin, English, French, Spanish, and Russian.

The importance of Arabic rests not only in the hundreds of millions of people who speak it, but also in the vital historical role it has played in the Arabic-Muslim society. In addition to being ancillary to Islam, Arabic has constituted the medium of cultural and national revival in the Arabic-speaking countries.

The Spread of Arabic

Arabic was not originally the language of what is commonly known today as the Arab world, extending from Morocco to the Persian Gulf. Two thousand years ago, it was but one of many Semitic languages with its locus in central Arabia. It was not until the Islamic conquests following the birth of Islam in the 7th century that it reached a position of cultural dominance. By the 11th century, Arabic had become the chief medium of everyday use from Persia to the Pyrenees, superceding the old culture languages like Aramaic, Coptic, Greek, and Latin.

Today, the Arabic language is on far more tongues than, for example, is French. It is the official language of the Fertile Crescent (Iraq, Jordan, Lebanon, and Syria) and the Gulf states (Kuwait, Bahrain, Qatar, the United Arab Emirates, Oman, North Yemen, South Yemen, and Saudi Arabia). It is also the language of such African countries as Egypt, Libya, Tunisia, Algeria, Morocco, Mauritania, Sudan, Djibouti, and Somalia.

Religious Significance

Arabic myth has it that the Arabic language had its beginning at the time of Creation when God placed it in the mouth of Adam. But when Adam disobeyed God, he was deprived of this privilege and had to learn Syriac instead. According to the myth, Arabic has ever since remained the language of the people of paradise; it is God-given and is the mother of all tongues.

The religious significance of Arabic reached its peak when Islam was born, and Arabic became the language of the Quran, Islam's holy book.

The Arabic language may be viewed as the Latin of Muslim countries with a population of about 800 million people, one fifth of mankind. Religious leaders as well as lay Muslims everywhere use Arabic for worship. Whereas religious leaders are expected to read and write Arabic and to be able to recite the text of the Quran, lay Muslims must be able to recite the Quran in their prayer even though many of them in such countries as Indonesia and Pakistan do not speak or understand Arabic.

The reason why all Muslims, regardless of their native tongues, must recite the Quran in Arabic derives from the Muslims' conviction that the Quran cannot be faithfully translated into any other language. The Quran is Islam's miracle; its ravishing language could not have been written by any human being, let alone by the Prophet Muhammad who was illiterate. To all Muslims, even as far away as the Philippines, the idea of translating God's Arabic appears impious. Because of the religious significance Arabic has for all Muslims, the 11th century great Islamic thinker and scientist, Al-Baruni (a Persian), was reported to have said that he "preferred being reviled in Arabic to being praised in Persian."[1]

To all Arabs, the language of the Quran is the best Arabic one could possibly imagine. As a model for every Arabic writer, it has never been equalled, nor can it be equalled. The Egyptian scholar, Taha Husain, educated in Paris and well known as a contemporary critic and writer, says: "There are three sorts of literary speech: poetry, prose, and the Quran."[2] Even to his critical mind, the Quran is a work with which no other literary monument can be compared. All Arabs consider the Quran as the ideal book on grammar and writing style. Consequently, it is impossible for an educated Arab to write without giving consideration for the Quran's grammatical, idiomatic, and stylistic requirements. If he did, he would run the risk of being denounced as ignorant, if not as an impudent abuser of the integrity of Arabic and the sacredness of the revealed word of God.

Cultural Significance

In medieval times, Arab scholars had classified peoples by what they considered to be their most characteristic trait. Thus, the Greek was characterized by the superiority of his brain, the Chinese by the dexterity of his hands, the Indian by his imagination, and the Arab by the eloquence of his tongue. In pre-Islamic times, eloquence (*fasaha* or the ability to express oneself correctly) had been considered one of the basic attributes of the perfect Arab. Arab tradition had fostered an attitude toward the Arabic language which was almost worship. Linguistic purity was valued, and meticulous use of the language was required by all.

The pre-Islamic Arabs hardly possessed any written tradition. The Arabs themselves call this period the "Age of Ignorance," as the light shed by the Prophet Muhammad's mission had not then dawned on the Arabian peninsula. The "Age of Ignorance" notwithstanding, the pre-Islamic Arabs had developed a remarkably rich poetic language and tradition. It was poetry characterized by elaborate and strict rules of prosody and rhyme, subtlety of an almost unlimited vocabulary, and a variety of rhythmic and tonal nuances. Poetry represented the "true expression of the life of the Bedouins, singing of wine, love, war, hunting, the terrible landscapes of mountain and desert, the martial valor of the tribesmen themselves, and the turpitude of their enemies."[3]

The creative power of those early Arab Bedouins, whose world consisted merely of sun, sand, rocks, and camels, was concentrated on one medium of expression, namely, language. Unlike the Greeks and the Romans who focused on sculture, music, and painting, the Bedouins used language as their primary medium of artistic expression. Indeed, the ancient Bedouin poets used neither pen nor parchment. Their poems, hundreds of them, were committed to memory and passed on from mouth to mouth and from one generation to the next. To some Western students of Arabic literatures, Bedouin poetry represents "one of those spiritual achievements of mankind which, following laws known only unto themselves that serve no practical purpose, can fill us with wonder."[4]

The Arab poet performed important political and social functions. In battle, his tongue was as effective as his people's bravery. In peace, he might prove a menace to public order by his fiery harangues. His poems might arouse a tribe to action in the same manner as the tirade of a demagogue in a modern political campaign. As the press agent, the journalist of his day, his favor was sought by princely gifts. His poems offered inavluable means of publicity. He was both a molder and agent of public opinion.[5]

The Arabs reserve the highest place in their culture for poets. Despite the passage of centuries, poets of the "Age of Ignorance" are still held in the highest esteem. Until fairly recently, reverence paid to the early poetic creations was so great that almost every poem written in Arabic had to be modelled after the old pattern. Ancient Bedouin poetry became the example to be emulated, the standard against which the quality of any literary composition was measured. Due to the high esteem the Arabic culture attaches to poets, it is not surprising to note that every educated Arab, at one time or another in his life, has tried to write poetry.

Today's Arab, like his counterpart of the past, displays strong attachment to his language. Arabic is important to him not only for religious reasons but also for cultural and nationalistic reasons. The Arab looks at Arabic as the language of his ancestors whose exploits made the history of which he is proud; it is a great honor to use the language of those great and illustrious forebearers. He also displays tremendous pride in the beauty and resonance of his language whose wealth of vocabulary is staggering. For example, while other languages might have one or two words to express one thing, Arabic has hundreds — 300 words for "camel," 800 for "sword," 500 for "lion," 200 for "snake," and so on.

Pride in ones' language as a cultural element is, of course, common. But some nations feel it more than others. While many Americans may take liberty with the spelling, pronunciation, and grammar of their English without undue criticism, it would be considered almost treasonable if an educated Arab were to misspell a word or break one of the intricate and numerous rules of Arabic grammar.

In modern history, the Arabic language has become one of the pillars of the Arabs' cultural and political resurgence. Arab governments in various countries have attempted diligently to give Arabic a prominent place in the national life. For example, in Iraq, the government has issued a decree requiring school teachers to use classical instead of colloquial Arabic in the classroom. In its struggle for independence, Algeria insisted that Arabic be the official language of the country. Today, Algerian children begin their classes with the chant: "Islam is my religion, Arabic is my language, Algeria my country."

Emotional Effect

The Arabic language has a bewitching emotional effect upon its users. Whether employed in poetry, sermons, songs, or political speeches, the word has entranced the Arabs throughout their history. In describing this phenomenon, H.A.R. Gibbs states: "The medium in which the esthetic feeling of the Arabs is mainly...expressed is that of words and language — upon the Arab mind the impact of artistic speech is immediate; the words, passing through no filter which might weaken their effects, go straight to the head."[6] Commenting on the same point, P.H. Hitti, the well-known historian, says:

> No people in the world, perhaps, manifest such enthusiastic admiration for literary expression and are so moved by the word, spoken or written, as the Arabs. Hardly any language seems capable of exercising over the minds of its users such irresistable influence as Arabic. Modern audiences in Baghdad, Damascus and Cairo can be stirred to the highest degree by the recital of poems, only vaguely comprehended, and by the delivery of orations in the classical tongue, though it be only partially understood. The rhythm, the rhyme, the music produce on them the effect of what they call "lawful magic."[7]

Arabic maintains a strong hold on the literate and the masses alike. Education does little in reducing the Arabs' susceptibility to the charms of a good sermon or a political harangue. Anyone who has witnessed a public address in an Arab setting will soon realize the powerful effect of language on its audience regardless of education. A public speaker — be he a politician, a preacher, or a charlatan — is able, with proper and correct Arabic, to captivate his audience. Frequently, an articulate speaker can keep a massive crowd spellbound not so much by what he is saying as by how the words roll off his tongue.

The Arabs' passionate response to their language is due mainly to the richness, majesty, and beauty of Arabic. Because of its intrinsic characteristics, the Arabic language makes for magnificent poetry, evoking splendid images and setting them to music. It is this quality that gives Arabic a musicality which exerts a great influence on the psychology of the Arabs. The hypnotic effect of words on the Arabs is also evident in the songs of popular male and female entertainers. Although Arabic music may sound monotonous to the educated ear of a Westerner, to the Arabs what counts in their music is not so much the sounds of the instruments as the magical sounds of words.

The Arabic language leads its user to become passionately, if unintentionally, carried away. When reciting Arabic poetry or prose, speaking literary Arabic and especially chanting the Quran, the literate Arab almost always has to show signs of emotion. Because of the endless rules of inflections and changing vowels and consonants as well as the ubiquitous accent marks, the simple act of reading or speaking in Arabic involves numerous voice changes accompanied by emotional and physiological changes. The emotionalism to which Arabic lends itself sometimes reduces the ability of the language users to think clearly and rationally. This may account for the empty arguments in which even those Arabs who are both intelligent and learned often engage. The interplay of the debators' mutual emotional effects leads to a vicious spiral of rising emotions which finally reduces reasoning to a minimum and contributes to controversy and quarreling.

Even when he speaks a foreign language, the Arab shows signs of emotion of which he may not even be aware. This can potentially be a source of considerable misunderstanding. A foreigner may think an Arab, from his manner of speaking, to be excited, angry, or affectionate when in fact he is not. On the other hand, an Arab may think a foreigner to be calm and serene when he is actually upset or annoyed.

Emphasis on Form

The language of literary Arabic is one in which the form seems to count far more than the substance. That is, the writer appears to concern himself more with the impact on his reader of word arrangements and sounds than with the meaning such words are intended to communicate. Consequently, the writer is compelled to fit the thought to the word rather than the word to the thought. In this manner, the words become the substitutes for thoughts and not their representatives.

The Arabs love fine and sonorous words for their own sake. They derive great pleasure from the sounds of rhythm and harmony produced by combinations of words. Arabic poetry is based to a larger extent than is English or French on the effects of these sound combinations. The rhythming is sometimes too important to leave much room for the consideration of meaning. Such preoccupation with word sounds is so great that many Arabs still prefer to write in a mild form of *saj'*, an old style of rhymed prose which resembles eupehmism in English, but with much less emphasis on alliteration and more stress on the rhyming of word-endings. No writer is considered good unless his prose evinces the harmony of words, and the words should convey some of their meanings through the effects created by their sounds.

As long as he pays attention to the grammatical and the idiomatic aspects of his writing, a successful Arab writer has only to make it diffusely comprehensible; his duty does not extend as far as making his meaning clear-cut and unequivocal. In most cases, he may occupy himself with the arrangement of word patterns in order to give expression to his thoughts. Instead of manipulating the linguistic tools to make them convey his thoughts in a clear manner, he tends to force his thoughts to accommodate themselves to the ready-made linguistic structures which he borrows from general use.

An extreme example of such a case is provided by a line of poetry which, if translated literally, would read something as follows: "There is no one like him among the people, except a crowned, his mother's father, his father, alive, resembles him." The line is intended to praise the maternal uncle of a sovereign, since there is nobody like him except the sovereign, his nephew.

The heavy emphasis placed on form and sounds produces a great deal of vagueness in meaning. Any Westerner who has attempted to comprehend Arabic will agree that thoughts expressed in that language are generally vague and hard to pin down. It is possible to understand an ordinary Arabic sentence as a unit, but when it comes to understanding it in a manner that fits all the details into a clear and well-integrated picture, then it is a different matter. Naturally, Arabic that deals with simple or familiar topics creates no difficulties. But the more novel or abstract the content, the more difficult it is to understand Arabic with accuracy.[9]

In dramatizing the communication problems stemming from the Arabs' preoccupation with form rather than substance, one Arab intellectual warns:

> Unless one is in full command of an idea, and unless he has it precisely articulated in his head, he should not attempt to publish it in Arabic — for somewhere on the way he will eventually lose it and find himself, to his surprise, writing thoughts he never dreamed of. Those who use the Arabic

language must be solid men, of disciplined mind, otherwise they will lose their ascendancy and succumb hopelessly to its seductive form. This fascination with the form, the outward, and the irrelevant is deeply rooted in our culture. Its bad air chokes our throats, and permeates our whole existence.[10]

Fascination with linquistic forms seems to have its own side effects in the Arabs' other aspects of life. A Christian missionary tells a revealing story of how he placed before an Arab audience the question as to which son in the New Testament parable (Matthew, 21:28) is better: the one who, when asked by his father to do something, replies that he will and then does not, or the son who replies that he will not and then does what his father asks. Virtually all Arabs said the son who answered that he would was the better since even though he did not carry out his father's wish, he showed proper respect in his reply. Respect, for the Arabs, consists in conforming to an ideal form of verbal acquiescence rather than in a real act of obedience.[11]

Another manifestation of this addiction to form is the Arabs' predilection for adopting plans — for economic development, domestic reforms, and so on — that are often not closely related to their capacity for carrying them out. But plans have that seductive quality which they can not resist. Unlike reality, a plan can be a perfect thing, complete, structurally neat, and self-contained, with emphasis on appearance and not meaning. There is also the feeling that one need not go beyond the plan, for the ideal picture is sufficient and is in any case esthetically far more pleasing than the uncertainty and disorderliness of reality.[12]

It would be misleading if we did not point out that Arab intellectuals have been exhibiting a growing tendency toward functionalism in their language usage. The huge numbers of Arabs who received their education in Western universities, have become aware of the value of objectivity not only in carrying out scientific investigations but also in communicating their research findings accurately and clearly. Many Arab scientists and scholars are now cognizant of the pitfalls of the traditional emphasis on form. Consequently, they have begun to exhibit greater caution in the type of words and expressions which they choose in conveying their meanings. The new spirit of scientific inquiry which is now prevalent among Arab scientists and scholars is no doubt responsible for their resistance to the traditional pull toward form in favor of substance in the communication of their ideas.

Tendency Toward Assertion

The Arabic language abounds with forms of assertion (*tawkid*) and of exaggeration (*mubalagha*). There is the doubling of the sounds of some consonants to create the desirable stronger effect. And there are such forms of assertion as repetition of pronouns and certain other words to get across their meaning or just to create the desirable impact on the reader. In addition to the grammatical types of overassertion, there are numerous stylistic and rhetorical devices to achieve even further exaggeration. Fantastic metaphors and similes are used in abundance, and long arrays of adjectives to modify the same word are quite frequent. Though gradually developing in the direction of brevity, the style of Arabic prose is still too florid (as judged by standards applicable to English prose) to be considered realistic.

The tendency toward assertion in Arabic becomes evident in translation. A simple statement in English cannot be translated into Arabic without losing part of its meaning. Those who read the same paragraph in both English and Arabic will get more from the English version, if the Arabic version contains no devices of assertion and exaggeration. It is significant to note that even Arabs whose English is inferior to their Arabic often prefer to read serious matter in English.[13]

Overassertion is most evident in the rhetoric of intra-Arab rivalry. In their frequent squabbles, the Arabs are prone to using highly offensive if not abusive verbal attacks. Such epithets as coward, agent, stooge, puppet, lacky, immoral, degernate, lunatic, traitor, and criminal are freely hurled at kings, heads of state, or political leaders at the slightest sign of disagreement. Equally offensive and abusive is the language used in attacking foreign governments. As one American observer of Arab politics noted: "It might be said of the Arabic language at least that it has a bountiful of invective. We have become accustomed to being denounced in the most horrible manner imaginable."[14]

That such vituperation is mostly a linguistic tendency is attested to by the fact that Arab leaders who vilify each other in the strongest possible terms on one occasion are quick to profess their brotherhood on the next. There are occasions, of course, when Arab rivalry derives from genuine ideological differences. But to a Westerner with no knowledge of the characteristics of the Arabic language, the exchange of violent verbal barrages among the Arabs over relatively minor issues appears incomprehensible.

The built-in mechanism of assertion in language affects the Arabs' communication behavior in at least two ways. First, an Arab feels compelled to overassert in almost all types of communication because others expect him to. If an Arab says exactly what he means without the expected assertion, other Arabs may still think that he means the opposite. For example, a simple "No" by a guest to the host's request to eat more or drink more will not suffice. To convey the meaning that he is actually full, the guest must keep repeating "No" several times, coupling it with an oath such as "By God" or "I swear to God." Second, an Arab often fails to realize that others, particularly foreigners, may mean exactly what they say even though their language is simple. To the Arabs, a simple "No" may mean the indirectly expressed consent and encouragement of a coquettish woman. On the other hand, a simple consent may mean the rejection of a hypocritical politician.

Classical and Colloquial Arabic

The Arabic language comes in two forms: the classical and the colloquial. The classical or written Arabic is common to all literate Arabs, regardless of their native country. It is also the language of piety for millions of Muslims in such non-Arab countries as Indonesia, Iran, Pakistan, and Turkey. Even though these Muslims are unable to speak or understand classical Arabic, they nonetheless use it for worship, since it is the language of the Quran.

There are twenty-eight letters in Arabic as compared to the English twenty-six. Nine consonant sounds are not present in English, and it normally takes a foreigner much practice to learn them. In fact, no one who is not born an Arab can get to the point where he can pronounce them properly in every position. Classical Arabic is rather difficult to learn. It would take a foreigner at least one year to become proficient enough to read it, and it might take him three to five years to be able to speak it.

A literate Arab can travel from one end of the Arab world to the other with no great linguistic difficulty as long as he communicates with other literate Arabs. However, when he attempts to communicate with the illiterate, he runs into difficulties. Local dialects are quite varied, and they differ not only from country to country but sometimes from one city to the next. Colloquial Arabic is often mixed with Persian, Turkish, English, French, Kurdish, or Berber words, depending on the speaker's country. This point is illustrated by a story which tells of the chagrin felt by a devout Arabian Muslim on his pilgrimage to Mecca when an Algerian Arab greeted him with "Bonjour *Alaikum,*" with the Arabic *Alaikum* meaning "unto you."

In general, there are four main groups of Arabic dialects:

1. The Syrian dialect. This dialect is spoken in western Jordan, Lebanon, and Syria.
2. The Arabian peninsula's dialect. Considered to be the most pure, this dialect is spoken in Saudi Arabia and the other states of the peninsula.
3. The Moroccan dialect. This dialect is spoken west of Tunis.
4. The Egyptian dialect. Divided from the Syrian and Arabian dialects by the Sinai peninsula, the Egyptian dialect is the most commonly understood dialect throughout the Arab world. This is due to such factors as the popularity of the Egyptian movies, TV and radio programs, and musical arts.

The educated Arab's use of the classical or the colloquial Arabic depends on the purpose and the occasion of communication. He is expected to use the classical Arabic in his written and other types of formal communication, but is not supposed to use the same language in his informal and daily conversations. Should he attempt to use the colloquial outside the area in which his dialect is used, he will not be understood. On the other hand, if he tries to use the classical in his everyday conversations, he will find himself misunderstood by the illiterate and ridiculed by all. Thus, whereas educated Arabs require every public speaker to use classical Arabic, they themselves make fun of anybody who uses it for practical everyday purposes.

The colloquial Arabic is used by the illiterate who comprise the majority of the population. This does not mean that these Arabs lack any knowledge of classical Arabic. In their everyday life, the illiterate come in touch with literary Arabic through listening to the radio, to public speakers, to sermons at the mosque, and to the ritualistic recital of the Quran. Consequently, they come to acquire some knowledge of literary Arabic, even though their understanding of it remains in the majority of cases vague.[15]

Implications for the Business Executive

The fact that Arabic is a relatively difficult language to learn and that it might take a few years before one can be adept at it is not an insurmountable obstacle; it should not discourage the business executive from applying himself to learning it. Many Western diplomats and business executives have done it with remarkably successful results.

Learning a foreign language is, of course, a matter of motivation; it is predicated on the intensity of an individual's felt need. The greater the intensity of the need, the stronger the motivation becomes. The executive's need to learn the language of those he seeks to influence, to do business with, is unarguable. Contracts worth millions of dollars, for which many other businessmen compete, are at stake and should, therefore, constitute a sufficiently strong motivation to learn Arabic.

It is true that many Arab officials and businessmen with whom the Western executive deals speak English. But these Arabs, having normal ego needs, would surely appreciate, respect, and be influenced by an executive who speaks their language or at least makes an earnest effort to speak it. An executive with facility in Arabic does more than just use the language as a vehicle for the exchange of ideas. He also sends out signals to the Arabs that he likes them, that he is interested in them, and that he is willing to please them. Considering the enormous pride they have in their language, the Arabs invariably respond in a positive manner to such ego-massaging overtures.

It should be emphasized that any executive who plans on doing business with the Arabs should, as a minimum, endeavor to develop a working familiarity with Arabic. This will enable him not only to get around in the Arab countries but more importantly to create the type of psychological climate that is conducive to constructive communication and productive business dealings. In this regard, the executive would do well to study the list of Arabic words and expressions at the end of this book, which can serve as a good starting point toward a higher facility in the use of the Arabic language.

Summary

This chapter deals with the Arabic language — its significance and impact on its speakers. The following statements summarize the chapter's major points:

1. Before the birth of Islam, Arabic was spoken only in the Arabian Peninsula. Following the Islamic expansion in the 7th century, it became the chief medium of communication in what is known today as the Arab world.

2. The Arabic language enjoys a special religious significance. It is the language of the Quran, Islam's holy book. All Muslims, regardless of their native tongues, must say their prayers in Arabic. The Muslims believe the Quran cannot be translated into other languages without losing the exceptionally powerful force of its language.

3. Arabic serves as an important cultural device. Unlike the Greeks and the Romans who focused on sculpture, painting, and music, the Arabs have traditionally used language as their primary medium of artistic and political expression.

4. Whether listening to or speaking the language, the Arabs act in an emotional fashion. This is due to the richness, majesty, musicality, and beauty of the language. Audiences can be stirred to the highest degree by the recital of poems, sermons, or political speeches. When speaking, the Arab almost always shows some signs of emotion, particularly while using classical Arabic.

5. The Arabs display a great fascination with language form (word arrangement) rather than substance (meaning). Such a tendency obscures the real intent of the message, thus leading to communication difficulties. The Arabs' emphasis on form frequently spills over into their use of foreign languages. One, therefore, may have to peer through the fog of the linguistic form to uncover the Arabs' real meaning.

6. The Arabic language abounds with forms of assertion. Metaphores, similes, long arrays of adjectives, and repetition of words are frequently used by the Arabs in communicating their ideas. Repetition of words is especially common in extending or rejecting invitations for coffee, dinner, and the like. When an Arab extends an invitation, he typically repeats the invitation several times. By the same token, when an Arab says, "No, thank you," he expects the other person to repeat the invitation; and in all probability, the Arab ends up accepting the invitation.

7. Although rather difficult, learning or acquiring a working knowledge of Arabic can be an asset to the business executive. Facility in Arabic has the practicable value of enabling the executive to get around in the Arab countries. It can also create a positive psychological atmosphere that is conducive to more successful business relations with the Arabs.

Footnotes

[1]Anwar Chejne, "The Role of Language in the Growth of Arab Nationalism," in Abdeen Jabara and Janice Terry (eds.), *The Arab World: From Nationalism to Revolution* (Wilmette, Il.: The Medina University Press International, 1971), p. 17.

[2]Arnold Hottinger, *The Arabs: Their History, Culture and Place in the Modern World* (Berkeley: University of California Press, 1963), p. 24.

[3]Bernard Lewis, *The Arabs in History* (New York: Harper and Row, Publishers, 1960), p. 131.

[4]Arnold Hottinger, 1963, *op. cit.*, p. 19.

[5]Philip K. Hitti, *History of the Arabs* (London: Macmillan and Company, Ltd., 1963), pp. 94-95.

[6]H.A.R. Gibbs, *Modern Trends in Islam* (Chicago: The University of Chicago Press, 1947), p. 5.

[7]Philip K. Hitti, 1963, *op. cit.*, p. 90.

[8]Elie Salem, "Forms and Substance: A Critical Examination of the Arabic Language," *Middle East Forum,* Vol. 33, No. 7, July 1958, p. 18.

[9]This material heavily depends on E. Shouby's article "The influence of the Arabic Language on the Psychology of the Arabs," *The Middle East Journal,* Vol. 5, No. 3, Summer 1951, pp. 284-302.

[10]Elie Salem, July 1958, *op. cit.,* pp. 17-18.

[11]Morroe Berger, *The Arab World Today* (New York: Doubleday and Company, Inc., 1964), pp. 160-161.

[12]*Ibid.*

[13]E. Shouby, Summer 1951, *op. cit.,* pp. 299-300.

[14]C. Leiden, "Middle East Misconceptions," *National Review,* Vol. 16, No. 2, January 28, 1964, p. 69.

[15]E. Shouby, Summer 1951, *op. cit.,* p. 290.

Chapter 6

Cultural Patterns of the Arabs

In Chapter 1, culture was defined as "that complex whole which includes knowledge, belief, art, morals, law, customs, and any other capabilities and habits acquired by man as a member of society."[1] This definition is broad enough to encompass much of our discussion in the previous three chapters. In other words, what we said about Islam, Arab nationalism, and the Arabic language represents certain aspects of the Arabic culture. In this chapter, we will focus on specific cultural patterns of the Arabs, with a view toward providing the reader with a fuller picture of what might be termed the "Arab personality."

To some observers of the Arab world, the Arab is a riddle; he is a "peculiar" creature and is too difficult to understand. One observer, for instance, cites the following parable to illustrate this point:

> A tired and dusty desert traveler stopped beneath a tree to inquire of an Arab: "Where am I?" The Arab rose from his patch of shade, unfurled the long folds of his robe, touched his forehead, his lips and his heart, and with a steady gaze and an air of profound frankness replied: "You are neither in the East nor in the West, neither in the North nor in the South. You are at the center of the world."[2]

This and other similar parables notwithstanding, the Arabs are no more "peculiar" than any other cultural group when perceived by an outsider. The apparent difficulty in understanding the Arabs may not be anything more than a reflection of the perceiver's lack of knowledge of the cultural setting in which they function. The Arabs act as they do because they are a people whose thoughts and behaviors are molded by the circumstances in which they live, their convictions, and their language. It is in such determining factors, rather than in the human essence of the Arabs, that an explanation of Arabs' behaviors should be sought.

Some other observers of the Arab world make the claim that there are no common cultural patterns among the Arabs. To such observers, there seems to be no apparent affinity among the purebred Bedouins of the Arabian Peninsula, the mixed-blood Egyptians, the veiled horsemen of Algeria, and the Christians of Lebanon. As an evidence of the Arabs' cultural disunity, these observers state that the Arab world "is perpetually in a shamble; it is always at odds and always shifting its loyalties, its alliances, and its ideologies. It is rocked by incurable rivalries and hamstrung by an evidently congenital disability to make a common cause and stick to it."[3]

Despite the outward appearances of disunity or the lack of commonalities among the Arabs, a closer socio-historical examination of the Arabs would readily reveal the presence of an unmistakable cultural unity. As we pointed out previously, the Arabs have a common language (Arabic), a common faith (Islam), a common historical tradition, and a common territory. Furthermore, the same architecture and the same passions and temperaments are evident from Baghdad to Marrakesh. It may, therefore, be said that the cultural unity of the Arabs is almost their strongest and most solid tie. Actually, "Today's Arabs are culturally more cohesive than Western Europe."[4] If you ask a man in Algeria, Syria, or Kuwait what he feels himself to be, he is likely to reply: "I am an Arab."

Genesis of the Arabic Culture

A number of forces have contributed to the crystallization of the Arabic cultural patterns. The most potent of these is the value system of the nomadic Bedouins of the Arabian Peninsula.

The Bedouin's character and traditions are a faithful reflection of the aridity of his desert habitat. Endurance seems to be his supreme virtue, and individualism is deeply ingrained in his attitude. The *ghazwa* (or raid) is raised by the economic and social conditions of desert life to the rank of a national sport. Although a raider, the Bedouin can be extremely hospitable; and within his laws of friendship, he can be a loyal and generous friend.

Following the birth of Islam, the Bedouins were drawn to the new faith in large numbers. Skillfully blending the Bedouins' traditional values with the mission of Islam, the Prophet Muhammad began urging the believers to spread the new faith to the neighboring countries. And in less than a decade, the Bedouins brought Arab Muslim rule over the entire Fertile Crescent.

The Islamic conquests brought about a fundamental transformation of the population of the conquered provinces. The conquered peoples, with a few scattered exceptions, gradually began to absorb the Bedouins' language, customs, and traditions. Later, as the Arabs invaded North Africa, a similar process of Arabization took place. In importance, this Arabization process ranks higher than the military conquest, and may be considered as one of the most significant accomplishments of Islam.

Among all the groups who, as a result of the Islamic expansion, came to call themselves Arab, the desert Bedouins were the one group that continued to possess a unity and uniformity of cultural patterns; they were the purest of all Arabs.

This is due to the fact that their peninsula, being uninviting to alien colonists and difficult to conquer and rule, offered little to foreign invaders and thus remained thoroughly Semitic in culture. Equally important is the fact that the peninsula constituted a wellspring that replenished the Arabized provinces in the Middle East. The unfailing source of Arab blood, language, and customs overflowing the lands bordering on the desert counteracted whatever effects alien invaders might have had on the Middle East. Consequently, such Bedouin ideals as hospitality, generosity, chivalry, and bravery continued to be prevalent throughout the Middle East and North Africa.

In short, it can be stated that contemporary Arabic culture is to a large measure a Bedouin culture.

Cultural Patterns

Before we probe the specific cultural patterns characterizing the Arabs, it is important to make the following observations:

1. It is not our intention to come up with a summary statement that describes the Arabs in all their individuality. Rather, our purpose is to delineate a group of patterns encompassing the Arabs in their variety, a kind of modal point which they approximate in varying degrees.
2. The intensity of some of the cultural patterns presented below varies from country to country and from one locality to another within the same country. In such tradition-bound societies as Saudi Arabia, Kuwait, and some other Gulf states, the ancient Bedouin customs are still observed rather strictly. In the more Westernized countries of Egypt, Lebanon, Syria, Algeria, and Iraq, certain aspects of such patterns as honor and vengeance are showing signs of weakness. Even in these more Westernized societies, Bedouin customs tend to be more visible and more deeply rooted as one moves from cities to rural areas.

Hospitality

To a foreigner, the Arabs' outstanding trait may well be hospitality. As hosts, the Arabs are entirely charming, and the generosity of their hospitality can be overwhelming. They are a people who like to please, and who are always warm hearted and cordial to their guests. A guest is considered almost a sacred trust to be treated as well as or better than one's own immediate family.

The legendary Arab hospitality has its roots in the nomadic Bedouin lifestyle. Pre-Islamic poets never tired of singing the praises of *diyafa* (hospitality) which is considered one of the Arabs' supreme virtues. The pagan Arab's idea of morality is expressed in the word *muruwwa* (manliness) which consists mainly in courage and generosity. His courage is shown not only by his readiness to defend his own clan, but also by the chivalrous treatment of his foes, very much akin to that of the medieval knight. The Arab's "generosity appears in his being always more ready to join in the fray than to share the spoil, in his readiness to slaughter his camels for behoof of the guest and of the poor and the helpless, and in his being generally more willing to give than.to receive."[5]

As is the case with the customs of other societies, Arab hospitality did not come about by accident. It grew out of human helplessness in the desert, the utter dependence of man upon other men. The stranger you offer coffee to today may feed you tomorrow if you lose your way in the bleak and dangerous desert. Such is the importance of hospitality to the Arabs that certain superstitions began to develop about the mysterious powers of strangers. A stranger may have an evil eye, be capable of magic, or bring evil as well as good. So he must be appreciated and special care must be taken to avoid making the stranger-guest angry, for he can easily bring a curse down upon the tent.

Hospitality is granted not only to travelers but also to those in need of protection from an avenger or an oppressor. None may refuse such a request for protection but must admit the pursued man and offer him food and a place to sleep; sometimes, the pursued man may pitch his own tent alongside his protector's. In some cases, a whole clan may seek refuge with another clan. So strong is the right of a Bedouin to protection by another that it is respected even by the pursuer.

The protection system (called *Al-Aman* or safety) is clearly useful and practicable in a desert environment. In the absence of specialized agencies to protect the rights of the accused persons and in view of the ease with which revenge may be carried out, this practice softens the rigor of an excessively individualistic approach to law enforcement. It provides the accused both a refuge and an advocate in his host. It also permits a third party to come between disputants and to seek an honorable settlement.

In today's Arab society, hospitality is strongly felt and closely adhered to in rural areas which still show an historic affinity for desert values. The guest is always shown great honor. Each village has a guest house for visitors with no families to stay with. The village mayor, like the *shaikh,* entertains as lavishly as his means permit. Indeed, one of the qualifications for the post is possession of the means to entertain in a manner pleasing to villagers who enjoy the hospitality themselves and who like to see their leader able to extend proper treatment to visitors.

In the cities, the display of hospitality is also common. It is a symbol of man's status and personal quality to be hospitable to others. City dwellers display their hospitality by providing their guests with lavish dinners and spending a considerable portion of their incomes on elaborate weddings where there is an opportunity to be hospitable to a large number of people.

Since everyone understands the hospitality impulse on the part of everyone else, each person is constrained not only to offer but also to accept hospitality. To refuse another's hospitality is to insult him by denying him the opportunity to display his valued qualities of character: generosity, fellowship, and a certain ability to spend. Even when it is inconvenient, one is under compulsion to accept another's hospitality. A refusal to do so may lead to a counterrefusal by another to accept one's own hospitality when it is offered.

Just as an Arab is willing to extend hospitality to others, he expects them to be hospitable to him also. For example, when an Arab businessman comes to the U.S. and calls an American executive, he expects an Arab type of hospitality. If the American says: "I am free for lunch a week from today," or "I'll be free for 30 minutes in the office tomorrow," he might just have lost a lucrative deal. To an Arab, hospitality implies an immediate and extensive welcome.

Pride

A tremendous sense of pride can be easily seen in the conduct of Arabs. Like hospitality, pride is basically a Bedouin trait and can be traced back to the pre-Islamic times. The Bedouin had always displayed a great deal of self-exaltation and looked down on the outside world. The Bedouin viewed himself as the embodiment of the consummate pattern of creation. To him, the Arabs were the noblest of all peoples. In the purity of his blood, his eloquence and poetry, his sword and horse, and above all in his noblest ancestry, the Bedouin took infinite pride. He was excessively fond of prodigious geneology and often traced his lineage back to Adam. "No people other than the Arabians have raised geneology to the dignity of science."[6]

Then came Islam, and with it came an even greater sense of pride and superiority. According to the Islamic historical view of prophecy, the mission of Muhammad is the last link in the chain of revelations of which Judaism and Christianity were the earliest links. Consequently, the Muslim Arab came to regard the Jew and the Christian as the possessors of early but imperfect versions of something which he alone possessed in its perfection.

Unlike Christianity, which for centuries was the religion of the humble and the dispossessed before becoming the state faith of the Roman Empire, Islam became, during the lifetime of its founder, the guiding code of an expanding and victorious community. The immense conquests of Islam in the first formative generations imprinted on the minds of the Believers a conviction of divine favor as expressed by the power and success in this world of the "only community" that lived by God-given law. The Arabs saw the finger of God in all their successes.

In recounting their past glories, the Arabs are quick to remind us that while Europe was struggling through the Dark Ages, the Arab Empire encouraged scholarly inquiry and learning. When Charlemagne, Emperor of the Franks, could barely write, Arab scholars in Baghdad were studying Aristotle. Today's Arabs are proud of their ancestors who developed algebra, discovered logarithms, introduced a numerical system that became the basis of modern mathematics, and measured the earth's circumference with amazing accuracy at a time when most Europeans thought it flat.

Caught between their past glories and present frustrations over their political disunity and economic backwardness, today's Arabs are extremely sensitive to outside criticism. Westerners are often puzzled by the Arabs' deep sense of injury and need for dignity. The Arabs have a tendency to see the slightest skepticism in another person as a grave insult. This tendency has prompted one observer of the Arab world to note that "since the Arabs are vain, one must flatter them, tell them how mighty their past, and how glowing their future."[7] Although highly sensitive to outside criticism, the Arabs do not shy from criticizing themselves or engaging in self-condemnation. In any informal gathering, the Arabs are quick to condemn themselves for the centuries of stagnation and the humiliation suffered at the hands of their conquerors. They also condemn themselves for their present political disunity, their military weakness, and their slow economic resurgence.

Honor

Honor plays an important part in the Arabs' life and is related to almost every aspect of their behavior. In early Arabic poetry, glorification of honor comes before everything else. Honor does not derive only from wealth or power over others. True, to own thoroughbred horses, many camels, valuable weapons, or to have numerous kinsmen and fine clothes can enhance a man's honor. He boasts of such possessions. But his honor might also consist in the fact that he can manage without any of these things.

It is honor, and not any feeling of friendship, which bids a Bedouin to undertake a blood feud against enemies of his clan. It is due to honor, and not to any human sympathy, that he shows hospitality to strangers, indeed wastes his substance on strangers not caring whether the following day might bring poverty or hunger to himself and to his family.

One area where honor takes on a special significance is the sexual conduct of women. Actually, the word "honor" (*ird*) and the words "wife" and "sister" are used synonymously. So, a man's honor is literally his wife or sister (that is, the conduct of his wife or his sister). In the past, when a woman tarnished her family's or tribe's honor, her punishment was often death. Actually, this practice is still observed by the traditional elements in Arab society, particularly in the rural areas.

Protection of one's honor is so intense that jealousy has become one of the Arab male's strongest impulses. Since the honor of a husband, a father, or a brother is tied up with a woman's sexual behavior, men tend to be highly suspicious of women. This is one reason why, in a traditional society such as that of Saudi Arabia, women are carefully guarded and secluded to their own company.

In the metropolitan areas of the more Westernized countries of Egypt, Lebanon, Syria, Iraq, and others, many of the restrictive codes governing women's social behavior have been relaxed. Women are free to go out unveiled and uncloaked, wear the latest Western fashions, get a college education, and mingle with and even date men (though often secretly).

These behaviors, however, are not always met with the blessings or approval of the woman's parents or older brothers who tend to be traditionally bound. In fact, the conservative elements in Arab society have, within the past decade, been experiencing a considerable conflict over what woman's behavior actually is and what it ought to be. It is perhaps this type of conflict which, in some way, has contributed to the growing popularity in the Arab world of the Islamic revivalist movement which aims, among other things, at redefining the woman's social role in a manner consistent with the traditional Islamic values which are designed to protect man's honor.

Rivalry

The Arabs are plagued by excessive rivalry, bickering, and backbiting. In describing the relationship among the tribes of the Persian Gulf area, one writer notes that "the Beni Kitab hate the Sheik of Sharja, and the Al-Bu Shamis hate the Naim, and the Naim hate themselves, and the Beni Kaab hate everyone else."[8]

Intra-Arab rivalry dates back to pre-Islamic times when various tribes continually raided one another; the raid was almost a national institution with these desert dwellers. In listing some of the virtues most prized by pre-Islamic Arabs, Reynold Nicholson included "bravery in battle, patience in misfortune, persistence in revenge, protection of the weak, and defiance of the strong."[9] Most of these are virtues exemplified above all in the mutual antagonism of tribes, clans, and families in the desert. It was only for a relatively brief period that Islam was able to contain the conflicts among various families and tribes and between the desert and the settled areas.

Arab rivalry may be partially explained in terms of a concept known as the *noyau* or "society of inward antagonism" which was advanced by Robert Ardrey in his book, *The Territorial Imperative.* According to Ardrey, certain animal groupings may be regarded as "societies of outward antagonism" because hostility to alien groups is a basic attitude among them and has as its complement friendly relations within the group. In contrast, the *noyau* concept is based on an attitude of intense mutual animosity among its subdivisions.[10] One feature of the *noyau* is that members of a group are so engrossed in their mutual rivalry that they pay little attention to external enemies.

There is, of course, something of the *noyau* in all human societies, although in varying degrees. Among the Arabs, however, the *noyau* is a highly visible, if not a dominant, cultural trait. Rivalry is such a dominant cultural trait among the Arabs that even their common enmity to Israel, a country which according to the Arabs poses a grave threat to their very survival, has not thus far proven a sufficiently strong motive to unite the Arabs in a common front.

Revenge

The Arabs are known for their characteristic thirst for revenge. The following incident, told by General Glubb Pasha who commanded Jordan's

Arab Legion for nearly two decades, illustrates the intensity of this trait:

> When I first went to Jordan, I was traveling in the desert and had stopped
> to spend the night in the tent of a headman of a small Bedouin tribe. We
> had dined lavishly on boiled mutton and rice, and were sitting in a small
> circle round a fire of sticks in our host's tent, smoking, drinking coffee,
> and talking. Outside lay the desert in darkness and silence, beneath clear-
> cut Arabian stars. Suddenly, our host said, "I'll get some tea and we'll
> make a fresh pot on the fire.' He rose and slipped out of the tent into the
> night. Within a few seconds, a shot rang out, almost deafening in the still
> of the night. We jumped up and ran out of the tent. One of us stumbled
> over something. It was the body of our host, who had left us scarcely a min-
> ute earlier. He was already dead, and the blood was pouring from his
> mouth. 'It must have been Anda,' said one of the tribesmen. 'We killed
> one of his tribe five years ago.'[11]

Blood, according to the law of the desert, calls for blood; no chastisement
is recognized other than that of vengeance. A blood feud may, therefore,
last for a long time before it is settled. Blood vengeance was devised by early
desert dwellers as a mechanism to ward off social anarchy. The system
imposed on the kin of a murdered man the duty of exacting vengeance from
the murderer or one of his fellow tribesmen. If a member of a clan commits
murder inside the clan, none will defend him. In case of escape, he becomes
an outlaw. If the murder is outside the clan, a vendetta is established, and
any fellow clan-member may have to pay for it with his own life.

In today's Arab society, vengeance killing, as a means of settling personal
or family feuds, is more common in a traditional country such as Yemen
than in a Westernized country like Egypt; and, in the latter, it is more
evident in the countryside than in the city. Not too many educated Arabs
would be inclined to take the law into their own hands to settle personal
disputes. Rather, they would be more apt to avail themselves of the modern
criminal justice systems which have replaced the old tribal laws. It must be
remembered, though, that vengeance murder as a means of settling political
disputes is still in evidence throughout the Arab world.

Nonverbal Behaviors

We stated in Chapter 1 that each culture has its own distinct system of
nonverabl communication. This consists of such clues as spatial distances,
glances, postures, smiles, emblems, clothes, colors, and so on. Some of the
nonverbal communication patterns characterizing the Arabic culture have
already been touched upon throughout the previous chapters. As a way of
emphasizing their importance, we will repeat some of them and add a few
more.

Physical Proximity

When two Arabs engage in conversation, they usually stand close to each
other. Only two feet usually separates the Arabs in contrast to the five feet

which separate the Americans while conversing. The Arabs also frequently touch each other while talking. President Sadat of Egypt, for example, is known for his tendency to place his hand on the knee of the person he is talking with. Actually, in any Arab setting, it is quite common to see two Arab males holding hands while walking in the street.

Eye Contact

When talking, the Arabs constantly look each other in the eye instead of letting their gaze drift to the side as the Americans do. By watching the pupils of the eyes, the Arabs attempt to judge the other person's responses to different topics.

The validity of such a technique has been borne out by psychologists who have discovered that the pupil of the eye is a very sensitive indicator of how people respond to a situation. When we are interested in something, our pupils dilate; and when we are not interested or when we are bothered, our pupils contract. Since we cannot control the response of our eyes, the shape of our pupils is a dead giveaway.[14]

Americans are taught not to stare, not to look at the eyes very carefully, for that may be construed as too suggestive or too hostile. The Arabs, it seems, have known about the importance of the pupil response for hundreds, if not thousands, of years. By watching the pupils, the Arabs seek to pick up clues about the other person so as to be able to respond rapidly to his mood changes. This is one reason why Arabs use a closer conversational distance.

Gestures

For Arabs of all social levels, gestures are an indispensable part of any conversation. To tie an Arab's hands while he is speaking is tantamount to tying his tongue.

Greetings

Whenever Arabs meet and depart, hands are shaken and greetings and pleasantries are exchanged. Stereotyped greetings, coupled with many inquiries, are almost inexhaustible, and each has its own stereotyped response. "Welcome, welcome," "How are you," "How is the family," "How is everything," "We pray that you are well," "May the Lord bless you," "We are honored by your presence," "We are delighted to see you" are all forms of greeting repeated several times before the Arabs settle down to talk about other topics. When meeting a complete stranger, an Arab still uses some of these greetings; they provide him with a useful means of sizing up the stranger.

Even in a casual encounter, the Arabs almost always shake hands when they meet and depart. Such a practice is observed even when the same persons had met each other the day before. This prompted an American executive operating in the Middle East to inquire of an Arab acquaintance: "What office are you running for?"[15]

Coffee Drinking

Drinking coffee (or tea) is a widespread custom in many Arab countries. Arab etiquette dictates offering it to all visitors. Customarily, a member of the family or a servant holds a tray with a pot of coffee and only one cup which he fills with coffee and offers to each person in turn.

Everyone is expected to drink the Arabic coffee which is usually flavored with the herb stimulant cardomon. Refusal to drink is tantamount to a slap on the face; it is an insult to the host. While Arab etiquette dictates the offering of coffee, it also dictates that one should not drink more than three cups at a time. When the Arabs drink, they usually "slurp" which is a sign of enjoyment.

Eating

When an Arab finds himself in a situation where food is about to be served, and for which he had not received a prior invitation, he will decline to eat even though he might be very hungry. It is the host's duty to repeat the invitation several times as the guest repeatedly declines the invitation. While eating, the Arab tends to chew his food noisily; he "chomps," which is his cue to the guest that he is enjoying the food. After the meal, the Arab "belches," a sign that he is full; otherwise, the guest will continue to offer more food.

Alcohol

In Saudi Arabia, and a few other Gulf states, liquor is banned. But even in this most straitlaced of all Arab countries, prohibition against alcohol is only slightly more effective than it was in the U.S. a half century ago. At official parties, only fruit juice is served. Unofficially, the Saudis have learned to wink at their own laws—especially when a foreign visitor who likes to drink visits them at home. The cabinets of many Saudi businessmen and government officials are always well stocked with liquor. In legal terms, though, the manufacturing and sale of liquor are prohibited and are punishable by jail sentence and flogging.

Admiring Possessions

A visitor to the Arab world should exercise caution in admiring any Arab's possessions. Arab etiquette requires that the item being admired be given to the person admiring it on the spot or soon thereafter as a present. One of the authors recalls an incident in which he admired a tie which an Arab friend was wearing. The Arab immediately took the tie off and gave it to him as a present. Upon the persistent refusal of the author to accept the tie, the Arab unhappily put the tie back on. After the Arab, who was spending his vacation at the author's home, had departed, the author discovered the tie lying on the couch in the living room. The visitor to the Arab world can save himself and his Arab acquaintances a good deal of embarrassment by refraining from admiring an Arab's possession, especially if it is expensive.

Treatment of Women

Among all Arab countries, Saudi Arabia maintains the harshest rules concerning women. They are not permitted to drive or to work. Also, women are not supposed to wear short dresses, defined as anything that shows the ankles. American women who have lived in Saudi Arabia tell stories of how they have been flogged on the legs by Saudi policemen because their dresses were too short. If a woman is fortunate enough to escape this type of punishment, she cannot escape contemptuous stares of the Saudis.

Smoking

Arab custom dictates that no one should smoke in the presence of older people or people in a position of authority. Smoking is a sign of disrespect. One should, therefore, refrain from smoking in the presence of a king, a president, or a prime minister. Custom also dictates that one should not light his cigarette from the fire bowl of a water pipe (*narjila*) while it is being used by another person.

Appointments

Arabs are rarely on time for an appointment. Appointments are frequently broken with no thought of apology. The Arabs, however, become upset when a foreigner fails to show up on time.

Posture

When sitting and engaging in conversation, an Arab will not consciously point the sole of his shoes at another person. Doing so is regarded as a worse insult than finger-pointing.

Summary

The purpose of this chapter is to provide the reader with a composite picture of some of the cultural patterns characterizing the Arabs. Here is a summary of the major points covered in the chapter:

1. Today's Arabic cultural patterns have their roots in the value systems of the Bedouins of the Arabian Peninsula.
2. The Arabs' most outstanding cultural trait is hospitality. A guest is considered almost as a sacred trust to be treated as well as or better than one's own immediate family.

3. The Arabs exhibit a tremendous sense of pride. They pride themselves on the purity of blood, eloquence, poetry, bravery, chivalry, and nobility of their ancestors before the birth of Islam. They also boast of the religious, military, scientific, and literary accomplishments of the Arabs after Islam.

4. Honor occupies a special place in the Arab world. No aspect of the Arabs' life is more affected by honor than women's sexual behavior. A family's honor can forever be tarnished by a woman who violates the acceptable norm of conduct.

5. Rivalry is a dominant cultural trait. The bickering and backbiting which characterize the Arabs' political relations are but an expression of this trait.

6. The Arabs are known for their vengeful tendencies. This is most evident in tradition-bound societies and rural areas where tribal heritage is entrenched.

7. Arabs' behavior shows alternating patterns of extremes. Pride can quickly turn to self-condemnation, openness to secretiveness, and friendliness to hostility.

8. The Arabic culture manifests itself in certain types of nonverbal behavior. A sample of such behavior follows:

    a. The Arabs use a closer conversational distance than, say, the Americans; and they tend to look each other in the eye.

    b. Gesturing is always used by the Arabs even when making simple points.

    c. When meeting or departing, the Arabs engage in rather elaborate systems of greetings and pleasantries.

    d. Drinking coffee or tea (particularly coffee) has an etiquette of its own. For example, a guest's refusal to drink coffee is considered an insult to the host.

    e. While eating, the Arab tends to chew his food noisily. After the meal, he usually "belches," a sign that he is full.

    f. In some traditional societies, such as Saudi Arabia, liquor is banned, and its manufacturing or sale is punishable by jail sentence and flogging.

    g. Admiring an Arab's possession can, at times, be a discomforting experience. Arab etiquette requires that the admired item be offered as a present to the person admiring it.

    h. In some Arab countries, particularly Saudi Arabia, women cannot wear short dresses and are not permitted to drive or to hold a job.

    i. Arab custom dictates that no one should smoke in the presence of older people or individuals in a position of authority.

    j. Arabs rarely show up for an appointment on time, even though they expect foreigners to do so.

    k. It is considered a serious insult when someone points the sole of his shoes at an Arab.

Footnotes

[1]E.B. Taylor, *Primitive Culture* (London: John Murray, 1871), p. 1.

[2]Osgood Caruthers, "Enigma that is the Arab," *The New York Times Magazine,* October 20, 1957, p. 18.

[3]James Morris, "What is an Arab?" *Horizon,* Summer 1971, p. 6.

[4]Ahmed Baha El-Din, "Arab Cultural Image in World Context," *Journal of World History,* 1972, p. 828.

[5]"Djahilliya," *Encyclopedia of Islam*, Vol. 1, p. 999b.

[6]Philip K. Hitti, *History of the Arabs* (London: Macmillan and Company, Ltd., 1963), p. 90.

[7]Sania Hamadi, *Temperament and Character of the Arabs* (New York: Twayne Publishers, 1960).

[8]James Morris, "What It Means to be an Arab," *The New York Times Magazine,* November 16, 1958, p. 84.

[9]Reynold Nicholson, *A Literary History of the Arabs* (London: Cambridge University Press, 1930), p. 79.

[10]Robert Ardrey, *The Territorial Imperative* (London: Collins, 1967), pp. 167-188.

[11]John B. Glubb, "Glubb Pasha Analyzes the Arab Mind," *The New York Times Magazine,* November 18, 1956, p. 36.

[12]Hamad Ammar, *Growing Up in an Egyptian Village* (London: Routledge and Kegan Paul, 1954), p. 10.

[13]Sania Hamadi, 1960, *op. cit.,* p. 30.

[14]Edward T. Hall, "Learning the Arabs' Silent Language," *Psychology Today,* August 1979, p. 47.

[15]F.S. Yousef, "Cross Cultural Communication: Aspects of Contrastive Social Values Between North Americans and Middle Easterners," *Human Organization,* Vol. 33, Winter 1974, p. 383.

Chapter 7

Determinants of the Arabs' Perception of the West

The executive's success in communicating with a different cultural group depends in large measure on his knowledge of the forces which shape the manner in which the group perceives him. Such knowledge can provide him with valuable insights into the group's sensitivities. It can also enable him to anticipate its behaviors and deal with them appropriately by, for instance, not saying or doing something which could injure the group's feelings or bring about its hostility. In this chapter, we will seek to identify the general forces which condition the Arabs' perception of the West.

Let us point out at the outset that the Arabs generally exhibit mixed feelings toward the West. These feelings are at once an admiration and resentment or love and hate.

Most Arabs show a great admiration for Western ways. They admire the West's educational system, affluence, and technological advances. They even admire many of the West's values, including fashion, women's equality, consumer goods, and numerous other things. Actually, the trappings of Western life-style are springing up throughout the Arab world, with the oil riches serving as facilitators of social emulation.

The Arabs' admiration of the West is, however, tinged with deep resentment. The roots of such resentment may be traced back to several factors, five of which are: (1) Western colonialism, (2) the creation of the State of Israel, (3) the Anglo-French-Israeli invasion of Egypt in 1956, (4) the West's negative image of the Arabs, and (5) the superior attitude Westerners have generally exhibited toward the Arabs at the interpersonal level.

Western Colonialism

One of the principal factors influencing the Arabs' perception of the West is their history of subjugation to Western colonialism. As we pointed out in chapter 4, following the disintegration of the Islamic Empire, the Arabs came under the Turkish rule. When Turkey entered World War I on the side of the Central Powers, leaders of the Arab nationalist movement realized that the defeat of Turkey and her allies would result in the partition of the Ottoman Empire. So that their lands would not be divided as spoils of war and in order to realize their aspirations for independence, the Arabs reached an understanding with Great Britain, the world's superpower at the time. Accordingly, Great Britain promised to grant the Arabs their independence in return for the Arabs' military support for the Allies in the Middle East.

While Great Britain was negotiating with Sherif Husein, the Arabs' leader, a secret political arrangement known as the Sykes-Picot Agreement had been reached among the Allies to carve up the Ottoman Empire. When the war ended with the defeat of Turkey, all Arab provinces were placed under British and French control.

The Sykes-Picot Agreement became known to the Arabs when its contents were revealed by the Bolshevik government of Russia. A pall of disillusionment fell over the Arabs when they discovered that promises of freedom made during the war were now to be sacrificed to European political claims in the region. World War I emphasized in the Arabs' mind the Machiavellian characteristic of Western power politics, namely, readiness to promise anything to further a Western cause. The aftermath of the war left on the Arabs profound negative impressions of Western policy and behavior.

It was against many contrary influences that Sherif Husein of Mecca was able to gain support from the Muslim Arabs to revolt against their coreligionist Turks. The appeal of the revolt lay in the promise it gave of Arab independence. The Arabs were willing to trust the pledged word of the British that it was their intention to create an independent Arab kingdom. That the war ended with Arab lands divided into British and French spheres of influence "seemed to most Arabs to provide clear and incontrovertible proof of British, indeed of Western, perfidy."[1]

The Arabs felt double-crossed; they were indignant, and their struggle for independence now shifted from the Turks to the British and the French. Agitation against European domination intensified and became increasingly open. Although the Arabs finally managed to rid themselves of the new colonial domination, they have not forgotten the West's "broken promises." The West came to be perceived as untrustworthy and unreliable.

The Creation of Israel

While Arab nationalists were striving to extricate themselves from the Turkish hold, Zionist Jewish leaders were diligently working to obtain the right to establish a Jewish state in Palestine.

Like the Arab nationalists, the Zionists realized that to achieve their end, they had to secure the official backing of one or more of the great powers. Basing their plans on the assumption that the Allies would win World War I, the Zionists in England set about winning British support for Zionism.

This the English Zionists successfully accomplished in 1916 in the form of a secret gentlemen's agreement. Several months later, the agreement was publicly confirmed in the famous Balfour Declaration of 1917. The Declaration took the form of a public letter from Lord Balfour, the British foreign minister, to Lord Rothchild, a prominent English Jewish leader. The letter stated:

> His Majesty's Government views with favor the establishment in Palestine of a national home for the Jewish people, and will use their best endeavors to facilitate the achievement of this object, it being clearly understood that nothing shall be done which may prejudice the civil and religious rights of existing non-Jewish communities in Palestine, or the rights and political status enjoyed by Jews in any other country.[2]

The proclamation of the Balfour Declaration was designed "to win world-wide Jewish backing for the war effort at a time when Great Britain urgently needed every possible source of support."[3] The British thought that if an alliance could be contracted with world-wide Zionist interests, it might strengthen the pro-Allied sentiments of many influential Jews in Europe and in the U.S. Later, in 1936, the British wartime Prime Minister, David Lloyd George, revealed that "the Zionists had promised to rally Jewish pro-Allied sentiments if they received commitment for establishing a Jewish national home in Palestine. They were helpful, he commented in the House of Commons, both in America and in Russia, which at the time was walking out and leaving England alone."[4]

Wtih the tremors of the Sykes-Picot Agreement still being felt throughout the Arab world, the Arabs received another jolt when they learned of the West's scheme to establish a Jewish state in their midst. When Sherif Husein sought clarification from the British regarding the Balfour Declaration, he was assured that Great Britain's promise to the Zionists would be implemented only in so far as it did not impinge on the right and freedom of the inhabitants of Palestine.

The ultimate establishment of the State of Israel in 1948 hurt the Arabs deeply. To the Arabs, Israel symbolized the last trace of the hated Western influence and the chief base of Western imperialist interest in the Middle East. The Arabs blamed the retreating West for leaving behind an imperialist beachhead of Western Jews that posed a grave threat to the Arabs' political and territorial integrity. With their suspicion of the West now reinforced, the Arabs became convinced of the West's "treacherous" true self.

The U.S. was not spared the Arabs' wrath. The strong support the Zionists received from both the American government and the American public in the first Arab-Israeli war of 1948 seriously compromised the U.S. standing with the Arabs. President Truman's immediate recognition of Israel in May 1948 and the subsequent U.S. technical, military, and economic assistance to the new state added to the Arabs' bitterness. Later on, suspicion of the U.S. was compounded by the continued American alliance with Great Britain and France, the two most distrusted Western powers.

The Invasion of Egypt

In November 1956, Great Britain, France, and Israel jointly engineered a coordinated attack on Egypt. The avowed purpose of the invasion was to regain control of the Suez Canal, nationalized a few months earlier by Egypt's President Gamal Abdul Nasser.

After coming to power in 1952, Nasser sought to assert Egypt's sovereignty by pursuing a policy of what he termed "positive neutralism" and by building a strong national army. To achieve the latter objective, Nasser turned to the West, principally the U.S., for help. After failing repeatedly to obtain arms from the U.S., Nasser began, in 1954-55, to negotiate an arms agreement with the Communist block. Russia, eagerly awaiting an opportunity to press its cause in the Arab world, welcomed the Egyptian initiative. Soon, extensive military and economic assistance began to flow into Egypt from several Communist countries.

The Egyptian-Soviet ties grew closer and were accelerated by the political and psychological advantages the Communists had over the West. For one thing, the Communists were free of any record of Middle Eastern colonialism. For another, they were avowed opponents of Western imperialism, with no stake in the status quo of the pro-West, conservative Arab regimes existing at the time. The Communists were, therefore, in a position to support any revolutionary tendency of Arab nationalists, encouraging the impression of having a common interest in breaking the grip of Western imperialism on the emerging nations. Added to this was the Soviet Union's unwavering support of the Arabs in their feud with Israel. Although the Russians gave initial support to Israel, they later abandoned it in favor of upholding the Arab postion.

Arms provided by the Communists appealed to other Arab states, since the Communists attached no political, economic, or military strings to such assistance as the West customarily did. Even Syria, which had at first been reluctant to take foreign assistance, now accepted aid from the Soviet Union. Thus, as the Arabs were trying to reduce their dependency on the West, they consciously sought to increase their association with the Soviet bloc.

At the time the Communist influence in Egypt was on the rise, Nasser was nearing agreement with the U.S. to finance the building of the Aswan Dam, urgently needed to increase Egypt's productivity. Embittered at the friendly ties between Egypt and the Communists, John Foster Dulles, Secretary of State, informed Nasser that the U.S. had reconsidered the matter and could not, under the existing conditions, provide credits formerly agreed to. In a retaliatory move, Nasser nationalized the Suez Canal Company, owned mostly by the British and the French. Feeling that their national pride had been severely wounded by the nationalization act and reluctant to give up their control of the strategic waterway, England and France decided to topple Nasser, by force if necessary.

Aside from Nasser's nationalization of the Suez Canal, other factors contributed to the tripartite attack on Egypt. Great Britain was annoyed by Nasser's encouragement of anti-British sentiments in Jordan and in the Arabian coastal sheikdoms. France was eager to end Egyptian assistance to the Algerian nationalist movement engaging its forces in North Africa. And Israel feared the rapid growth of Egyptian military strength and the increase of Egyptian harassment of the Israeli border. In short, Nasser's presence in power posed a serious threat to the Western-Israeli interests in the Middle East. And his removal became an objective in itself that was no less significant to the three invading powers than regaining control of the waterway.

The Anglo-French-Israeli attack on Egypt failed to achieve its objectives. The United Nations ordered the invaders to evacuate their forces from Egypt immediately. More importantly, Russian threats to use rockets and to send volunteers to fight the invaders added to the potential danger of the situation. By the end of 1956, the British and French forces had retreated; and Israel, coming under heavy pressure from the U.S., withdrew its troops from the Gaza Strip early in 1957. The Suez Canal remained under Egyptian control, and Nasser not only survived the attack but emerged as a hero throughout the Arab world.

The invasion of Egypt rekindled Arab resentment and served to convert dark suspicions of the West and Israel into hard realities. It was commonly believed in the Arab world that the attack was directed not against Egypt alone but against all Arabs, with the purpose of re-establishing Western dominance in the area. To the Arabs, the attack revealed another aspect of the Machiavellian characteristic of the Western powers: the ruthless preoccupation with military force.

The West's Negative Image of the Arabs

The Arab's perception of the West is in some ways a reaction to the West's perception of him. The Arab who travels to the West for the first time becomes dismayed at the distorted picture Westerners have of the Arabs. As he watches TV, attends movies, and reads newspapers and magazines, the Arab is inundated with unflattering images in which he is portrayed either as a wastrel oil sheik with overflowing harem, a camel jockey, or a blood-thirsty killer. As a member of a highly proud culture, the Arab reacts angrily to such a distorted picture, and his anger often translates into bitterness and hostility toward the West.

To be sure, some Westerners harbor a number of positive images of the Arabs. There is the image of the noble desert Bedouin, devoted to his thoroughbred mare. And there is the image of the Arabian nights and the tales of Scheherazade. On the whole, though, the Westerners' image of the Arabs tends to be highly distorted.

There are at least three factors which may account for the West's negative picture of the Arabs: (1) the religious conflict between Christianity and Islam, (2) the idological difference between many Arab countries and the

West, and (3) the role which Western communication media have played in creating, perpetuating, and dramatizing many of the stereotyped Arab images.

The Role of Religion

The relationship between the Arabs and the West goes back at least 1300 years when Islam was born among the Arabs. From the very start, Islam and Christianity were at cross-purposes. The Muslims believe that the patriarch Abraham founded a forerunner faith to Islam, and that the coming of the Prophet Muhammad in the 7th century was foretold in the Old and the New Testaments. But the prophecy was either ignored or falsified by both the Jews and the Christians.

Muhammad preached a universal doctrine designed to perfect Christianity and Judaism. The Christians and the Jews, however, did not see themselves in need of perfection. Rather, they saw in Islam a threat to and denial of their own faith. On their part, the early Muslims who accepted the prophet-hood but not the divinity of Christ felt rebuffed in what they must have regarded as a friendly overture to the Christians.

This doctrinal incompatibility was soon compounded by territorial rivalries when Arab Muslims broke out of their desert to conquer Christian lands to the North and to the West as far as Spain. The Europeans responded defensively, creating of their conquerors an unflattering picture which came to govern European notions of Islam for centuries.

In the great medieval French epic of wars between Christians and Muslims in Spain, the Chanson de Roland, the Christian poet, endeavored to provide some idea of the Islamic religion. According to him, the Muslims worshipped a trinity consisting of three persons: Muhammad, founder of their religion; and two others, both of them devils, Appolin and Tervagant. Since Christendom worshipped its founder in association with two other entities, the Muslims also had to worship their founder, and he too had to be one of a trinity, with two demons coopted to make the numer complete.

It was a long time before Christendom was even willing to give the Muslims a name with a religious meaning. For many centuries, Western Christians called the followers of the Prophet Muhammad Saracens, a word of uncertain etymology but clearly of ethnic and not religious connotation. In the Iberian peninsula where Christians met Muslims who came from Morocco, the Muslims were called Moors.

In most of Europe, Muslims were called Turks, after the main Muslim invaders, and a convert to Islam was said to have "turned Turk" even if the conversion took place in Marrakesh or in Delhi. Even after Europe began to recognize the fact that Islam was a religion and not an ethnic community, it expressed this realization in a sequence of false analogies beginning with the name given to the religion and its followers. Thus, Islam was called Muhammadanism and the Muslims Muhammadans.[5] The Muslims do not and have never called themselves Muhammadans nor their religion

Muhammadanism, since Muhammad is not considered by the Muslims to be divine or the Son of God as Christ is by the Christians.

For hundreds of years, medieval divines, building on conceptions created by their predecessors living under Muslim rule, repeated and invented notions and incidents to prove that the Prophet Muhammad was an imposter, the Quran false, and Islam a sinister invitation to immorality. Early in this century, an American missionary graciously conceded that "the Prophet was not an imposter; rather he was a 'pathological case,' a 'trance-medium' who yielded to temptation and forged the awful machinery of divine inspiration to serve his own ignoble and selfish purposes."[6]

In recent times, a new stereotype of Islam, couched in the secular guise of social science, has emerged. With little or no knowledge of Islamic doctrines, Western academic experts follow one another in branding Islam as a "barrier" to economic and social development in the Arab world.

Perhaps the one facet of Islam which Westerners find most difficult to understand is the fusion of religious belief and civil power in one system. Westerners are simply unable to imagine the circumstances in which they would lodge religious beliefs not only at the center of their individual conduct, but also at the center of their politics. A country like the U.S., which is founded on the separation of religion and civil power and created in large part by people who had in common nothing but their flight from religious oppression elsewhere, is not exactly the best setting for a sympathetic grasp of Islam.[7]

Faced with so many misconceptions and falsehoods about Islam, the Arab reacts indignantly; he perceives the Westerners' distortion of his religion as an indication of their hatred of the Muslims. Echoing the views of most Arabs, Saudi Arabia's Minister of Oil, Sheik Ahmed Zaki Yamani, said in a speech delivered on April 24, 1981 before the Foreign Policy Association: "...quite simply, it is America's hatred for Moslems that makes it help Israel seize their land and expel the Palestinian nation."[8]

Unfortunately, Arabs as well as Muslims, for a variety of reasons, have done little, if anything, to dispel the Westerners' misconceptions of Islam. They have failed in drawing sufficient attention to the cultural and historical affinities between Islam and Christianity.

The Role of Ideology

Although European influence in the Arab world started in the 19th century, it did not peak until after World War I when the European powers (mainly Great Britain and France) carved up the Arab World following the collapse of the Ottoman Empire. By the 1920's, Great Britain and France were directly or indirectly in control of most of the Arab countries.

Unwilling to exchange one master with another, the Arabs turned their ire from the Turks to the British and the French, and within less than four decades, the Arabs were able to push out the last vestige of European colonial domination. Fearing that the Soviet Union might take advantage of the resultant "power vacuum," the U.S. felt obliged to step in and assume many of the European commitments in the area.

Instead of resorting to direct military occupation, as the British and the French did, the U.S. adopted a more subtle approach to draw the Arabs back into the Western sphere of influence. By playing up the threat of the Communists' expansionist schemes in the Middle East and by promising economic and technical assistance, the U.S. sought to persuade the Arabs to join the West in a series of mutual defense treaties. Although it met with some initial success, the U.S. policy ultimately failed to achieve its intended purpose when key Arab states opted to pursue a policy of nonalignment in the East-West cold war.

The West had difficulty resigning itself to the decolonization process and to the notion that it no longer had a commanding role to play in that strategic part of the world. With its military, economic, and political presence severely weakened, the West reacted with anger to the "ungrateful" attitude of the Arabs who did not know what was "good for them." After all, so the argument went, it was the West that taught the Arabs the meaning of nationalism and helped them make a fresh start with education, health, justice systems, public administration, agriculture, transportation, and communication. It was also the West that introduced modern technology, found oil, marketed it, and shared the profits with the legal rulers. Were it not for the West, it was maintained, the Arabs would still be sand poor. Many Westerners were convinced that the knowledge and skills they had provided the Arabs far outweighed whatever advantages and special privileges their governments had enjoyed.

The West's ego was dealt another jolt when the revolutionary regimes in Egypt, Iraq, Syria, Algeria, and Libya rejected Western political and economic ideologies. In their internal politics, the Arabs discarded the multi-party system after it had collapsed in a number of Arab countries in the 1950's. Maintaining that the Western-style democracy had been entirely imposed upon them by the West, the Arabs felt that the system did not suit their need for political stability so vital for the nation-building process in which they were engaged.

In their international politics, several Arab states adopted a policy of neutralism in the cold war raging at the time between the West and the Communist block. The political wedge between the Arabs and the West progressively widened as an increasing number of Arab states began to side with the Communists in supporting "revolutionary movements" throughout the world and in agitating against "conservative and reactionary" regimes which consistently received Western backing.

Economically, many Arab rulers turned their back to the free-enterprise system, another of the West's cherished institutions. Terming it exploitative and unjust, several Arab governments opted for socialism which they came to see as being more consistent with their avowed goal of establishing economic and social justice in their emerging nations.

Embittered with the Arabs' rejection of its ideology, the West could not conceal its pleasure whenever the Arabs faltered in their political, economic, and military endeavors. Such an attitude was perhaps no more evident than in the victories the Israelis continually scored in their military confrontations with the Arabs. To the West, the Israeli triumphs signified the superior form of Western institutions, present in Israel and absent in most of the Arab countries. On their part, the Arabs became increasingly indignant at the West's persistent military, economic, and moral support to their enemy, Israel. As a consequence, the Arabs began to view the West as an adversary.

The Role of the Communication Media

No single factor has conditioned the average Westerner's attitude toward the Arabs as the communication media have. The media are largely responsible for inventing and perpetuating a host of distorted images of the Arabs.

From the 1920's silent movies to today's wide-screen spectaculars, hundreds of movies with Arab themes have been made. With a few exceptions, the movies are mostly exotic melodramas in which swarthy Arabs abduct white women or attack the valiant foreign legion. The Arabs are generally depicted either as fools, pleasure seekers, or blood thirsty desert killers. In today's movies dealing with the Arab-Israeli conflict, the Arab is invariably cast in the role of a villain who—through ignorance, arrogance, or pure racial hatred—aggresses upon the Israelis who are portrayed as peace-loving, courageous, khaki-shirted citizen soldiers.

Perhaps the worst culprit in misrepresenting the Arabs' cultural image has been TV. Today, an erroneous image of the Arabs and their life style is offered to TV viewers on a continuing basis; the Arab has become the latest subject of TV stereotyping. As any TV fan knows, a villain is needed in conflicts that pit good against evil. Today's TV villain is the Arab, simplistically and unfairly portrayed.

Depicted as the murderous white-slaver, the dope dealer, the rich kid who thinks money can buy love, the TV Arab is about as close to being a real Arab as Rudolf Valentino was. The Arab is also portrayed as a terrorist or participant in political intrigue. He is concerned about political issues, but that concern is expressed largely through murder, kidnapping, and other forms of terrorism. Apparently, it is still socially permissable to accept these degrading caricatures as TV continues to foster the myth that there are no human Arabs.[9] The U.S. Commission on Civil Rights attacks the unfair depiction of Blacks, Hispanics, Asians, Jews, and Indians, but not Arabs.

Books and magazines have made their own contributions in the portrayal of a distorted picture of the Arabs. Ahmed Baha El-Din, Editor-in-Chief of *Al-Musawwar*, an Egyptian newsmagazine, could not help noticing this picture during his visit to the U.S. With obvious bewilderment, Baha El-Din writes:

> When I first visited the United States in 1960, I was interested in the litera-
> ture of the Beat Generation and read *On the Road* by Jack Kerouac. I was
> struck by the sentence saying, 'We were like a band of Arabs coming to
> blow up New York' and another saying 'Dean drove into a filling station...
> noticed that the attendant was fast asleep...quietly filled the gas tank and
> rolled off like an Arab.' I thought then that Kerouac had probably never
> met an Arab in his life, and his image had been dragged up from the pit
> of his subconscious.[10]

The press has been equally guilty in its erroneous depiction of the Arabs.
Studies made of the American press treatment of the Arab-Israeli conflict,
for example, have revealed a consistent anti-Arab bias. This has led one
researcher to conclude that much of the anti-Arab treatment in the
American press is purely racist in tone.[11]

The Arab defeat in the 1967 war with Israel let loose in Europe and in the
U.S. a flood of disparaging jokes that astonished many Arabs who were
pro-Western and who were even willing to see an end to the Arab-Israeli
hostilities. European and American cartoonists and stand-up comedians
made a daily practice of denigrating the Arabs, their culture, and their
heritage. The overwhelmingly negative Arab caricature depicted by the
media prompted one American writer to remark: "I do not think this
wholly owing to the absence of a big enough Arab-American political con-
stituency to raise hell. There is a dehumanizing, circular process at work
here. The caricature dehumanizes. But it is inspired and made acceptable by
an earlier dehumanizing influence, namely, the absence of feeling for who
the Arabs are and where they have been."[12]

Within the past few years, there has been a noticeable improvement in the
American media treatment of the Arabs. A number of forces have
combined to produce the new trend, one of which has undoubtedly been
President Sadat's dramatic visit to Jerusalem. Urbane, pipe-smoking,
English-speaking, Sadat not only looked "Western" but sounded
statesmanlike when he talked of peace. Sadat's demeanor shattered many of
the myths which the media themselves have helped spread in the West.
The improved treatment notwithstanding, anyone exposed to American TV
and newspapers cannot help forming an image of the Arab either as a
terrorist and a plane hijacker, or as an oil sheik threatening to strangle the
West by raising oil prices or shutting off the oil pipelines.

The West's images of the Arabs—images born out of differences in
religion and ideology and dramatized by the communication media—injure
the Arabs in the deepest sense. Like Baha El-Din, the Egyptian journalist,
the Arabs who visit Europe and the U.S. experience a feeling of bewilderment and shock at the disparaging manner in which their culture is portrayed. Here are people who grow up in a society that instils in them the
notion that they belong to a great culture with great traditions and unsur-
passed accomplishments. They are told how superior they are to other
cultures, and how proud they should be in their race and in their religion.
Yet as soon as the Arab steps out of his cultural setting into the Western

world, he is confronted with a different and painful reality. His self-esteem is challenged, his time-honored values distorted, his religion downgraded, and his culture denigrated.

In the face of such challenges, the Arab reacts defensively; he begins to develop negative images of his own about the West which he comes to perceive as a hostile world and Westerners as bigoted people.

These reactive perceptions of the West exert strong influence on the Arab's behavior long after he returns home. Westerners are often at a loss to understand why some Arab leaders, who had received their education in the West, speak and act with so much hostility toward the West. Such Westerners fail to realize that a great deal of the Arabs' hostility is but a reflection of the anger and frustration the Arabs feel over the manner in which they are perceived in the West. The Arabs' sensitivity to outside skepticism and their need for dignity are very much at play here. In their dealings with the West, some Arab leaders often act emotionally with no apparent purpose other than to humiliate the West or to "put it in its place."

In short, whatever negative perception the Arabs have of the West is, at least in part, a reaction to the West's negative perception of the Arabs.

The Westerners' Superior Attitude

Undoubtedly, the four factors discussed above (Western colonialism, the creation of Israel, the invasion of Egypt, and the West's negative image of the Arabs) account for most of the resentment the Arabs feel toward the West. There is yet another factor which has served to foster such a resentment. This can be found in the air of superiority which many Westerners operating in the Middle East have often displayed in their interpersonal communication with the Arabs. The Arabs' resentment here is also a reactive behavior; it is a type of defense mechanism which the Arabs resorted to as a means of dealing with the West's sense of superiority.

Many British and French officials, who served in the Arab world during the colonial period, were neither able nor well-balanced individuals. They were largely second-raters who, unable to better themselves at home, took minor posts in the Arab countries where they thought they could do better for themselves with much less effort. Foreign service afforded these officials an opportunity to appease their own sense of inferiority by lording it over the Arabs.[13]

The contemptuous attitude of Western officials is evident in the books some of them wrote detailing their impressions of the Arabs. In one such book called *Egypt and the English*, the author states:

> To hear the Egyptian talk, you would imagine that his one desire was to improve his mind, to raise his level to the equal of a highly-educated European. As a matter of fact, the Egyptian has no mind. There are gentlemen in Egypt as in other countries...But it cannot be denied that the ordi-

nary Egyptian has the ordinary faults of hybrids in an intolerable degree. He is a liar, a rogue, an assassin as needs be and opportunities arise. As the boy cheats over his work, so the man cheats over his business. Taking a mean advantage is, to him, a commendable strategy.[14]

Egyptians and other Arabs have not failed to notice that many Westerners who visted the Middle East had in their bags books similar to *Egypt and the English.* Most of these books contained outlandish stories of the experiences of Westerners who made their long years in the Arab coun- tries tolerable by seeing the amusing side of the antics of the natives with whom they came into contact.

In thê personal experiences of many Arabs are recollections of contemp- tuous and uncivil treatment by Westerners who regarded themselves superi- or to the Arabs by virtue of their being Western. Even members of the Arab educated class and those who became deeply attached tó Western culture were denied membership in Western communities based in the Arab world. After giving their best efforts to penetrate the secrets of Western culture, these Arab imitators of the West suffered a sense of betrayal when Westerners rejected them. The bitterness was compounded when Western- ized Arabs lost contact with their own society. It was only natural, there- fore, that many Westernized Arabs, convinced that there was no place for them in Western culture, should seek redemption by returning to their roots and becoming Arab nationalists.

Edward Attiyah, a Lebanese, is one of those educated Arabs who became disillusioned with the West. After becoming deeply attached to the British culture, Attiyah went to live in the British-occupied Sudan where he taught English. Later, he wrote an autobiography detailing the sense of rejection and resentment the educated Arabs in the Sudan felt. The Westernized Arab had revolted, Attiyah says, "not against oppression, injustice or economic exploitation...but against spiritual arrogance, racial haughtiness, social aloofness, and paternal authoritarianism."[15]

Attiyah tells how he, long a devoted Englophile educated in England, became an Arab nationalist and eventually a sympathizer with the Soviet Union. The break came when the British Governor-General came to visit Gordon College in the Sudan:

> One day his excellency came to visit the college. The British staff lined up to receive him and were one by one introduced to him. The non-British staff were required to remain in their Common Room; there was no part in the ceremony for them. We sat in the Common Room like a poor relation banished to the kitchen during the presence in the house of the distinguished guest...I walked home disgusted and angered by this humiliation.

> Thus I was liberated, not by an intellectual process, but by the force of an emotional reaction, originating in my own wounded feelings...I found myself understanding and sympathizing with that host of longings...which comes under the designation of "the Arab Awakening." My whole life went into reverse gear. I became myself an Arab nationalist.[16]

Conclusion

Despite their resentment and suspicion, the Arabs have a deep reservoir of goodwill toward the West. The slightest sign of understanding exhibited by Westerners often produces a remarkable change in the Arabs' attitude.

The oil boom, with its attendant massive economic development programs in many Arab countries, has brought the Arabs closer to the West than at anytime since the old days of colonialism. The Arabs now possess the power of oil money which the West eagerly seeks. They have also been experiencing a heightened sense of psychological confidence since attaining their full sovereignty. Combined, these factors will make the Arabs increasingly secure in the realization that they can deal with the West on an equal footing.

Summary

The Arabs' perception of the West is a mixture of admiration and resentment. Although they admire many of the West's values, the Arabs' admiration is tinged with resentment and suspicion. In this chapter, we point out that the Arabs' resentful attitude toward the West is attributable to at least five factors:

1. Western Colonialism. During World War I, the Arabs received promises of freedom from Great Britain in return for the Arabs' support for the West. When the war ended, the Ottoman rule was replaced by Western rule. The Arabs felt double-crossed; and even long after gaining freedom, the Arabs continued to view the West within the context of its "broken promises."

2. The Creation of Israel. To the Arabs, the establishment of Israel is another indication of the West's untrustworthiness. The Arabs blamed the retreating West for leaving behind an imperialist beachhead of Western Zionists, directed at undermining the Arabs' political and territorial integrity.

3. The Invasion of Egypt. The British, French, and Israeli invasion of Egypt in 1956 served to rekindle Arab resentment of the West. The invasion was viewed as an effort by the West to re-establish its dominance in the Arab world.

4. The West's Negative Image of the Arabs. The Arabs' resentful attitude toward the West is, in part, a reaction to the West's negative perception of the Arabs. The generally negative Western picture of the Arabs is due to three factors:

   a. Religious Differences. The Muslims believe that the Prophet Muhammad preached a universal doctrine designed to perfect Christianity and Judaism. Early Christians and Jews viewed Islam as a threat to their own religions. Reacting to the Muslim conquest of

Spain, the Europeans invented notions to prove that Muhammad was an imposter, the Quran false, and Islam a sinister invitation to immorality. The Arab perceives the Westerners' distortion of his faith as in indication of their prejudice against the Muslims.

   b. Ideological Differences. The Arabs have generally chosen economic and political systems at variance with those of the West. Politically, most Arab governments have instituted dictatorial or one-party rules in their internal politics and pursued a neutralist stance in their international relations. Such divergent economic and political paths have been instrumental in engendering a climate fraught with bitterness and hostility on both sides.

   c. The Role of the Communication Media. Whether in movies, TV, books, or magazines, the Arabs have largely been portrayed either as fools, pleasure-seekers, blood-thirsty killers, dope-smugglers, white-slavers, or plane-hijackers. The Arabs who become exposed to such images about them in the West react indignantly, and their resentment of the West continues long after they return to their countries.

5. The Westerners' Superior Attitude. Most Westerners who operated in the Arab world acted in a superior fashion in their interpersonal relations with the natives. In the personal experiences of many Arabs are recollections of contemptuous and uncivil treatment by Westerners.

Footnotes

[1] Charles Cremeans, *The Arabs and the World* (New York: Frederick A. Praeger, 1963), p. 124.

[2] J.C. Hurewitz, *The Struggle for Palestine* (New York: Norton, 1950), p. 26.

[3] Don Peretz, *The Middle East Today* (New York: Holt, Rinehart and Winston, Inc., 1963), p. 107.

[4] *Ibid.,* p. 108.

[5] Bernard Lewis, "Return of Islam," *Commentary,* Vol. 61, January 1976, p. 39.

[6] Morroe Berger, "Arabs' Attitude to the West," *Yale Review,* Vol. 61, December 1971, p. 219.

[7] Meg Greenfield, "Islam and Us," *Newsweek,* March 26, 1979, p. 116.

[8] *The New York Times,* April 24, 1981, pp. 1 and 5.

[9] Jack G. Sheehan, "The Arab: TV's Most Popular Villain," *Christian Century,* December 13, 1978, pp. 1214-1218.

[10] Ahmed Baha El-Din, "World Media and the Arabs: An Arab Perspective," in Abdeen Jabbara and Janice Terry (eds.) *The Arab World: From Nationalism to Revolution* (Wilmette, Il.: The Medina University Press International, 1971), p. 85.

[11] Janice Terry, "A Content Analysis of American Newspapers," in Abdeen Jabbara and Janice Terry (eds.), 1971, *ibid.,* p. 100. Also, see: Michael W. Suleiman, "An Evaluation of Middle East News Coverage in Seven American Newspapers, July-December 1956," *Middle East Forum,* Autumn 1965, pp. 5-30; American Institute for Political Communication, "Domestic Communications Aspects of the Middle East Crisis, A Special Report," Washington, D.C., APIC, July 1967; and Leslie Farmer, "All We Know is What We Read in the Papers," *Middle East*

Newsletter, February 1968, p. 105.
[12]Meg Greenfield, "Our Ugly Arab Complex," *Newsweek,* December 5, 1977, p. 110.
[13]Charles Cremeans, 1963, *op. cit.,* p. 49.
[14]Douglas Sladen, *Egypt and the English* (London: Hurst and Blackett, 1908), p. 73.
[15]Edward Attiyah, *An Arab Tells His Story: A Study in Loyalties* (London: John Murray, 1946), p. 165.
[16]*Ibid.,* pp. 147-149.

Part II

Profiles of Selected
Arab Countries

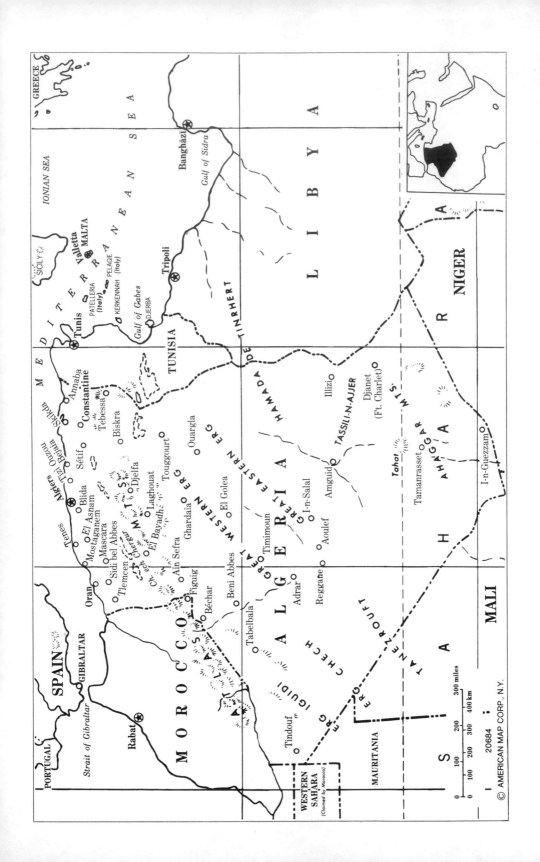

Chapter 8

Algeria
(Algerian Democratic Popular Republic)

Size and Location

The total area of Algeria is 2,381,741 sq. km. (919,592 sq. miles) of which a large part is desert.

Algeria is the largest of the three countries in northwest Africa that comprise the Maghreb, or the Arab West, which lies between the Mediterranean Sea and the Sahara desert. Algeria is located between Morocco and Tunisia with a Mediterranean coastline of nearly 1000 km. The country is bounded to the east by Tunisia and Libya, to the south by Niger and Mali, and to the west by Mauritania and Morocco. The physical geography of Algeria is the mountainous, relatively humid terrain of the north, and the vast expanse of lower, flatter desert to the south which is part of the Saharan tableland.

Climate

The climate of northernmost Algeria is of "Mediterranean" type with hot, dry summers and mild, wet winters. Typical summer temperatures range from 24° C to 26° C (75° F to 79° F) and winter temperatures from 10° C to 12° C (50° F to 54° F). Rainfall varies in amount with an average annual rainfall of 38 cm (15 in.).

To the south, in the high plateau region, the continental climate is dominant with great daily temperature ranges. Rain is scanty. The Sahara has a true desert climate with temperatures going to 50° C (122° F) on most days in summer. The climate of Saharan Algeria is characterized by extremes of temperature, wind, and aridity.

Population — Millions: Mid-Year Estimates[1]

1976 17.30
1977 17.91
1978 18.51
1979 19.13

The great majority of the inhabitants live in the northern part of the country, particularly along the Mediterranean Coast.

Religion

Islam is the official religion, and the whole Algerian population, with a few exceptions, is Muslim. The Christian population is almost entirely foreign.

Language

Arabic is the official language of Algeria and is spoken by more than 80 percent of the population. However, French is the language of the administrative and intellectual elite and is considered the semi-official language of Algeria. French is widely used in the educational institutions of higher learning.

Principal Towns — Mid-Year Estimates, 1973

Algiers (Capital)   1,200,000
Oran   440,000
Constantine   324,000

Education

Education is free, compulsory, and universal for 8 years from age 6 to 14. The literacy rate is estimated to be at 26 percent. Adult illiteracy is being combatted by a large-scale campaign. Since independence, Algeria's educational system has grown at a remarkable rate. Algeria has placed special emphasis on establishing technical institutes for training in the skills necessary to operate the country's burgeoning industrial sector. The main institutions of higher learning are the University of Algiers, the University of Oran, the University of Annaba, and the University of Constantine.

The Economy

The economy of Algeria is based on oil. To a large extent, the economy is centrally planned and is dominated by the public sector. Algeria has varied natural resources. In the coastal region are highly fertile plains and valleys where profitable returns are made from cereals, wine, olives and fruits. Mineral resources are abundant and are the mainstay of Algeria's foreign trade. Revenues from oil and gas are being used to finance ambitious industrialization plans. Algeria is still mainly an agricultural country. The most valued crop is the grape harvest which represents 66 percent of total agricultural exports by value. Wheat, barley and oats are grown for local consumption. Other crops include maize, millet, rye, rice, olives, figs, dates and tobacco.

Minerals. Algeria has rich mineral resources. Before the Petroleum era, Algeria had mined and exported high-grade iron ore, phosphates, lead, zinc, and antimony.

Petroleum and Natural Gas. Production of crude petroleum reached 53.3 million tons by 1977 (with the daily average being 1,140,000 barrels). The government has set up its own company (SONATRACH) which has complete control of the domestic distribution network.

Natural gas is becoming more valuable than oil to Algeria, which is expected to be the world's biggest natural gas exporter. Algeria is expected to export 80,000 million cubic meters per year by the early 1980's. Reserves are currently estimated at three to four million cubic meters. Contracts for sales of natural gas to Western Europe and the U.S.A. have shown a spectacular increase in size in recent years.

Industry. Manufacturing contributes about 12 percent to the Gross Domestic Product. The share of the industrial sector is expected to increase. The Algerian government has embarked upon a massive program of rapid industrialization; that is, industrialization is becoming the keynote of the government economic policy. Under the second Four-Year Plan (1974-77), industry has received 43.5 percent of the total budgetary allocations.

Principal Economic Indicators — Billions of Dinars

	1975	1976	1977
Gross Domestic Product	56.3	68.5	81.9
Per Capita GDP	3,355	3,960	4,573
Per Capita GDP in U.S. Dollars	833	908	1,133
Private Consumption	26.8	31.9	38.9
Gross Fixed Capital Formation	24.4	31.2	39.3
Consumer Price Index	100.0	113.9	116.3

Gross Domestic Product by Economic Activity, 1976

	% of GDP
Agriculture & Fisheries	7.4
Oil and Natural Gas	30.1
Mining & Energy	1.7
Manufacturing	11.4
Building & Public Works	13.1
Trade & Transport	25.2
Other	11.1

Foreign Trade—Millions of U.S. Dollars

	1977	1978	1979
Merchandise			
Exports fob	6,008	6,340	9,485
Imports fob	6,197	7,293	7,797
Services			
Exports	375	394	612
Imports	2,792	3,297	4,344

Finance

Currency—Algerian Dinar
1 Algerian Dinar = 100 centimes
Coins: 1, 2, 4, 10, 20 and 50 centimes, 1 and 5 dinars
Notes: 5, 10, 100 and 500 dinars
Exchange rate: U.S. $1 = 4.0385 dinars as of June 1978

Money Supply—Millions of Dinars: End of Period

	1977	1978	1979
Currency outside banks	21,957	28,765	35,882
Demand Deposits at banks	23,299	27,342	28,700
Total	45,256	56,107	64,582

Weights and Measures

The metric system is in force.

Banks and Other Commercial Organizations

Banque Centrale d'Algerie: 8 Blvd., Zirant-Youcef, Algiers
Banque Exteriere d'Algerie: 11 Blvd., Colonel Amirouche, Algiers.
    (Concerned with foreign trade and the financing of industrial development.)
Banque Nationale d'Algerie: 12 rue Hassiba Ben Bonali, Algiers
Export Institute—Institut National Algerien du Commerce Exterieur:
    6 Blvd., Amilcar, Cabral, Algiers
Jeune Cambre Economique D'Alger: Rue de Nimes, Algiers

Industrial and State Organizations

Societe Nationale de Constructions Mecaniques: 1 Route Nationale,
    Birkhadem, Algiers. (Manufacturer and importer of motor vehicles and
    agricultural equipment.)
Societe Nationale de Construction Metalliques: 38 Rue Didouche, Mourad,
    Algiers. (Production of metal goods.)
Societe Nationale de la Siderurgie: 5 Rue Abou Moussa, Algiers. (Steel, cast
    iron, zinc and products.)

Office Algerian Interprofessional des cereales: 5 Rue Ferhat Bousaad, Algiers. (Has a monopoloy of trade in wheat, rice, maize, barley and products derived from these cereals.)

SONATRACH: 80 Avenue Ahmed Ghermoul, Algiers. (A State-owned organization for exploration, exploitation, transport, refining and marketing of oil and gas and their products.)

Office Nationale des Ports: 2 rue d'Angkor, B.P. 830, Algiers. (Responsible for management of port facilities and sea pilotage.)

Government

Algeria attained its independence in 1962. The state is socialist. The Algerian Constitutional system rests on the principle of a single-party state. The ruling party is the National Liberation Front (FLN). The governmental structure is comprised of three branches: the executive, legislative, and judicial.

The Executive Branch. The President of the Republic is the Head of State and Head of Armed Forces. He is elected by universal, secret, direct suffrage.

The Legislative Branch. The National Popular Assembly prepares and votes the law. Its members are nominated by the party (FLN) and are elected by universal, direct, secret suffrage for a five year term.

The Judicial Branch. This consists of the Supreme Court and the Higher Judicial Council. The judges obey only the law. The right of the accused to a defense is guaranteed. The Supreme Court regulates the activities of the courts and tribunals. The Council is presided over by the President of the Republic, with the Minister of Justice serving as Vice-President of the Council. As of 1981, Benjeddid Chadi is the Head of State.

Office Hours

Summer: 0800-1600 Saturday-Wednesday
0800-1200 Thursday

Winter: 0800-1200
1430-1800 Saturday-Wednesday
0800-1200 Thursday

Public Holidays

January 1	New Year's Day
May 1	Labor Day
June 19	National Day
July 5	Independence Day
November 1	Revolution Day

Muslim Holidays

They are determined by sightings of the moon which may vary each year by a day or two. For 1980, the religious holidays were:

January 30   Birthday of the Prophet Muhammad
June 11   Ascension of the Prophet[2]
August 13   Eid Al-Fitr—End of Ramadan[3]
October 20   Eid Al-Adha—End of the Pilgrimage[4]
November 9   Al-Hijra—The Muslim's New Year[5]
November 18   Ashura—Day of mourning for Shi'ite Muslims[6]

Tourist Information

Office Nationale Algerien du Tourisme: 25-27 Rue Khelifa Boukhalfa, Algiers
Societe Nationale Algeriene de Tourisme et d'Hotellerie: 8 Rue du Dr., Saadane, Algiers—General Affairs
Air Algerie: 1 Place Maurice Audin, B.P. 858, Algiers

Visa Requirements

In addition to a valid passport, one must obtain a visa. Normally it takes three days to obtain a visa.

Hotels

Algiers: Hotel el Aurassi: Ave Franz Fanon, Te. 64 82 55/55
                  Hotel St. George: 24 Ave Sauidani Boudjema, Tel. 60 4164
                  Hotel Aletti: Rue Hocine Asselah, Tel. 63 50 50/48
                  Hotel Albert 1er: 5 Ave Pasteur, Te. 63 00 20/22
                  Hotel Angleterre: 11 Rue Ben Boulaid, Tel. 63 65 40/41
Annaba: Hotel Plaza: Rue Ste Monique, Tel. 82 35 77/79
Constantine: Hotel Cirta: 1 Ave Rahmani Cherif, Tel. 93 34 64
Oran: Hotel Grand: 5 Place du Maghreb, Tel. 33 15 33
                  Hotel Royal: 3 Blvd de la Saummain

Press

Arabic Dailies: *Al Shaab* (The People): 1 Place Maurice, Audin, Algiers
                  Al Joumnhouria (The Republic): 6 Rue Bencenousi Hamida, Oran
                  Al Nasr: 100 Rue Larbi Ben M'hidi, Constantine
French: *Al Moudjahid*: 20 Rue de la Liberte, Algiers

Selected Embassies

Canada: 27 bis Rue d'Anjou, Hydra, Algiers
China, People's Republic: 34 Blvd., des Martyrs, Algiers
France: Rue Larbi Alik, Hydra, Algiers

Germany, Federal Republic: 165 Chemin Findja, Algiers
India: 119 Didouche Mourad, Algiers
Japan: 3 Rue du Dr. Lucien Reynaud
U.S.S.R.: Chemin du Prince d'annam, El-Biar, Algiers
U.K.: 7 Chemin des Glycines, Algiers
U.S.A.: 4 Chemin Bachir Brahimi, Algiers

[1] Including more than 800,000 Algerian nationals living abroad.
[2] The Muslims believe the Prophet Muhammad was instantly transported from Mecca to Jerusalem, and from there he ascended to the seventh heaven. This explains why Jerusalem is as sacred to the Muslims as it is to the Christians and the Jews.
[3] Ramadan is the ninth month of the Islamic year in which all Muslims are required to fast from dawn to dusk. For 1980, it was July 14-August 13.
[4] All able-bodied Muslims, with the financial means, are required to make the pilgrimage to Mecca at least once in a lifetime.
[5] Al-Hijra marks the year in which Muhammad emigrated from Mecca to Medina.
[6] Every year, the Shi'ite Muslims commemorate the death of Husein, the Prophet's nephew, in a battle with Mu'awiyah, Syria's governor. The feud revolved around the legitimacy of Mu'awiyah's rule.

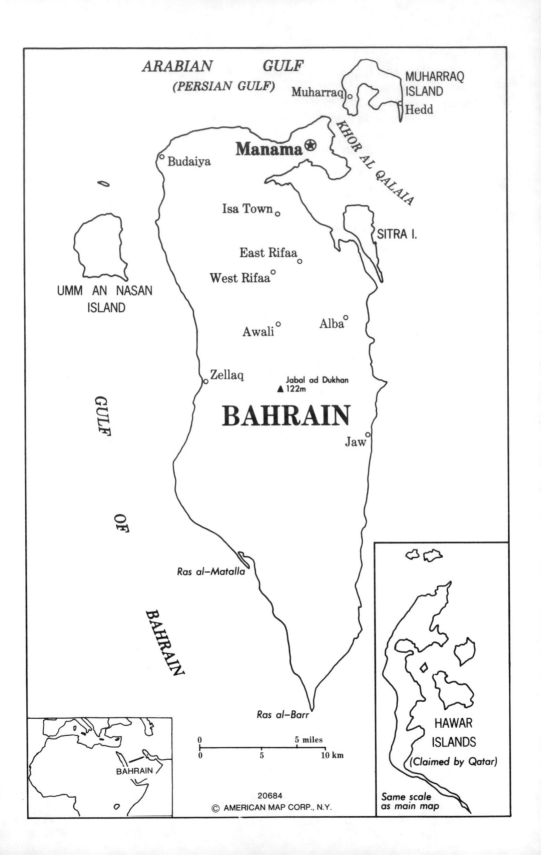

ARABIAN GULF
(PERSIAN GULF)

MUHARRAQ ISLAND

Muharraq

Hedd

Manama ⊛

KHOR AL QALAIA

Budaiya

Isa Town

SITRA I.

East Rifaa

West Rifaa

UMM AN NASAN ISLAND

Awali

Alba

Zellaq

Jabal ad Dukhan
▲ 122m

GULF

BAHRAIN

Jaw

OF

Ras al-Matalla

BAHRAIN

Ras al-Barr

HAWAR ISLANDS

(Claimed by Qatar)

0   5 miles

0   5   10 km

BAHRAIN

20684
© AMERICAN MAP CORP., N.Y.

Same scale
as main map

Bahrain

Size and Location

The total area of the Bahrain group of islands is 660.4 sq. km. (258.5 sq. miles). Bahrain itself, the principal and largest island, is 40.2 km (30 miles) long and 14.5 km (10 miles) wide. To the northeast of the Bahrain island, and linked to it by a causeway and motor road, lies Muharraq island which is approximately four miles long. A causeway linking Bahrain to Saudi Arabia is scheduled for completion in 1981.

The State of Bahrain consists of a group of 33 islands situated midway down the Arabian Gulf, 18 miles from the east coast of Saudi Arabia and about 20 miles from Qatar. Only six of the islands are of significant size: Bahrain, Muharraq, Sitra, Hawar, Nabih Salih, and Umm Suban.

Climate

In general, Bahrain's climate is harsh. In the summer months (May - October), it is hot and humid with maximum temperatures in July reaching 44° C (111° F) with 80 percent humidity. The most pleasant time of year lasts from December to March with temperatures ranging between 10° C to 20° C (50° F to 68° F).

Population — Thousands: Mid-Year Estimates[1]

1976	265
1977	274
1978	283
1979	292

Religion

The national religion is Islam of both Sunni and Shi'ite sects. The vast majority of Bahrainis are Sunni Muslims. The number of Christians is small, estimated at 7,000.

Language

Arabic is the official language. English is widely spoken and also dominates the media. Persian is the language of numerous Bahrainis of Iranian origin.

Principal Towns

Manama (Capital) 150,000
Muharraq   50,000
    Recently, a new center, Isa Town, has been constructed as a residential area. Awali is the oil town in the center of the main island.

Education

Education is free and universal but not compulsory. The literacy rate is 40 percent. The medium of instruction is Arabic. English is taught as a second language. The educational administration is centralized in the Ministry of Education. There are three higher educational institutes:
    Men's Teacher Training College
    Women's Teacher Training College
    Gulf Technical College

The Economy

Bahrain has a free market economy and is considered one of the high-income countries of the world. Traditionally, Bahrain's wealth has come from its pearling industry. However, in more recent years, Bahrain's economy has been largely based on oil, trades, and service industries. Bahrain has begun to diversify its economy to make it less dependent on oil whose known reserves are expected to run out before the end of this century.
    Agriculture and cattle breeding are practiced throughout the islands. The main crops are vegetables, lucerne, fodder crops, some dates, bananas, figs, and almond.
    Oil in commercial quantity was found in 1932. The Bahrain Petroleum Company (BAPCO) was formerly owned jointly by the Standard Oil Company of California and Texaco, Inc. In March 1975, the Bahrain Government announced that it would take over full ownership of BAPCO. The take-over was accomplished in early 1978. Crude oil production was averaging 58,000 barrels per day in 1978.
    In April 1978, the Bahrain National Oil Co. and the Japan Gas Co. signed an agreement under which previously flared gas would be processed to make 80,000 tons of propane per annum and 75,000 tons of butane as well as 125,000 tons of natural gas.
    In 1969, the Aluminum Bahrain Company (Alba) was established and started production in 1971. The aluminum smelter is the biggest not-oil related industrial project in the Gulf, producing 120,000 tons of aluminum annually.

Among the industries now firmly established are manufacturing of building materials, flour mills, clothing, plastics, the manufacture of air-conditioning equipment and fish-processing.

A drydock project, backed by the Organization of Arab Petroleum Exporting Countries, costing U.S. $340 million, was officially opened in December 1977.

In December 1971, the new Bahrain International Airport Terminal Building was opened, designed specifically for jumbo jets. The Port of Mina has nine berths for general cargo for ocean vessels. It also has storage and refrigeration facilities for the transit trade.

Principal Economic Indicators — Millions of Bahrain Dinars

	1975	1976	1977
Gross Domestic Product	364.1	538.0	655.3
Per Capita GDP	1,422	2,030	2,392
Per Capita GDP in U.S. Dollars	3,595	5,131	6,046
Consumer Price Index	100	122.6	144.3

Foreign Trade: Millions of Dinars

	1977	1978	1979
Exports fob	730.1	733.1	949.5
Imports fob	807.6	792.3	945.3

Finance

Currency — Bahrain Dinar
1 Dinar = 1000 fils
Coins: 1, 5, 10, 25, 50, 100, 250 and 500 fils
Notes: 100, 250 and 500 fils; 1, 5, and 10 dinars
Exchange rate: U.S. $1 = 377.0 fils as of June 1980

Money Supply — Millions of Dinars: End of Period

	1977	1978	1979
Currency outside banks	43.78	44.14	49.90
Demand Deposits at banks	108.71	127.20	136.21
Total	152.49	171.34	186.11

Weights and Measures

The metric system is in force.

Banking

Bahrain's broad industrial base, good telecommunication facilities, steady economic development, Bahrain's International Airport the best equipped and managed in the Middle East, and other facilities have made Bahrain a major international banking base by using Arab oil-surpluses as a source for short and medium term loans. Hence, Bahrain can be considered the financial capital of the Middle East. Financial services form an important sector of the economy of Bahrain. In 1975, the Bahrain Monetary Agency decided to set up Offshore Banking Units. An offshore banking unit is permitted to accept deposits from governments and large financial organizations in the area and to make medium-term loans for regional capital projects. By the end of 1977, 36 international banks were operating and seven more licensed.

Banks and Other Commercial Organizations

Bahrain Monetary Agency (Central Bank): P.O.B. 27, Manama
Locally incorporated banks:
National Bank of Bahrain: P.O.B. 106, Manama
Bank of Bahrain and Kuwait: P.O.B. 597, Manama
Continental Bank Ltd.: P.O.B. 5237, Manama
Gulf International Bank: P.O.B. 1017, Manama
Foreign banks:
Algemene Bank Nederland (Amsterdam): P.O.B. 350, Manama
Arab Bank Ltd. (Amman): P.O.B. 395, Manama
Bank Melli Iran (Teheran): Sheik Mubarak Bldg., P.O.B. 785, Manama
Banque du Caire (Cairo): P.O.B. 815, Manama
Banqe de Paris et des Pays — Bas, FCB (Paris): P.O.B. 5241, Manama
British Bank of the Middle East (London): P.O.B. 57, Manama
Chase Manhattan Bank (New York): P.O.B. 368, Manama
Citibank N.A. (New York): P.O.B. 548, Manama
Habib Bank Ltd. (Karachi): Government Road, P.O.B. 566, Manama
Bahrain Chamber of Commerce and Industry: P.O.B. 248, Manama
Bahrain National Oil Company: P.O.B. 504, Manama
Bahrain National Gas Company: P.O.B. 477, Manama

Government

Bahrain attained its independence in 1971. Since the 18th century Bahrain has been ruled by the Khalifa family. The ruler is called an Emir. The power of the Emir was absolute until 1973 when a new constitution was ratified. The constitution states that "all citizens shall be equal before the law." It guarantees freedom of speech, press, and religious beliefs. It also provides for a National Assembly, composed of elected members and cabinet ministers who are appointed by the Emir. Suffrage is restricted to men over 21. Despite these provisions, power is closely held in the hands of the Khalifa family.

Office Hours

Government: 0700-1300 Saturday - Thursday
Banks: 0730-1200 Saturday - Wednesday
       0730-1100 Thursday
Private Firms: 0700-1200
            1430-1700 Saturday - Thursday

Public Holidays

January 1   New Year's Day
December 16   National Day

Muslim Holidays

Variable Islamic festivals based on the sighting of the moon. For 1980, these holidays were:

January 30   Birthday of the Prophet
August 13   Eid al Fitr — End of Ramadan[2]
October 13   Eid al Adha — End of the Pilgrimage
November 9   Al Hijra — The Muslim New Year
November 18   Ashura — Day of mourning for Shi'ites

Tourism

Tourism in Bahrain is practically nonexistent. Foreigners go to Bahrain for business purposes. Most inhabited areas of Bahrain are linked by roads. Public transport consists of taxis and privately owned bus services.

Visa Requirements

In addition to valid passports, visitors need entry visas which can be obtained from a Bahrain embassy or consulate. Transit visas for 72 hours are obtainable from the immigration officials at the airport if an onward ticket is held. There is no requirement to obtain an exit visa.

Airline Services

Bahrain is served by the following foreign airlines: Air India, Alia (Jordan), British Airways, Egypt-Air, Iran Air, Iraqi Airways, KLM (Netherlands), Pan American (U.S.A.), Quantas (Australia), TWA (U.S.A.), and UTA (France).

Hotels

Because of the shortage of hotel rooms, it is advisable to book in advance.
Bahrain Hilton: P.O.B. 1090, Tel. 250000, Telex 8288
The Gulf Hotel: P.O.B. 580, Tel. 712881, Telex 8241

Royal Hotel: P.O.B. 154, Tel. 714901, Telex 8777
Delman Hotel: P.O.B. 26, Tel. 254761, Telex 8224
The Tylos Hotel: P.O.B. 1086, Tel. 252600, Telex 8349
Omar Khayam Hotel: P.O.B. 771, Tel. 713941
The Moon Plaza Hotel: P.O.B. 247, Tel. 8263, Telex 8308
Ramada: Tel. 714821, Telex 8855
LeVendome: Tel. 257777, Tel. 8811

Press ,

Arabic: *Akhbar Al-Bahrain*
             Akhbar Al-Khalij
English: *Awali Daily News*
             Gulf Daily News

Selected Embassies

Canada: Kuwait City, Kuwait
France: Mahooz 1785/7, P.O.B. 1034, Manama
Germany, Federal Republic: Kuwait City, Kuwait
India: Wolverthampton Bldg., Mahooz 1736/7, P.O.B. 26106, Manama
Japan: Kuwait City, Kuwait
U.K.: Government Road, Manama
U.S.A.: Sh. Isa Rd., P.O.B. 26431, Manama

[1]The State has one of the highest population densities in the world with more than 1100 inhabitants per square mile.
[2]For an explanation of the meaning of religious holidays, see the section on Algeria.

Egypt
(The Arab Republic of Egypt)

Size and Location

Egypt's total area is 997,667 sq. km. (835,201 sq. mi.). However, more than 90 percent of the land is desert. Egypt is located at the northeastern corner of Africa, extending across the Gulf of Suez into the Sinai region. The country is bounded by the Mediterranean to the north, by the Red Sea to the east, by Sudan to the south, and by Libya to the west.

Climate

The climate is arid, with 3-8 inches of rain annually. With a deficient rainfall, the entire country depends on irrigation from the Nile, and about 99 percent of the population live in the valley and delta of the Nile. Summers are hot, with the temperatures reaching a maximum of 43°C (110 F). Winters are mild, with an average day temperature of about 18° C (65° F).

Population—Millions: Mid Year Estimate

1976	37.87
1977	38.74
1978	39.64
1979	40.98

Religion

Over 90 percent of the population is Muslims. The remainder is mainly Christians.

Language

Arabic is the official language and is the language of almost all Egyptians. However, English, and to a lesser extent French, are widely spoken by most educated Egyptians.

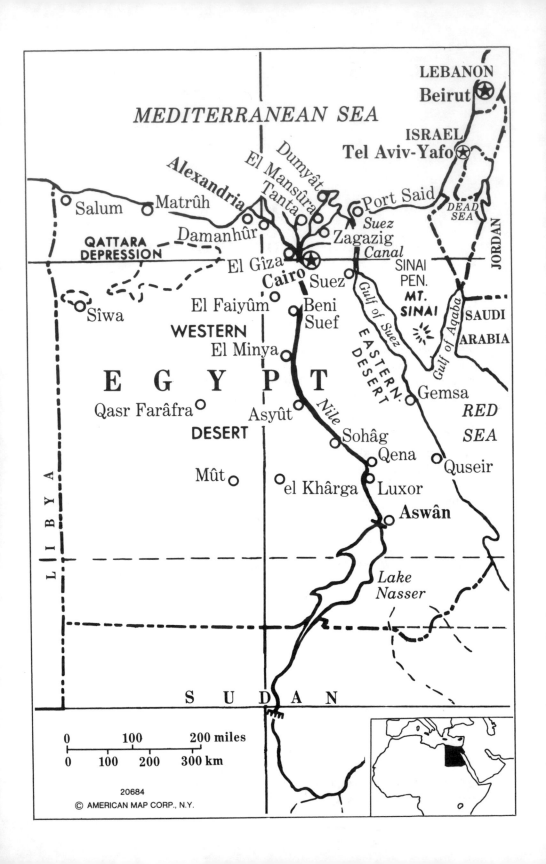

Principal Towns — Census Population: November, 1976

Cairo (Capital)	5,084,463[1]
Alexandria (Chief Port)	2,318,655
El-Girza	1,246,713
Subra El-Khema	393,700
Port Said	262,620

Education

Education is free at all levels. Primary education is compulsory, extending to all children between the ages of 6 and 12. There are eight universities in Egypt.

The Economy

More than 40 percent of the labor force is engaged in agriculture. The chief crops are cotton, onions, wheat, maize, rice and sugar cane. The country depends largely on the waters of the Nile. The completion of the Aswan High Dam in 1970 increased the fertile land of Egypt by one third.

Industry is the second major economic sector. About 15 percent of the labor force are engaged in manufacturing, mining and petroleum production. Petroleum is small but on the increase. At the end of 1979, Egypt produced 600,000 barrels per day.

Civilian Labor Force — 1977 ('000 employed)

Agriculture, forestry and fishing	4,200.9
Manufacturing and mining	1,247.4
Construction	593.7
Housing	145.2
Electricity and public utilities	106.8
Transport and communications	472.5
Finance and Commerce	1,044.1
Other services	2,187.6
Total	9,987.6

Principal Economic Indicators — (Millions of Pounds)

	1975	1976	1977
Gross National Product	4,738	6,118	7,139
Per Capita GNP	127	162	184
Per Capita GNP in U.S. Dollars	325	413	471
Gross Domestic Product	4,886	6,276	7,341
Private Consumption	3,281	3,863	4,505
Gross fixed capital formation	1,228	1,385	1,769
Consumer Price Index	100	110.3	124.3

Foreign Trade—U.S. $ million

Merchandise	1975	1976	1977
Exports, fob	1566.0	1609.3	1992.6
Imports, cif	4387.9	4366.9	4715.6
Services			
Exports	1079.7	1976.5	2551.8
Imports	723.2	796.1	1088.4

Finance

Currency—Egyptian Pound
1 pound = 1,000 milliemes = 100 piastres = 5 tallaris
Exchange rate: U.S. $1 = 700 milliemes or 0.7 pound as of Feb., 1980

Money Supply—Millions of Pounds—end of the year

	1977	1978	1979
Currency outside banks	1,749.5	2,183.7	2,656.9
Demand deposits at banks	1,193.5	1,369.1	1,697.3
Total	2,943.0	3,552.8	4,354.2

Weight and Measures

The metric system is in force.

Banks and Other Commercial Organizations

Central Bank of Egypt: 31 Kasr-el-Nil St., Cairo
Chase National Bank: 12 El Birgas, Garden City; P.O.B. 2430, Cairo
Cairo Barclays International Bank: 12 El-Sheikh Youssef Square, Garden City; P.O.B. 2335, Cairo
Misr International Bank: 14 Ally St., P.O.B. 631, Cairo
Misr America International Bank: 1Mamar Bihlar, Kasr El-Nil St., Cairo
Cairo Stock Exchange: 4 El Sherifein St., Cairo
Egyptian Chamber of Commerce: Alexandria, El-Ghorfa Eltegareia St., Alexandria
Cairo Chamber of Commerce: 4 Midan El Falaki St., Cairo
American Express of Egypt Ltd.: 15 Kasr-el-Nil St., Cairo
Thomas Cook Overseas Ltd.: 4 Sharia: Champalion, Cairo
Investment and Free Zone Authority: 8 Adly St., P.O.B. 1007, Cairo
Egyptian General Petroleum Corporation: P.O.B. 2130, Cairo

Government

Egypt attained its independence in 1922. The official title is the Arab Republic of Egypt. The legislative power is held by the unicameral People's Assembly with 382 elected members and 10 nominated by the President.

The President is elected by popular referendum for six years. The President has executive power and appoints one or more vice-presidents, a prime minister and a council of ministers. Hosni Mubarak is the President of Egypt.

Office Hours

0830-1300 Monday-Thursday, Saturday and Sunday

Public Holidays

January 1	New Year
May 1	Labor Day
June 18	Evacuation Day
July 23	Revolution Day
October 6	Armed Forces Day
October 24	Popular Resistance Day

Muslim Holidays

These are determined by sightings of the moon which vary each year by a day or two. For 1980, the religious holidays were:

January 30	Birthday of the Prophet
August 13	Eid al-Fitr — End of Ramadan[2]
October 20	Eid al-Adha — End of the Pilgrimage
November 9	Al Hijra — The Muslim New Year

Tourism

Egypt has always been a considerable tourist center. Historical remains of ancient civilizations include the pyramids and the Temples at Abu Simbel. The River Nile is popular for cruises. Cairo is an important air center and Egypt-Air has branches all over the world. The area of the Nile Delta is well served by railways. Roads link major towns.

Tourist Information

Ministry of Tourism: 110 Sh. Kasr el-Nil, Cairo. Branches at Alexandria, Port Said, Suez, Luxor and Aswan.
Egyptian General Company for Tourism and Hotels: 4 Latin America St., Garden City, Cairo
Egyptian Air: Cairo International Airport, Heliopolis, Cairo

Visa requirements

It is preferable to obtain tourist and business visas in advance. Visas are available at the airport. Vaccination for smallpox is mandatory.

Hotels

Cairo: Sheraton, P.O. Box 11, Galae Square, Giza Tel. 98300
                Nile Hilton, Nile and Liberation Square Tel. 811811
                Meridian, Corniche El-Nil St. Tel. 845444
                Shepheards, Corniche El Nil St. Tel. 33800
                Mena House Oberoi, Pyramids Road Tel. 853779
Alexandria: Palestine, Montaza Palace Tel. 66799
                Cecil, 26 July Street Tel. 807532
                San Stephano, El-Geish Street Tel. 63580

Press

Major Arabic Newspapers: *Al-Ahram:* Galla a St., Cairo
                         Al-Akhbar: Dar-Akhbar Al-Yom, Sharia Al-
                             Sahafa
                         Al-Gomhouriya: 24 Sharia Zakaria Ahmed
English Daily: *Egyptian Gazette:* 24 Sharia Galal, Cairo

Selected Embassies

Canada: 6 Sh. Muhammad Fahmy, El-Sayed, Garden City, Cairo
China, People's Republic: 14 Sh. Bahgat Aly-Zamalek, Cairo
France: 29 Sh. Giza, Cairo
Germany, Federal Republic: 20 Boulos Hanna St. — Dokki, Cairo
India: 5 Aziz Abaza St., Zamalek, Cairo
Japan: 10 Sh. Ibrahim Naguib, Garden City, Cairo
U.S.S.R.: 95 Sh Giza, Cairo
U.K.: Kasr El-Doubara, Garden City, Cairo
U.S.A.: 5 America El Latinia St., Garden City, Cairo

[1]As of the end of 1980, Cairo population was estimated at 8.5 m.
[2]For the meaning of religious holidays, see the section on Algeria.

Iraq
(The Republic of Iraq)

Size and Location

Iraq's total area is 434,924 sq. km. (167,925 sq. miles). Iraq is an almost landlocked country with a narrow outlet on to the Arabian Gulf. The country is bounded to the east by Iran, to the north by Turkey, to the west by Syria and Jordan, and to the south by Saudi Arabia and Kuwait.

Climate

The climate is extreme with hot, dry summers (lasting from May to October) when temperatures rise to 49° C (120° F) and cold winters with mean minimum temperature of − 14° C (6° F). Most of the rainfall occurs from December through March. To a very large extent, the country depends on irrigation from its major rivers, the Tigris and the Euphrates.

Population — Millions: Mid-Year Estimates

1976	11.51
1977	12.03
1978	12.33
1979	12.77

Religion

Islam is the state religion, adhered to by about 95 percent of the population. Christians account for about 4 percent of the population.

Language

Arabic is the official language of Iraq and the mother tongue of 80 percent of the people. Kurdish, a co-official language since 1966, is spoken by 16 percent of the people. English is the most common foreign language used by the educated elite, and it is employed in institutions of higher learning and in scientific publications.

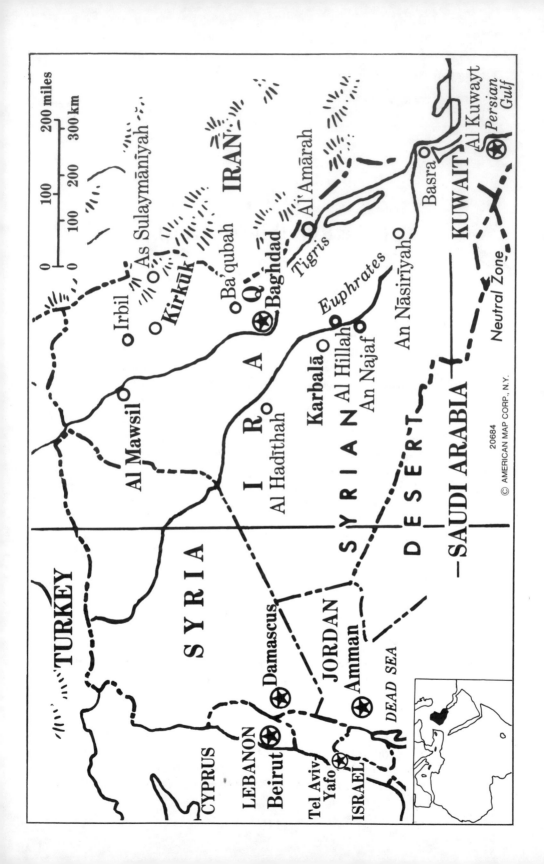

Principal Towns — Population of 1976 Census

Baghdad (Capital) 2,800,000
Basra   854,000
Mosul   892,000

Education

Education is universal and free at all levels. Primary education, lasting six years, is compulsory. The literacy rate is 26 percent. The educational administration is centralized in the Ministry of Education. The medium of instruction is Arabic, but English is taught from grades 5 and 6 on. There are six universities.

The Economy

Iraq is traditionally an agricultural country. Agriculture is the main source of employment and next to oil, the most important sector. The principal crops are wheat, barley, rice, dates, cotton, maize, and millet. Generally, the agricultural output varies according to rainfall, flooding, and political disturbances.

Although it employs close to half of the labor force, agriculture contributes less than 15 percent of the gross domestic product. The economy almost totally depends on oil, and the economic development programs have largely been attributable to the oil industry. In 1973, the oil industry was nationalized.

As a founding member of OPEC, Iraq has favored steep oil price increases, and the government policy is to increase oil production. The total oil production was 22 million tons in 1957 and 47.3 million tons in 1960. By 1970, the output reached 76.5 million tons; and in 1976, it amounted to 104 million tons.

Iraq is using its increased oil revenues in a massive program of industrialization. More than 40 percent of planned development expenditure is allocated to industrial development. In recent years, Iraq has moved into a wider range of secondary industry directed towards import substitution. The latest developments in the manufacturing sector have been in the production of pharmaceuticals, electrical goods, telephone cables, and plastics.

Principal Economic Indicators (Millions of Dinars)

	1974	1975	1976
Gross National Product	3136.0	3907.4	4736.8
Per Capita GNP	291.2	351.4	411.5
Per Capita GNP in U.S. Dollars	986.0	1190.0	1394.0
Gross Domestic Product	3378.0	4022.4	4856.8
Government and Private Consumption	1418.2	2051.4	---
Gross Fixed Capital Formation	628.6	1068.0	---
Consumer Price Index	91.3	100.0	111.4

Foreign Trade—Millions of U.S. Dollars

	1974	1975
Merchandise		
Exports fob	6,980	8,301
Imports fob	2,754	4,162
Services		
Exports	554	543
Imports	1,927	1,712

Finance

Currency—Iraqi dinar
1 Dinar = 1,000 fils = 20 dirhams
Coins: 1, 5, 10, 25, 50, and 100 fils
Notes: 1, 5, 10, and 100 dinars.
Exchange rate: U.S. $1 = 295.3 fils as of Feb., 1980.

Weights and Measures

The metric system is in force.

Banks and Other Commercial Organizations

All banks and insurance companies were nationalized in July 1964.
Central Bank of Iraq: Banks St., Baghdad. Branches in Mosul and Basra.
Rafidain Bank: New Banks St., P.O.B. 35, Baghdad, 152 branches.
Agricultural Bank of Iraq: Rashid St., Baghdad. 24 branches.
Industrial Bank of Iraq: Industrial Bank Building, Khullani Square. 7
     branches.
Iraq National Oil Company: P.O.B. 476, Kullani Square, Baghdad.
Federation of Iraqi Chambers of Commerce: Mustausir St., Baghdad.
Baghdad Chamber of Commerce: Mustausir St., Baghdad.
General Establishment for Industry: Baghdad.
Iraqi Dates Administration: Museum Square, Baghdad.
State Organization for Minerals: P.O.B. 2330, Alwiyah, Baghdad.

Government

Iraq is ruled by the Baath (Renaissance) Socialist Party. The principal
features of the constitution are: the Iraqi Republic is a popular, democratic, and sovereign state. Islam is the state religion, with the political
economy of the state founded on socialism. Power rests with the president
and a revolutionary command council of 17 members. The day-to-day
running of the country is carried out by a council of ministers. As of 1981,
Saddam Hussein is President, Prime Minister, and Chairman of the Revolutionary Command Council.

Office Hours

Summer: 0800-1400 Saturday - Sunday
Winter: 0830-1430 Saturday - Sunday
All offices close an hour earlier on Thursday.

Public Holidays

January 1	New Year's Day
January 6	Army Day
February 8	Baathist Revolution (1963)
May 1	Labor Day
July 14	Republic Day
July 17	Peaceful Revolution Day (1968)

Muslim Holidays

Islamic festivals are based on the sighting of the moon and are thus variable. For 1980, these holidays were:

January 30	Birthday of the Prophet Muhammad
August 13	Eid al-Fitr — End of Ramadan[1]
October 20	Eid al-Adha — End of the Pilgrimage
November 9	Al-Hijra — The Muslim New Year
November 18	Ashura — Day of mourning for Shi'ites

Tourism

Iraq is the ancient Mesopotamia of early history and one of the oldest centers of civilization. The ruins of Ur of the Chaldees, Babylon, Nineveh, and other relics of the Sumerian, Assyrian, and Persian Empires are of interest to the tourist. The country has 11,000 km. of roads linking major towns. In addition, the Iraqi rail system consists of 1,130 km. (700 miles).

Tourist Information

Ministry of Information, Tourism, and Resorts Administration: Ukba bin Nafi Square, Baghdad.
Iraqi Republic Railways: Baghdad Central Station Building, Baghdad
State Organization of Iraqi Ports: Basra, Iraq.
Iraqi Airways: Al-Karkh, Baghdad.

Visa Requirements

All non-Arabs require visas which must be obtained before departure. Applications may take some time to be processed.

Hotels

Al-Abbasi Palace, Sa'adoun Street, Baghdad. Tel. 9438416
Al-Khayam Hotel, Sa'adoun Street, Alwiyah, Baghdad. Tel. 96176
Carlton Hotel, Aqaba ibn Nafi Square, Baghdad. Tel. 96091
Dar al-Salam Hotel, Sa'adoun Street, Baghdad. Tel. 93733
Ambassador Hotel, Abu Nawas Street, Baghdad. Tel. 96105
Baghdad Hotel, Sa'adoun Street, Baghdad. Tel. 89031
Sahara Hotel, Andalus Square, Nidhal Street, Baghdad. Tel. 90003
Tigris Palace, Rashid Street, Baghdad. Tel. 87624

Press

Main Arabic Dailies: *Al-Jumhuriyah*—Waziriya, Baghdad
                      Al-Thawra—Aqaba bin Nafi Square, P.O.B. 2009,
                      Baghdad
English: *Baghdad Observer,* P.O.B. 257 Karantina, Baghdad

Selected Embassies—Baghdad

Canada: Mansour, P.O.B. 323
China, People's Republic: 82/l/la Jadriya, P.O.B. 223
France: Kard Al-Pasha 9G/311
Germany, Federal Republic: Al-Karada Al-Sharquiya 224/225/337
India: Taha Street, Najib Pasha, Adhamiya
Japan: 41/7/35 Al-Karada Al-Sharquiya
U.S.S.R.: 140 Mansour St., Karadat Mariam
U.K.: Shari Salah Ud-Din, Karkh
U.S.A.: (Belgium Embassy—U.S. Interest Section) Al-Karada Al-
    Sharquiya, Masbah 52/5/35

---

[1]For the meaning of religious holidays, see the section on Algeria.

Jordan
(Hashemite Kingdom of Jordan)

Size and Location

The total area of Jordan is approximately 96,000 sq. km. (37,500 sq. miles). Close to 8 percent of the land is part of the Great Syrian Desert. Jordan is located in Southwest Asia and is an almost landlocked state. The country is bounded by Syria to the north, by Iraq to the east, and by Saudi Arabia to the south. The port of Aqaba in the far south gives Jordan a narrow outlet to the Red Sea.

Climate

The climate is a modified Mediterranean type with hot, dry summers (temperatures reach 38°C or 100°F), and cool winters (4°C or 25°F). August is the hottest month, and January is the coolest. The average annual rainfall is 30 cm (12 in.). The rainy season is the period between November and March. The principal river is Jordan which rises inside the frontiers of Syria and Lebanon, flows through Jordanian territory for 156 m, and empties into the Dead Sea.

Population — Millions: Mid-Year Estimates

1976	2.78
1977	2.89
1978	2.98
1979	3.09

Religion

Islam is the official religion of Jordan, and over 90 percent of the population is Sunni Muslims. There are small communities of Christians and Shi'ite Muslims.

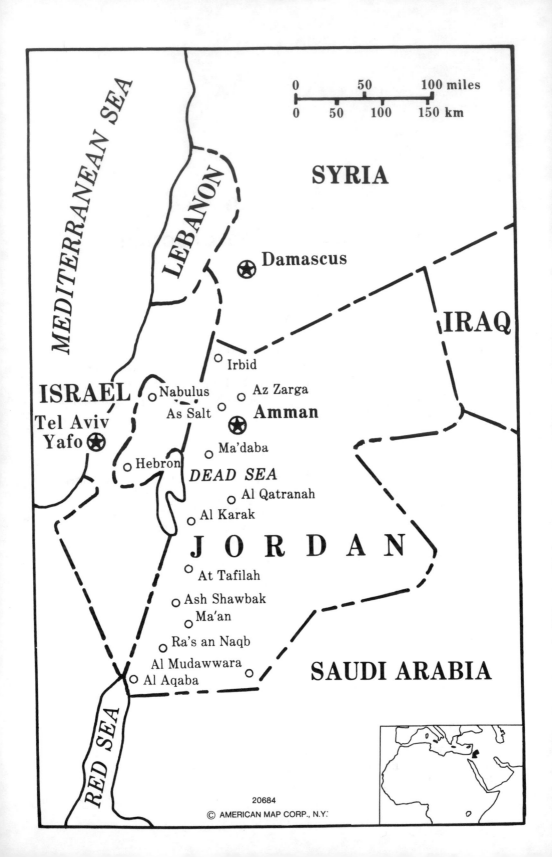

MEDITERRANEAN SEA

LEBANON

SYRIA

⊛ Damascus

IRAQ

0   50   100 miles
0   50   100   150 km

○ Irbid

ISRAEL

○ Nabulus   ○ Az Zarga
As Salt   ⊛ **Amman**

Tel Aviv
Yafo ⊛

○ Hebron   ○ Ma'daba

DEAD SEA

○ Al Qatranah

○ Al Karak

J O R D A N

○ At Tafilah

○ Ash Shawbak
Ma'an

○ Ra's an Naqb

Al Mudawwara
○ Al Aqaba   ○

SAUDI ARABIA

RED SEA

Language

Arabic is the official language of Jordan. English is widely spoken and is taught in the schools as a second language.

Principal Towns: Estimated Population — 1977

Amman (Capital)	732,587
Zarka	269,780
Irbid	139,780

Education

Education is free and compulsory for nine years from age 6 to 14. Basically, education in Jordan is centralized. The Ministry of Education prescribes textbooks and curricula for all schools. The medium of instruction is Arabic, and English is taught from the fifth grade up. The literacy rate is estimated at 32 percent. Jordan has two universities: the University of Jordan at Amman, and Yarmuk University at Irbid.

The Economy

Agriculture is a major sector of the Jordanian economy. Howeer, only 11 percent of Jordan's total land is arable. Cultivation is of a subsistence type. Agricultural sector contributes a little over 10 percent to the Gross Domestic Product, although it employs about one third of the labor force. Principal crops are wheat, barley, lentils, citrus fruits, and vegetables.

Jordan is short of natural resources. The industrial sector is small, and its growth it limited. The major industrial income is derived from three heavy industries, namely, phosphates, cement, and oil refining. Phosphate is the country's only mineral wealth.

Jordan has had to rely heavily on foreign aid which in recent years has been coming increasingly from oil-rich Arab governments.

Principal Economic Indicators (Millions of Denars)

	1977	1978	1979
Gross National Product	612.5	713.0	771.9
Per Capita GNP	212	239	250
Per Capita GNP in U.S. Dollars	673	815	848
Gross Domestic Product	477.6	576.7	632.8
Private Consumption	416.8	509.5	609.3
Gross Fixed Capital Formation	197.0	229.1	278.4
Consumer Price Index (1975 = 100)	127.8	136.6	156.1

Foreign Trade—Millions of U.S. Dollars

	1977	1978	1979
Merchandise			
Exports fob	248.9	296.5	401.8
Imports fob	1,225.4	1,334.6	1,741.9
Services			
Exports	920.8	728.8	818.5
Imports	433.1	662.0	1,043.6

Finance

Currency—Jordanian Dinar
1 Dinar = 1,000 fils
Coins: 1, 5, 10, 25, 50, 100 and 250 fils
Notes: 500 fils, 1, 5, 10 and 20 dinars
Echange rate: U.S. $1 = 313.0 fils as of April 1978

Money Supply—Millions of Dinars: end of the year

	1977	1978	1979
Currency outside banks	188.25	219.46	275.39
Demand Deposits at banks	139.81	149.98	182.00
Total	328.06	369.44	457.39

Weights and Measures

The metric system is in force.

Banks and other Commercial Organizations

Central Bank of Jordan: P.O.B. 37, Amman
Arab Bank Ltd.: King Faisal St., P.O.B. 68, Amman
Bank of Jordan Ltd.: P.O.B. 2140, Jabal Amman on 3rd Circle, Amman
British Bank of the Middle East: P.O.B. 444, Amman
Chase Manhattan Bank: P.O.B. 20191, On the First Circle, Jabal Amman
Jordan Stock Exchange: Amman
Amman Chamber of Commerce: P.O.B. 287, Amman
Chamber of Industry: P.O.B. 1800, Amman
Jordan Phosphate Mines Co. Ltd.: P.O.B. 30, Amman

Government

Jordan attained its independence in 1946. Jordan is a constitutional monarchy—the Hashemite Kingdom of Jordan. The legislative power is vested in a bicameral National Assembly. The Senate has 30 members appointed by the King for eight years (half retiring every four years), and the House of Representatives has 60 members, including 50 Muslims and 10 Christians, elected by universal adult suffrage for four years. The executive power is vested in the King, who governs with the assistance of an appointed Council of Ministers, responsible to the Assembly. King Hussein Ibn Talal, proclaimed King on August 11, 1952.

Office Hours

Government: 0830-1430 Saturday - Thursday
Banks: 0800-1330 Saturday - Thrusday
Business: 0800-1300 and 1530-1930 Saturday - Thursday (Summer)
            0830-1330 and 1500-1830 Saturday - Thursday (Winter)

Public Holidays

March 22	Arab League Day
May 1	Labor Day
May 25	Independence Day
August 11	King Hussein's Accession
November 14	King Hussein's Birthday

Muslim Hoidays

These are determined by sightings of the moon which vary by a day or two each year. For 1980, they were:

January 30	Birthday of the Prophet
June 11	Ascension of the Prophet[1]
August 13	Eid al-Fitr — End of Ramadan
October 20	Eid al-Adha — End of the pilgrimage
November 9	The Muslim New Year

Tourism

The ancient cities of Jerash and Petra, and Jordan's proximity to biblical sites, have encouraged the recent growth of tourism. The expansion of hotel accommodation and other facilities is barely keeping pace with demand.

Tourist Information

Ministry of Tourism and Antiquities: P.O.B. 224, Amman
Alia (The Royal Jordanian Airline): Head Office — P.O.B. 302, First Circle, Jabel Amman, Amman.

Airline Services

The following airlines serve Jordan: Air France, British Airways, Egypt Air, Iraqi Airways, KLM (Netherlands).

Visa Requirements

Visitors need an entry visa. A seven-day tourist visa can be obtained at the airports. A residence permit is required for a stay longer than three months.

Hotels

Intercontinental (Al-Urdan): P.O.B. 1827, Jabel Amman, Amman, Tel: 41361
Grand Palace: P.O.B. 6916, University Avenue, Amman, Tel. 61121.
Ambassador: P.O.B. 19014, Shmeisani, Amman, Tel. 65161.
Philadelphia: Amaneh Street, P.O.B. 10, Amman, Tel. 25191.
Note: It takes at least two weeks for advance booking.

Press

Arabic: *Al-Destur:*P.O.B. 591, Amman
          Al-Rai: P.O.B. 6710, Amman
          Ash-Sha'ab: P.O.B. 3037, Amman
English: *The Jordan Times:* P.O.B. 6710, Amman

Selected Embassies

Canada: Diplomatic functions are handled through its embassy in Beirut, Lebanon
China, People's Republic: Amman
France: Amman
Germany, Federal Republic: Amman
India: P.O.B. 2168, Amman
Japan: Amman
U.S.S.R.: Amman
U.K.: 3rd Circle, Jabel Amman
U.S.A.: Amman

[1]For the meaning of religious holidays, see the section on Algeria.

Kuwait

(State of Kuwait)

Size and Location

Kuwait is a small state with an area of 19,940 sq. km. (7,700 sq. miles), roughly rectangular in shape. To the south of Kuwait, along the Gulf is a Partitioned Zone of 5,700 sq. km. (3,560 sq. miles) which is divided between Kuwait and Saudi Arabia. However, the oil wealth of the whole zone remains undivided and production is shared equally between the two states.

Kuwait is located in the northwest corner of the Arabian Gulf, sharing borders with Iraq and Saudi Arabia. The country is bordered on the south by Saudi Arabia and on the north and west by Iraq.

Climate

The territory of Kuwait is mainly flat desert with a few oases. Kuwait has an arid, subtropical climate, with an annual rainfall of 1 to 37 centimeters, almost entirely between November and April. Summer, which lasts from May to October, is extremely hot with temperatures ranging from 43°C (110°F) to 54°C (130°F). Sand and dust storms are frequent in the summer. Winter, lasting from November to April, is generally pleasant. January is the coldest month with night temperatures occasionally touching the freezing point. Kuwait has no rivers, and there is little drinking water within the state. Water supplies are largely distilled from sea water and brought by pipeline from Shattal-Arab.

Population

Kuwait's population has been increasing very rapidly. It is estimated to have been 152,000 in 1950, 321,621 in 1961, 738,662 in 1970, and 1,355,827 in 1980. The average rate of increase in the 1960s was approximately 10.0 percent, the highest growth rate recorded in any country. Much of this growth stemmed from immigration. Less than half the population is Kuwaiti, the remainder being other Arabs, Pakistanis, Iranians, and Indians.

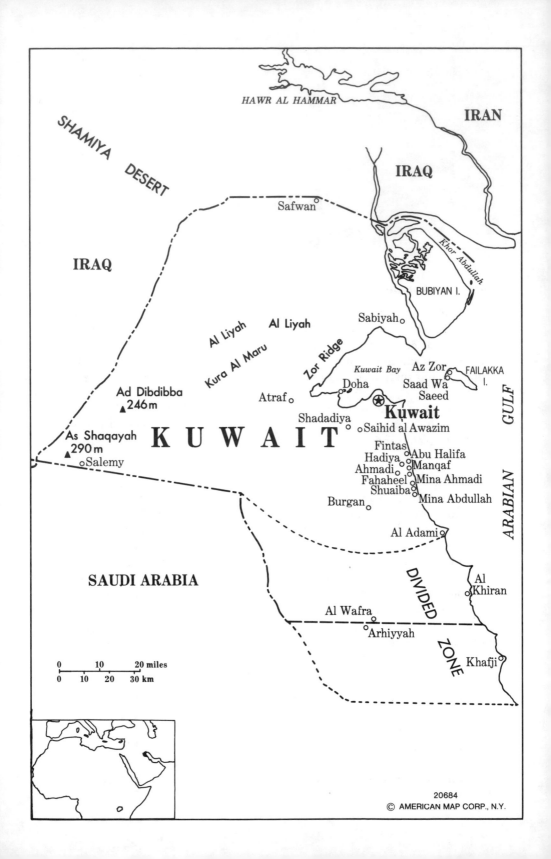

HAWR AL HAMMAR

IRAN

IRAQ

SHAMIYA DESERT

IRAQ

Safwan

Khor Abdullah

BUBIYAN I.

Sabiyah

Al Liyah   Al Liyah

Kura Al Maru

Zor Ridge

Kuwait Bay   Az Zor   FAILAKKA I.

Doha   Saad Wa Saeed

Atraf   **Kuwait**

Ad Dibdibba
▲246 m

Shadadiya

Saihid al Awazim

As Shaqayah
▲290 m
Salemy

K U W A I T

Fintas
Hadiya   Abu Halifa
Ahmadi   Manqaf
Fahaheel   Mina Ahmadi
Shuaiba   Mina Abdullah

Burgan

Al Adami

SAUDI ARABIA

DIVIDED

Al Khiran

Al Wafra
Arhiyyah

ZONE

Khafji

GULF

ARABIAN

0   10   20 miles
0   10   20   30 km

20684
© AMERICAN MAP CORP., N.Y.

Population — Millions: Mid-Year Estimates

1977	1.130
1978	1.200
1979	1.270
1980	1.356

Religion

Islam is the state religion, adhered to by 94.7% of the population. The Christians comprise 4.6% of the population.

Language

Arabic is the official language of Kuwait. English is the second language. It is taught in schools and is widely used as a medium of commercial communication. A few merchants speak Urdu and/or Persian (Farsi).

Principal Towns

The population of Kuwait is overwhelmingly (90%) urban, since areas outside the towns and cities are virtually uninhabitable.

Population of 1975 Census[1]

Kuwait City (Capital)	78,116
Hawali	130,565
Saliniya	113,943
Araq Kheetan	59,443

Education

Education is free, universal, and compulsory between the ages of 6 and 14. The literacy rate is 55%. Kuwait has one of the most developed educational systems in the world. The government policy is to provide free education to all Kuwaiti children from the kindergarten stage to the university level. Pupils are provided, free of cost, food, textbooks, clothing, and medical treatment. The educational administration is centralized in the Ministry of Education.

The medium of instruction is Arabic. English is taught as the second language. Schools are segregated by sex. Girls constitute 45% of enrollment. A high proportion of teachers are foreigners, mostly Egyptians and Jordanians. Scholarships are granted to students to study abroad, mainly in Egypt, France, U.K., and the U.S.A. Kuwait University, founded in 1966, has become a major institution of higher learning in the Middle East. Kuwait University has over 17,000 students and provides scholarships for a number of Arab, Asian, and African students.

The Economy

The Kuwaiti economy is almost totally based on the petroleum industry and the returns on foreign investment of oil revenues. In 1979, Kuwait's oil production was the seventh largest in the world, and oil revenue was estimated at U.S. $16,000 million. In 1978, the World Bank estimated Kuwait's per capita GNP at $14,890, the highest in the world.

Agriculture is the smallest economic sector, employing 2% of the labor force and contributing 0.03% to the gross national product. Agricultural development is very limited by the infertility of the land and the lack of water. As a result, most of the food consumed in Kuwait has to be imported. However, the government has done much to encourage animal husbandry, fishing of shrimps and prawns on the Arabian Gulf, and developing an experimental farm on land owned by the government.

Industry. Kuwait has no natural resources other than crude petroleum and natural gas. Oil is the cornerstone of the Kuwaiti economy. However, the government supports various measures to foster the growth of other industries in order to diversify the economy and to provide an alternative source of employment to oil. The oil industry employs less than 5% of the population. Most native Kuwaitis are employed in the government and service sectors of the economy, and a sizable proportion is engaged in trade and commerce. Non-Kuwaitis make up 77% of the country's labor force employed in the private sector.

Oil-related economic activities still contribute an overwhelming proportion of the total industrial output. In 1963, a Petrochemical Industries Company was formed; and in 1964, a larger concern, Kuwait Chemical Fertilizer Company, was set up. In 1965, a law was passed empowering the government to grant exemption from import duties on capital goods, subsidize rates for water and power, and give preference in government purchases for locally manufactured products. In 1974, the government established the Industrial Bank of Kuwait to finance the industrial sector. In 1979, the Industrial Development Committee was established with a far-reaching authority over regulating industry, issuing licenses, and imposing protective tariffs.

There are several factories in Kuwait to meet consumer demand for processed food and soft drinks. There is also a flour mill company. The construction industry is important, owing to the vast amount of houses and office buildings, as well as roads, power stations, schools, and hospitals.

Welfare Services. The Kuwait economy is a welfare economy. Education is completely free, and this includes free food and clothing. Medical attention is also free to all, and the health service is considered to be of a very high standard. A heavily subsidized housing program has provided accommodation for most residents and even local telephone calls are free. Low-cost loans are available to Kuwaitis who want to start a business or to get married. Pensions are provided to widows and their dependents and to the handicapped.

Investment Abroad. Kuwait's first priority for spending its oil revenue is the development of its own economy and the provision, through the investment of surplus funds, of an income for its citizens in the future when oil wells have run dry. Kuwait's total state investments and foreign reserves passed $40,000 million by the end of 1979. The Kuwait Investment Office (KIO) in London, an arm of the Ministry of Finance, handles much of the state's investments in Europe and elsewhere. About 65% of Kuwait's long-term investments are in the U.S.A. Kuwait has holdings in almost every one of the top 500 U.S. companies. Kuwait also has major real estate projects, including Kiwana Island off the South Carolina Coast, on which a tourist and office complex have been built. Kuwaitis have shown interest in investment in other countries in Asia (South Korea, Hong Kong, Malaysia), in Africa, and in South America. Kuwait pioneered foreign aid in the Arab world by setting up the Kuwaiti Fund for Arab Economic Development (KFAED) in 1961.

Principal Economic Indicators — Millions of Dinars: Year Beginning April 1

	1977	1978	1979
Gross National Product	3,885	4,188	6,431
Per Capita GNP	3,438	3,490	5,064
Per Capita GNP in U.S. Dollars	12,274	12,840	18,542
Gross Domestic Product	4,054	4,210	6,436
Government Consumption	593	646	745
Private Consumption	1,265	1,457	1,641
Gross Fixed Capital Formation	854	785	691
Consumer Price Index (1975 = 100)	114.2	124.5	130.9

Foreign Trade — Millions of U.S. Dollars

	1977	1978	1979
Merchandise			
Exports fob	9,530	10,235	18,287
Imports fob	4,490	4,319	5,014
Services			
Exports	2,629	3,660	4,929
Imports	1,654	2,150	2,695

Finance

Currency — Kuwaiti Dinar
1 dinar = 1,000 fils = 10 dirhams
Coins: 1, 5, 10, 20, 50 and 100 fils
Notes: 250 and 500 fils; 1, 5, and 10 dinars
Exchange rate: U.S. $1 = 268.45 fils as of June 1980

Weights and Measures

The metric system is in force.

Money Supply—Millions of Dinars—End of Period

	1977	1978	1979
Currency outside banks	150.9	177.0	215.9
Demand deposits at banks	339.8	454.4	453.5
Total	490.7	631.4	669.4

Banks and Other Commercial Organizations[2]

Central Bank of Kuwait: P.O.B. 526, Kuwait City
Alahali Bank of Kuwait: P.O.B. 1387, Commercial Center 5, Kuwait City
Bank of Bahrain and Kuwait: P.O.B. 24396, Safat, Kuwait City
Bank of Kuwait and the Middle East: P.O.B. 71, Safat, Kuwait City
Commercial Bank of Kuwait: P.O.B. 2861, Mubarak Al Kabir St., Kuwait
    City
National Bank of Kuwait: P.O.B. 95, Kuwait City
Kuwait Petroleum Establishment: Kuwait City
Kuwait Chamber of Commerce and Industry: P.O.B. 775, Chamber's
    Bldg., Kuwait City
Kuwait Foreign Trading, Contracting and Investment Co.: P.O.B. 5665,
    Kuwait City
Kuwait Fund for Arab Economic Development: P.O.B. 2921, Kuwait City
Kuwait Planning Board: Kuwait City
Petrochemical Industries Co.: P.O.B. 1084, Kuwait City

Government

Kuwait attained its independence in 1961. Basically, Kuwait is a heredi-
tary emirate ruled by the Sabah family. In response to public opinion and
radical Arab criticism, the ruling family permitted a Constituent Assembly
to draft and to publish a constitution in 1962. The 1962 constitution
established a constitutional monarchy based on Arab traditions and Islamic
law. The constitution also contains a bill of rights.

Executive Authority. The executive power is vested in the Emir (title of the
rulers of Kuwait) who is also the supreme commander of the armed forces.
The Emir exercises his powers through a council of ministers headed by a
prime minister who is appointed by the Emir.

Legislature. A National Assembly of 50 members is elected for a four-year
term by all natural-born literate Kuwaiti males over the age of 21. The Emir
has the right to dissolve the Assembly. This right was exercised for the first
time on August 29, 1976.

Judicial Branch

The judiciary system is supervised by the minister of justice who is appointed by the Emir. Elements of British and French law have been incorporated in the judicial system. Kuwaitis are equal before the law in prestige, rights, and duties. Individual freedom is guaranteed. No one shall be seized, arrested, or exiled except within the rules of the law. Every person has the right to education and freedom to choose his type of work. Freedom to form peaceful societies is guaranteed within the limits of the law.

Office Hours

Government:	0700-1300 Saturday - Wednesday	(Summer)
	0700-1100 Thursday	
	0700-1330 Saturday - Wednesday	(Winter)
	0730-1130 Thursday	
Banks:	0800-1200 Saturday - Thursday	
Business:	0800-1200 Saturday - Thursday	
	1530-2030 and 0800-1200 Friday	

Note: The weekend begins Thursday afternoon and runs all day Friday.

Public Holidays

| January 1 | New Year's Day |
| February 25 | Kuwait National Day |

Muslim Holidays

Islamic festivals are based on the sighting of the moon and may vary from year to year by a day or two. For 1980, these holidays were:

January 30	Birthday of the Prophet
June 11	Ascension of the Prophet[3]
July 14	First day of Ramadan
August 13	Eid al-Fitr — End of Ramadan
October 20	Eid al-Adha — End of the Pilgrimage
November 9	Al-Hijra — The Muslim New Year
November 18	Ashura — Day of Mourning for Shi'ites

Visa Requirements

Visas are normally issued at Kuwait airport. However, it is advisable to obtain entry visas through the usual channels, i.e., a Kuwaiti embassy or consulate. If a visitor's passport shows evidence of a visit to Israel, it will be necessary to obtain a new passport in order to enter Kuwait. A certificate of vaccination against smallpox is required.

Airline Services

The Kuwait International Airways services all major cities in the Middle East: Amman, Baghdad, Cairo, Damascus, Jeddah, Karachi, Tehran. It also provides regular service to Athens, Copenhagen, Frankfurt, Geneva, London, Madrid, New York, Paris, Rome, and other European cities.

Kuwait is also served by Air France, Air India, Alia (Jordan), British Airways, Egypt-Air, KLM, Lufthansa, and other airlines.

Hotels

It is recommended that reservations be made well in advance of actual departure.

Ambassador Hotel: P.O.B. 2813, Kuwait Tel. 42528819
Bristol Hotel: P.O.B. 3531, Kuwait Tel. 439281-4, Bristotel KWT 2061
Carlton Hotel: P.O.B. 3492, Kuwait Tel. 423171, Telex 2064KT
Golden Beach Hotel: P.O.B. 3482, Kuwait Tel. 43951221, Telex 2231KT
Kuwait Hilton: P.O.B. 4996, Kuwait Tel. 533000, Telex 2039KT
Kuwait Sheraton: P.O.B. 5902, Kuwait Tel. 422055, Telex 2106KT
Universal Hotel: P.O.B. 5593, Kuwait Tel. 42536112, Telex 2347KT

Press

Main Arabic Dailies: *Al-Anba'*: P.O.B. 23915, Kuwait
                      Al-Qabas: P.O.B. 21800, Airport Rd., Shuwaikh, Kuwait
                      Al-Rai al-Amm: P.O.B. 695, Airport Rd., Shuwaikh, Kuwait
                      Al-Siyasa: P.O.B. 2270, Kuwait
English Dailies: *Arab Times*: P.O.B. 2270, Kuwait
                      Kuwait Times: P.O.B. 1301, Safat, Kuwait

Selected Embassies — Kuwait City

Canada: 28 Quraish St., Nuzha
China, People's Republic: P.O.B. 2346, Safat
France: Qabazard Bldg., Istiqlal
Germany, Federal Republic: Shamiya District, Al-Mamoun St., Villa Shaikh
India: 34 Shara, Istiqlal
Japan: House No. 5, Plot No. 1, Street No. 13, Rowdah Area
U.S.S.R.: Baghdad St., House No. 6
U.K.: Arabia Gulf St.
U.S.A.: Bneid Al-Gar

---

[1] In all towns, non-Kuwaitis (immigrants and resident alients) form a huge majority. The Kuwaitis contitute 15% of Kuwait City inhabitants, 8% of Hawali City, and 15% of the Saliniya City.
[2] No foreign banks are allowed to operate in Kuwait. The only foreign bank is the Bank of Bahrain and Kuwait which is 50% Kuwaiti-owned.
[3] The meaning of religious holidays can be found in the section on Algeria.

Libya
(The Socialist People's Libyan Arab Jamahiriya)

Size and Location

The total area of 1,759,540 sq. km. (679,360 sq. miles) makes Libya the fourth largest country in Africa; it is one-fourth the continental United States or 2.5 times as large as Texas. The whole area of Libya is part of the vast plateau of North Africa which extends from the Atlantic Ocean to the Red Sea.

Libya is located on the central Mediterranean coast of North Africa. Libya shares borders with six nations. The country is bounded by the Mediterranean Sea on the north, by Egypt and Sudan on the east, by Chad and Niger on the south and south-west, by Algeria on the west, and by Tunisia on the north-west.

Climate

Libya is almost entirely a desert country. The climate is characterized by wide alterations of temperatures. Lacking mountain barriers, the climate is directly influenced both by the Sahara and the Mediterranean Sea; and, as a result, weather transitions are abrupt and there are wide variations in temperature. Winter is fairly cold in the north with sleet and snow on the hills. Summer is extremely hot with temperatures ranging from 41°C (105°F) to 46°C (115°F) In the southern desert, conditions are hotter still.

A special feature of the weather is the hot and very dry, sand-laden, wind called ghibli that can raise temperatures by 30-40 degrees fahrenheit within a few hours. The northern highlands receive annually as much as 12 to 14 inches of rainfall, but in the remainder of the country, the amount is irregular, unreliable, and less than 8 inches. There are no perennial rivers but only water courses known as wadis that are dry in the summer but are flooded during rains.

Population

Relative to its enormous area, Libya's population (estimated at 3 million, 1979) is quite small. The Libyan Government favors a policy of population

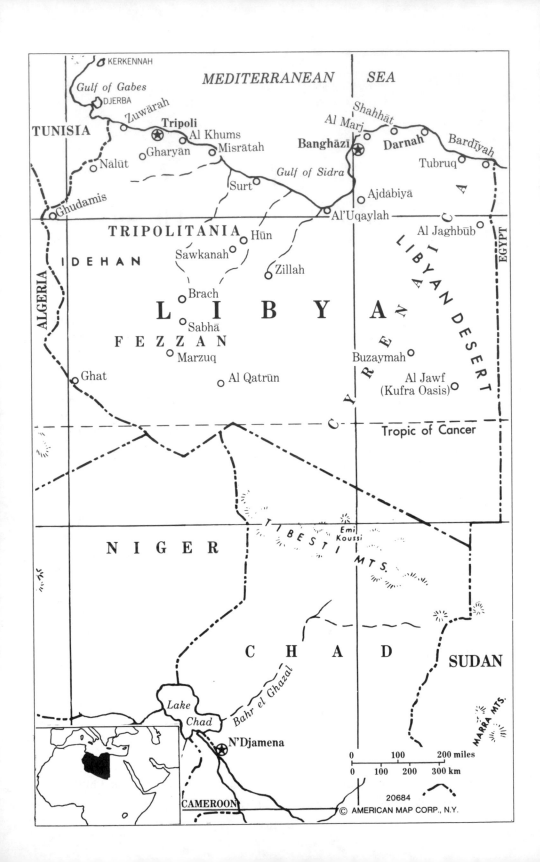

expansion for demographic as well as economic reasons. Other population policies are to stabilize the rural population and to stem the flow of migration to the cities. Given the fact that almost the whole country is desert, it is not surprising that the population is heavily concentrated in the northern part within 20 miles of the Mediterranean Sea. Nearly 90% of the population lives on 10% of the land area.

Population — Millions: Mid-Year Estimates

1976	2.51
1977	2.63
1978	2.75
1979	2.86

Religion

Islam is the state religion and is the religion of almost all Libyans. Identification with Islam has been traditionally strong in Libya. Since the military coup in 1969, the regime has converted religion into a keystone of state, domestic, and foreign policy by reaffirming Islamic values and establishing literal Quranic practices in national life at home and propagating Islam abroad. The Libyans, practically without exception, follow Sunni Muslim rites. The number of Christians in Libya is small and was estimated at 35,000 in 1978.

Language

Arabic is the official language of Libya since 1969. The return to the Arabic language and the rejection of external influences took several forms such as the use of Arabic in all official communications, street signs, private letterheads, and even the use of Arabic in foreigners' passports. The main minority language is Berber, a Semitic language related to Arabic. The use of foreign languages such as English and Italian is discouraged.

Principal Towns — Population of 1973 Census

Tripoli (Capital)	551,477
Benghazi	140,000
Misurata	103,302
Hans-Cussabat	88,095
Zawia	72,207
Tubruq (Tobruk)	58,869

Education

Schooling is free, universal, and compulsory for nine years from age 6 to 15. The academic year runs from October to June. The medium of instruction is Arabic, and the curricula and textbooks are designed to reflect the Arabic spirit and Islamic heritage. The study of foreign languages is, however, discouraged. Private schools operated by foreign communities

(Italian, French, German, and Greek) serve the children of resident aliens only. Because of an acute teacher shortage, the educational system continues to rely on foreign teachers, mainly Egyptians. The national literacy rate is 35%.

In 1958 the University of Libya opened in Benghazi. In 1973, the university was divided into two parts to form the universities of Tripoli and Benghazi, later renamed Alfateh and Ghar Yunis universities. A number of Libyan students are enrolled in institutions of higher learning abroad—the United States, France, West Germany, the United Kingdom, Italy, and Poland.

The Economy

When Libya was declared independent in 1951, she was regarded as one of the world's poorest and least endowed countries. But now, with an economy based on oil, Libya is considered one of the high-income countries in the world. Libya is the fourth largest oil producer in the Middle East and the second largest in Africa.

Plans for extensive economic development are being drawn up and implemented, with the aim of raising agricultural productivity; improving urban housing; introducing new social, educational, and medical amenities; and fostering consumer-goods industries. Roads, electricity, telephone facilities, better water supplies, and reorganized town planning are being achieved. Special attention is given to the diversification of the economy by investing in non-oil activities. Libya launched its first five-year plan in 1963 as oil revenues began to increase. A National Planning Council and a Ministry of Planning and Development have been set up to design and oversee long-term development programs.

Agriculture. Agriculture dominated the economy until the discovery of oil. At present only a very small proportion of the total area of Libya is cultivable. The area under irrigation is increasing, however. A number of very large contracts have been awarded for reclamation and irrigation work in various parts of the country. All projects are meant to be completely integrated, providing for the establishment of farms and the building of rural roads, irrigation, and drainage facilities.

Animal husbandry is still the basis of farming in Libya. Sheep and goats are used for meat, milk, and wool. Cattle is used for draft and transport, but in recent years breeding for dairy produce has been expanded.

Industry. The industrial sector is small and contributes 2% to the gross domestic product. Manufacturing is largely confined to the processing of local agricultural products, consumer items, textiles, construction materials, and such traditional crafts as carpet weaving, tanning, leather working, and shoemaking.

Industrial development has received a massive allocation under Libya's five-year plan (1976-80). Plans are being made for a whole range of factories to make such diverse articles as prefabricated construction materials and woolen and synthetic textiles, among other things. Industrial expansion is, however, limited by a small domestic market, lack of skilled manpower, and lack of raw materials.

Contracts for a large number of industrial projects have been awarded to European, U.S., and Japanese companies. In 1975 a joint venture agreement to manufacture carbon paper was signed with a Japanese firm, and another agreement to build an aluminum plant was reached with Yugoslavia. In 1976, a French firm was awarded a contract for the construction of two organic fertilizer plants at Tripoli and Benghazi. In 1977, an Italian firm won a contract for setting up a steel-frame factory. Also in 1977, a German firm won a contract to build a blanket factory.

By far the most important industrial project outside the oil and petrochemical sector is the steel complex at Misurata. Iron ore reserves, estimated at over 700 million tons, were discovered in 1974 at Wadi Shutti in the southern section of the country. Work began in 1979 to construct a steelwork plant at Misurata to be completed in 1985.

In light of the government's increasing attention to housing and industrial construction, cement-making is an industry with every likelihood of expansion. The existing cement plant at Homs has been expanded. Two more cement plants are being built at Sauk al-Khemis and Derna, and a new Benghazi cement plant was opened in 1978.

Principal Economic Indicators — Millions of Dinars

	1976	1977	1978
Gross National Product	4,389	5,182	5,407
Per Capita GNP	1,749	1,970	1,966
Per Capita GNP in U.S. $	6,608	6,654	6,641
Gross Domestic Product	4,907	5,750	5,912
Government Consumption	1,185	1,378	1,590
Private Consumption	1,337	1,490	1,657
Gross Fixed Capital Formation	1,226	1,368	1,450

Foreign Trade — Millions of U.S. Dollars

	1977	1978	1979
Merchandise			
Exports fob	10,405	9,900	15,915
Imports fob	4,929	5,764	6,160
Services			
Exports	379	468	559
Imports	1,607	1,815	2,102

Finance

Currency — Libyan Dinar
1 Dinar = 1,000 Dirhams

Coins: 1, 5, 10, 20, 50, and 100 Dirhams
Notes: 250 and 500 Dirhams; 1, 5, and 10 Dinars
Exchange rate: U.S. $1 = 296.05 Dirhams as of June 1980.

Weights and Measures

The metric system has been officially adopted, but traditional weights and measures are still used.

Money Supply — Millions of Dinars — End of Period

	1977	1978	1979
Currency outside banks	585.0	868.5	1,053.7
Demand deposits at banks	592.9	559.3	708.2
Total	1,177.9	1,427.8	1,861.9

Banks and Other Commercial Organizations

Central Bank of Libya: Shari' al-Malik Saud, P.O.B. 1103, Tripoli
Jamahiriya Bank: P.O.B. 3224, Shari' Emhamed al-Megarief, Tripoli
Libyan Arab Foreign Bank: 1 St. September St., P.O.B. 2542, Tripoli
National Commercial Bank: Shuhada Square, P.O.B. 4647, Tripoli
Wahda Bank: Jamal Abdul Nasser St., P.O.B. 452, Benghazi
National Oil Corporation (NOC): P.O.B. 2655, Tripoli
Chamber of Commerce and Industry for the Western Province: Al-Jomhouriya St., P.O.B. 2321, Tripoli
Chamber of Commerce and Industry for the Eastern Province: P.O.B. 208-1286, Benghazi
General National Organization for Industrialization, P.O.B. 4388, Tripoli.

Government

Libya attained her independence in 1951. The only political party in Libya is the Arab Socialist Union, formed in 1971. The Union, meeting in the General People's Congress in Sebha in March 1977, adopted a new name for the country, the Socialist People's Libyan Arab Jamahiriya. It also proclaimed its adherence to freedom, socialism, and a comprehensive Arab unity. A five-member General Secretariat was established with Colonel Muammar al-Quaddafi as General Secretary. A twenty-six-member General People's Committee (twenty-five secretaries plus the head of the committee) was formed, to replace the council of ministers. In 1979, the number of secretaries of the General People's Committee was reduced to 21. Theoretically, direct people's authority constitutes the basis of Libya's political order, with the Quran serving as a social code.

Office Hours

Summer: 0800-1230 Saturday - Thursday
             1600-1700 Saturday - Wednesday
Winter   0900-1300 Saturday - Thursday
             1600-1700 Saturday - Wednesday

Public Holidays

March 31	Anniversary of the Evacuation of British Troops
June 11	Anniversary of the Evacuation of American Troops
July 22	Anniversary of the Egyptian Revolution
September 1	Anniversary of the Libyan Revolution
October 7	Anniversary of the Evacuation of Fascist Settlers

Muslim Holidays

Islamic festivals are based on the sighting of the moon, and there may be variations of a day or two. For 1980, these holidays were:

January 30	Birthday of the Prophet
June 11	Ascension of the Prophet[1]
July 14	First day of Ramadan
August 13	Eid al-Fitr — End of Ramadan
October 20	Eid al-Adha — End of the Pilgrimage
November 9	Al-Hijra — the Muslim New Year

Tourism

There are a few sites of interest in Libya. These include the Phoenician and Carthagenian ruins, the Roman Cities of Sabratha, the Leptis Magna, and other ancient and medieval remains.

Tourist Information

General Board of Tourism and Fairs: Tripoli

Visa Requirements

Passports must be accompanied by an official Arabic translation of essential particulars. It is advisable to obtain entry visas well in advance.

Airline Services

The Libyan Arab Airlines provides regular passenger and cargo services from Tripoli and Benghazi to Algiers, Amman, Beirut, Casablanca, Damascus, Jeddah, Athens, Belgrade, Frankfurt, London, Madrid, Moscow, Paris, Warsaw, and Zurich. Libya is also served by: Aeroflat (U.S.S.R.), Air Algerie, Alitalia, KLM, Lufthansa, Swissair, and UTA (France).

Hotels

Tripoli: Beach Hotel: Tel. 71641/5
            Tourist Village: Tel. 71392, 71250
            Libya Palace: Tel. 41886
            Cleopatra: Tel. 41886
            Grand: Tel. 32509
            Marhaba: Tel. 36464
            Ennasser: Tel. 36478
Benghazi: Omar Khayyam: Tel. 4420
            Gesira Palace: Tel. 2144

Press

Al-Fajr Al-Jadid: P.O.B. 2303, Tripoli
Al-Jarida Al-Rasmiya (Irregular official state gazette), Tripoli

Selected Embassies

Canada: Cairo, Egypt
China, People's Republic, Tripoli
France: Shari' Ahmad Lutfi Said, Tripoli
Germany, Federal Republic, Shari' Hassan al-Masha, Tripoli
India: Shari' Mahmud Shaltut, Tripoli
Japan: 37 Shari' Ubei Ben Ka'ab, Tripoli
U.S.S.R.: Shari' Mustapha Kamel, Tripoli
United Kingdom: Shari' Gamal Abdul Nasser, Tripoli
U.S.A.: Shari' al-Nasr, Tripoli

[1]For the meaning of these holidays, see the section on Algeria.

Oman
(Sultanate of Oman)

Size and Location

Oman's area is estimated at 212,457 sq. km. (82,000 sq. mi.). The Sultanate of Oman is situated at the southeastern corner of the Arabian Peninsula, facing the Gulf of Oman and the Arabian Sea. The country is bounded by the United Arab Emirates on the north and west, by Saudi Arabia on the west, and by the People's Democratic Republic of Yemen (Southern Yemen) on the south-west. The country's frontiers with its neighbors are not clearly demarcated.

The landscape is a varied one, including stretches of desert, areas of rich vegetation, and mountain ranges. The country may be divided typographically into:

1. The tip of the Musandam Peninsula which touches the strait of Harmuz. It consists of low mountains.
2. The fertile plain, a narrow coastal plain, called Batinah.
3. The Muscat-Matrah coastal region bounded by cliffs.
4. The high table land of central Oman which blends into the great sandy desert of Rub al-Khali (the Empty Quarter).
5. The barren and forbidding coastline south of Dhofar.
6. The uninhabitable and inhospitable island of Masirah.
7. Dhofar's coastal plain (10 miles wide and 40 miles long), noted for rich vegetation and natural beauty.

Climate

Most of the country has an arid subtropical climate. The summer months run from April to October with an average temperature of 47.2°C (117°F) and humidity in excess of 85%. The summer is regarded as one of the hottest in the world, and temperatures as high as 54°C (130°F) have been recorded. The west wind blowing from the Rub al-Khali makes the heat more oppressive. The winter months from December until the end of March are the most pleasant with temperatures ranging from 16°C (60°F) to 32°C (90°F).

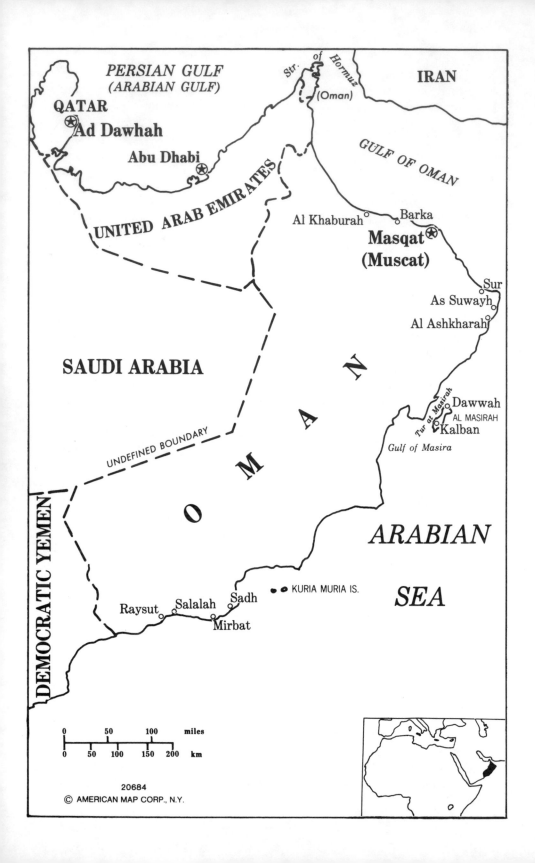

PERSIAN GULF
(ARABIAN GULF)

IRAN

Str. of Hormuz
(Oman)

QATAR
⊛ Ad Dawhah

Abu Dhabi ⊛

GULF OF OMAN

UNITED ARAB EMIRATES

Al Khaburah ○   ○ Barka

Masqat ⊛
(Muscat)

○ Sur
As Suwayh ○
Al Ashkharah ○

SAUDI ARABIA

O M A N

Dawwah ○
AL MASIRAH
Kalban ○
Tur at Masirah

Gulf of Masira

UNDEFINED BOUNDARY

ARABIAN

DEMOCRATIC YEMEN

SEA

○○ KURIA MURIA IS.

Raysut ○   ○ Salalah   ○ Sadh
○ Mirbat

0   50   100   miles
0   50   100   150   200   km

20684
© AMERICAN MAP CORP., N.Y.

The average annual rainfall is 5 cm. (2 in.) to 10 cm. (4 in.) with very wide regional variation. Some regions are well-watered, while other areas receive no rain at all in the course of a year. The south-western province of Dhofar receives abundant rain during the summer monsoon between June and September. By contrast, winter is the rainy season in the north.

Population

No census has ever been held in Oman, and estimates of the country's population are based on conjecture. The UN Population Division has put a total of 657,000 for mid-1970 and 766,000 for mid-1975. Preliminary surveys for a census were conducted in 1975, and the generally accepted estimate of 840,000 has been given for 1978.

Population — Millions: Mid-Year Estimates

1977	.810
1978	.840
1979	.860

Religion

Islam is the official religion. Ibadism, a strict and fanatical sect, is the dominant and official rite of Oman. The Ibadis regard all contacts with infidels as sinful and are notorious for their puritanism and doctrinal rigidity. There are a number of Sunni Muslims who are moderately orthodox. There is also a shi'a minority.

Language

Arabic is the official language of Oman. Due to its isolation, Oman has developed dialects which may cause difficulty even for other Arabs. Among the business community, there are sizable minorities of Iranians, Indians, and Pakistanis who speak their own languages. English is widely spoken and even used to some extent in government.

Principal Towns

The population is 90% to 95% rural. There are no towns with over 100,000 population. More than 75% of the population engage in subsistence agriculture. There has been little immigration from the countryside to the towns, except for the growth of the capital, Muscat, with an estimated population of 80,000. The other population centers are Matrah (20,000),

Salalah (10,000 — the capital of the southern province of Dhofar), Nizwa
(10,000), and smaller towns — Sohar, Rustaq, Sumail, and Sur.

Education

The primary education is a recent introduction to Oman. The literacy rate
is 5%. Oman has not introduced free, universal, and compulsory education. Until 1970 there were only three primary schools for boys only and no
schools for girls.

Since the coup of July 24, 1970, led by Sultan Qaboos deposing his
father, the country has made a major effort to expand education horizon-
tally as well as vertically all over the Sultanate. By 1978, a total of 266
schools had been built, of which 257 were primary and 9 were secondary; 58
schools for girls, and 77 coeducational schools. The number of students
attending schools in 1978 was put at 78,000. The large majority of teachers
are from other Arab countries such as Egypt, Jordan, and Sudan. The
recent establishment of a Teacher Training Institute is aimed at producing
100 teachers annually for primary school teaching.

Schooling is under the control of the Ministry of Education. The medium
of instruction is Arabic. English is taught from the secondary grades on.
There are plans to start an agricultural technical institute. Adult education
classes to combat illiteracy have met with success. For higher education,
Omanis have been sent to study abroad.

The Economy

Until 1967, when the production of oil began, Oman's economy was
overwhelmingly agricultural and of a subsistence type with negligible
growth. Since then the economy has been dominated by the oil industry
which provides almost all government revenue. Economic growth has been
sudden in the years following the dramatic increase in oil prices. With an
economy based on oil, Oman is considered on of the upper middle-income
countries in the world.

Agriculture and Fisheries. Oman is predominantly an agricultural country
with some 70% of the working population engaged in agriculture. The
Sultanate's long-term plans for development foresee a considerable
expansion in agricultural production that would result in greater self-sufficiency and in exportable surpluses. Because of the very wide variations in
rainfall from one year to another and between the main regions, water
supply becomes one of the key elements in the country's agricultural
development.

The 1976-80 development plan is aimed at increasing the cultivable land
and improving the utilization of water. A series of surveys of water
resources conducted by international consultants will be the basis for agricultural planning. Assisted by the American Farm Machinery Corporation,
the Department of Agriculture (which is part of the Ministry of Develop-

ment) has been able to develop a number of experimental farms and extension centers.

Of the total land under cultivation 50% produces dates. Other crops are limes, wheat, maize, lucerne, various fruits (mangoes, papaya, oranges, bananas), and vegetables (onions, peppers, cabbages, tomatoes, and cucumbers).

Livestock development is also under study. Several schemes are under way. Among existing projects is the Garziaz Cattle Station. It is managed by a Swiss firm as a joint venture, known as the Sun Farms of Oman, which controls a number of livestock projects in Dhofar, Sahnut, and Sohar.

The sea is important to Oman's economy. Fishing is a traditional occupation employing about 10% of the working population and a principal source of animal protein in the Omani diet. Here, too, the government is making considerable efforts to establish modern systems of commercial fisheries. Fish is abundant in the waters off the coast. The catch includes sardines, whitebait, crayfish, and sharks.

Individual fishermen are being trained and are offered loans for equipment. Cold stores and refrigerated transport are provided to improve the marekting of fish. Further developments, including canning plants, are under way. In 1979, the National Fishing Corporation was established to be responsible for concession agreements. Recently, the government has signed agreements with an American firm to develop commercial fishing.

Industry. At the present, petroleum is the main resource being commercially exploited. Before 1967 (when oil export began), the industrial sector was confined to small-scale food processing and traditional handicrafts. Oil has provided the basis for industrial development. Industry in Oman is still in its infancy and is directed solely for satisfying local needs. With the expected decline in oil revenues, limited mineral resources, a shortage of manpower, and a small local market, Oman will have a difficult task developing heavy industry or manufacturing on a large scale.

Government spending of oil revenues on infrastructure projects and private spending on housing has generated a boom in the construction industry. Also, in an attempt to diversify, the government has built two major petrochemical projects — one is a French natural gas fertilizer plant, and the other is a gas liquefaction built by an American firm. In 1977, a paint factory was opened under Danish supervision. There are also plants producing building materials, plastics, furniture, shoes, and soft drinks. Another major plant is the 150-ton-a-day flour mill.

In 1973, the government concluded a joint venture agreement with Canadian and American firms to carry out geological surveys to locate mineral deposits. Since then, important reserves of copper and chromite have been discovered. Saudi Arabia has given aid for the exploitation of these deposits. Other explorations have shown the presence of coal, asbestos, manganese, and other metals. No feasibility studies, however, have been made to assess the prospects of commercially exploiting these mineral deposits.

Principal Economic Indicators — Millions of Omani Riyals

	1977	1978	1979
Gross National Product	749.9	775.2	1,034.4
Per Capita GNP	926	923	1,203
Per Capita GNP in U.S. $	320	319	416
Gross Domestic Product	880.1	896.6	1,172.5
Government Consumption	223.0	250.0	283.5
Private Consumption	203.9	271.0	308.6
Gross Capital Formation	310.8	281.0	318.0

Foreign Trade — Millions of Omani Riyals

	1977	1978	1979
Exports	543.3	522.3	748.0
Imports	302.1	327.2	430.5

Finance

Currency — Omani Riyal
1 Omani Riyal = 1,000 baiza
Coins: 2, 5, 10, 25, 50 and 100 baiza
Notes: 100, 250, and 500 baiza; 1, 5, 10, and 20 Riyals
Exchange rate: U.S. $1 = 345.4 baiza as of June 1980

Weights and Measures

The metric system was adopted in 1974. Traditional measures are still in use.

Money Supply — Millions of Omani Riyals

	1977	1978	1979
Currency outside banks	55.1	64.4	74.3
Demand deposits at banks	54.4	56.2	49.9
Total	109.5	120.6	124.2

Banks and Other Commercial Organizations

Central Bank of Oman: P.O.B. 4161, Muscat
Arab Bank Ltd. (Jordan): P.O.B. 991, Muscat
Bank Melli Iran: P.O.B. 410, Muscat
Banque de Paris et des Pays-Bas (France): P.O.B. 425, Muscat
British Bank of the Middle East (London): P.O.B. 234, Muscat
The Chartered Bank (U.K.): P.O.B. 210, Muscat
Citibank NA (New York): P.O.B. 918, Muscat
Grindlays Bank Ltd. (London): P.O.B. 91, Muscat
Oman Chamber of Commerce and Industry: P.O.B. 4400, Muscat
Petroleum Development Ltd.: P.O.B. 81, Muscat

Government

Oman attained her independence in 1650. Oman has never been under foreign rule in modern times. Politically, Oman has come to be regarded as the least developed nation in the region if not in the world. The country has no constitution, no legislature, no political parties, and has never held an election. Many medieval prohibitions are in force. The Sultanate is ruled with absolute authority by Sultan Qaboos bin Said who holds the offices of prime minister, foreign minister, defense minister, finance minister, and supreme commander of the armed forces. All decrees of the Sultan have the force of law.

The judicial system of Oman is based entirely on the Islamic law (Sharia), and jurisdiction is exercised by the Sharia courts. The Sharia is interpreted by religious judges (qadis), appointed by the minister of justice. The Chief Court is at Muscat, but the ultimate court of appeal is the Sultan himself.

Oman is now a member of the United Nations, the International Monetary Fund, the Arab League, and other Arab organizations. It should be noted that Oman is not a member of the Organization of Petroleum Exporting Countries (OPEC).

Office Hours

Government: 0700-1300 Saturday - Thursday (Summer)
0800-1300 Saturday - Thursday (Winter)
Banks: 0800-1200 Saturday - Wednesday
0800-1130 Thursday
Business: 0830-1230 and 1600-1800 Saturday - Thursday

Public Holidays

November 18	National Day
November 19	Birthday of the Sultan
July 23	Accession of the Sultan

Muslim Holidays

Islamic festivals are based on the sighting of the moon and may vary from year to year by a day or two. For 1980, these holidays were:

January 30	Birthday of the Prophet
June 11	Ascension of the Prophet[1]
July 14	First day of Ramadan
August 13	Eid-al-Fitr — End of Ramadan
October 20	Eid al-Adha — End of the Pilgrimage
November 9	Al-Hijra — the Muslim New Year
November 18	Ashura — Day of Mourning for Shi'ites

Tourism

Oman is not open to tourism. A network of adequate graded roads links the main centers of population.

Visa Requirements

A visitor must obtain entry visa issued at Omani embassies. No Objection Certificate needs to be obtained from the Sultanate Immigration Department if a visitor is sponsored by an Omani citizen.

Hotels — Muscat Area

Intercontinental Hotel: Tel. 600500, Telex. 3491
Gulf Hotel: Tel. 600100, Telex. 3416
Ruwi Hotel: Tel. 702244, Telex. 3456
Al-Falaj Hotel: Tel. 702311, Telex 3229
Mina Hotel: Tel. 734226, Telex. 3350, Cable: ALMINA

Press

Al-Watan: P.O.B. 463, Muscat, weekly, Arabic
Oman: P.O.B. 600, Muscat, twice weekly, Arabic
Akhbar Oman: P.O.B. 3959, Muscat, weekly, English
Times of Oman: P.O.B. 3770, Muscat, weekly, English

Selected Embassies (in Muscat unless otherwise stated)

Canada: Tehran, Iran
China, People's Republic
France: P.O.B. 5252
Germany, Federal Republic: P.O.B. 3128
India: P.O.B. 4227
Japan: P.O.B. 900
United Kingdom: P.O.B. 300
U.S.A.: P.O.B. 966

[1]The meaning of religious holidays can be found in the section on Algeria.

Qatar

(State of Qatar)

Size and Location

The total area of Qatar is 11,000 sq. km. (4,257 sq. miles), roughly 160 km. (100 miles) in length, and a maximum width of 80 km. (50 miles). The terrain is flat, barren, stony, and sandy with a limited supply of underground water which is not suitable for drinking or agriculture.

Qatar is located on the peninsula projecting northwards from the mainland of Arabia into the Arabian Gulf. Low-lying and surrounded by shallow waters, the Qatar peninsula was ignored until it was chartered by naval surveyors in the 19th century. Its landward frontiers are with Saudi Arabia and the United Arab Emirates. Qatar has border disputes with all its neighbors—Saudi Arabia, Abu Dhabi, and Bahrain—over certain islands.

Climate

The climate is oppressively humid. Annual rainfall ranges between 25 mm. (1 inch) and 212 mm. (8.5 inches). Temperatures range from 6°C (43°F) in January to 48°C (118°F) in July. The winter months from December to March are pleasant. The summer months from May to September are extremely humid.

Population

No official census exists. But in January 1980, the population was estimated at 250,000. Only about a quarter of the total population is indigenous Qataris; the rest is immigrant workers: Indians, Pakistanis, Iranians, and other Arab nationals.

Religion

Islam is the official religion, and most of the indigenous population are Muslims of the Sunni sect. The smaller Shi'ite community is mainly of Iranian origin.

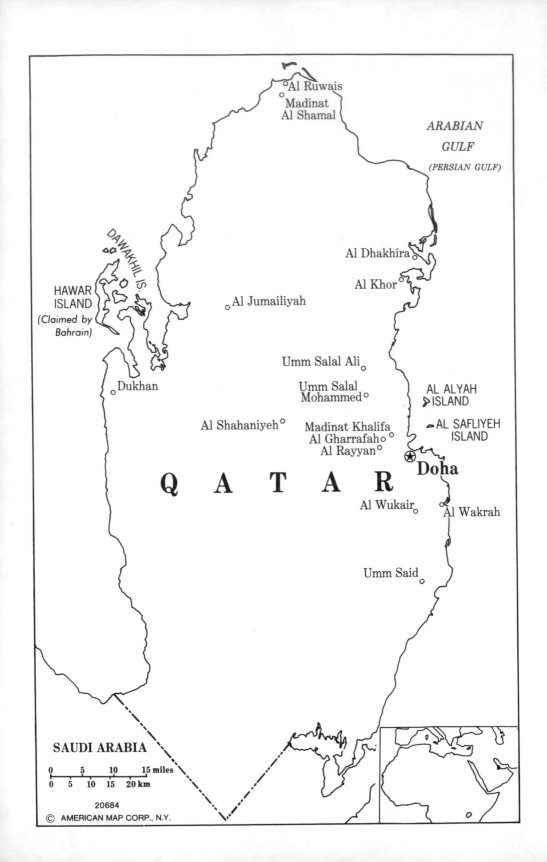

Language

The official language is Arabic, and the spoken dialect is the Gulf Arabic which is influenced by Farsi (Persian). English is widely understood, especially in the business community; and it is taught as a second language in secondary schools.

Principal Towns

The urban component of the estmated population is put at 88%, two-thirds of which are concentrated in the capital city of Doha, the deepwater commercial port. Two other towns (ports), Zakrit on the west coast and Umm Said (the deepwater port for oil shipments) on the east, owe their existence to the petroleum industry. Other towns are Khor, Wakrah, Ruwais, and Dukhan (where oil is produced).

Education

Schooling in Qatar is free but neither universal nor compulsory. The state does provide students with free books, clothing, food, and transportation. The national literacy rate is estimated at 10%. The Ministry of Education has overall control of the educational system. The medium of instruction is Arabic and English is taught as a second language. Increasing attention is being paid to the training of teachers. In 1976, the Teacher Training College was upgraded into the University of the Lower Gulf, with additional facilities for science, engineering, and administration. Numerous scholarships are awarded for study overseas.

The Economy

Qatar is very poorly endowed with natural resources. Even water is scarce. About half the water supply comes from artesian wells. The inhabitants have traditionally lived from pearl-diving, fishing, and nomadic herding. The discovery of oil has changed the picture, from a relatively simple life of fishing to a bustling urban life with a planned earth satellite station. Oil is the dominant factor in the economy, accounting for more than 90% of the country's income and 95% of export earnings. Qatar is the 16th largest oil producer in the world. With an economy based on oil revenues, Qatar is considered on of the high-income countries of the world.

Agriculture. Of the total area of the Qatar Peninsula, only about 5% is considered arable, and only 50% of the arable land is cultivated. In spite of the low agricultural potential, Qatar manages to be self-sufficient in vegetables. The government provides free tractor plowing, seeds, insecticides, and pesticides. Sheep, goats, cows, camels, and horses are bred. In 1976, the government established a sheep rearing station and a dairy farm.

Industry. In order to avoid complete dependence on oil, the government is using oil income to encourage the development of other industries. The consistent aim of development is to achieve an economy which will be viable when the oil runs out. The industrialization program is centered in the town of Umm Said. The main large-scale industrial plants are:

The Steel Works, built by Japanese firms, opened in 1978.

The Qatar National Cement Company at Umm Babe, with a production
    capacity of 600,000 tons.

The Qatar Fertilizer Company at Umm Said utilizes the lighter fractions of gas. It had an annual capacity of 371,00 metric tons of ammonia and
    497,000 tons of urea in 1979.

A polyethylene plant in Umm Said, being constructed by two French
    companies as the first part of a petrochemical complex.

A Refrigeration and Fish Processing Plant near Doha with a daily capacity
    of seven tons of shrimp.

The Qatar Flour Mills, a privately owned company, can process 100 tons of
    flour a day.

To meet the rising demand for electricity created by a growing population and expanding industry, the government has allocated one-third of its capital budget to the electricity sector. The electrification of the entire peninsula has essentially been completed. Just outside the capital, a new power station and desalination complex are being erected at Ras Abu Fontas at a cost of $242 million.

Principal Economic Indicators

No statistics are available on gross national product and its sectoral breakdown.

Foreign Trade — Millions of Riyals

	1977	1978	1979
Exports	7,888	9,202	14,217
Imports, cif	4,850	4,590	5,378

Finance

Currency — Qatar Riyal
1 Qatar Riyal = 100 Dirhams
Coins: 1, 5, 10, 25, and 50 Dirhams
Notes: 1, 5, 10, 50, 100, and 500 Riyals
Exchange rate: U.S. $1 = 3.66 Riyals as of June 1980.

Weights and Measures

Two systems, the imperial and the metric, are used. Full conversion to the metric system is planned.

Money Supply

	1977	1978	1979
Currency outside banks	505.0	573.3	715.1
Demand deposits at banks	1,582.1	1,733.2	1,776.4
Total	2,087.1	2,306.5	2,491.5

Foreign Investment

Regulations require at least 51% local participation in all undertakings. All foreign investments are coordinated by the Qatar Investment Board.

Banks and Other Commercial Organizations

Qatar Monetary Agency: P.O.B. 3144, Doha
Qatar National Bank, S.A.Q.: P.O.B. 1000, Doha
Arab Bank, Ltd. (Jordan): P.O.B. 172, Doha
Banqe de Paris et des Pays-Bas (France): P.O.B. 2636, Doha
British Bank of the Middle East: P.O.B. 57, Doha
Grindlays Bank, LTD. (U.K.): Rayan Rd., P.O.B. 2001, Doha
Citibank N.A. (U.S.A.): P.O.B. 2309, Doha
Qatar General Petroleum Corporation: P.O.B. 3212, Doha

Government

Qatar is an absolute emirate. In April 1979, a provisional constitution was announced which created a Council of Ministers and a 23-member Advisory Council (increased to 30 in December 1975). The cabinet of ministers is appointed by the emir. Most of the members of the cabinet belong to the ruling Al-Thani family.

Qatar became independent on September 1971, when the special treaty arrangement with Great Britain came to an end. In the same year, Qatar became a member of the United Nations and the League of Arab States.

In 1972 Shaikh Khalifa ibn Hamad Al-Thani took over control of the administration as emir and chief of state. To reduce the oligarchical nature of the government, Shaikh Khalifa adjusted the composition of the Advisory Council to reflect a variety of economic and family interests and loyalties. As its title indicates, the council's function is primarily an advisory one. In December 1975, the Advisory Council was granted power to summon individual ministers to answer questions on legislation before promulgation. Justice is administered by five courts on the basis of codified laws in addition to the traditional sharia courts applying Islamic laws. The constitution guarantees the independence of the judiciary.

Office Hours

Government: 0700-1300 Saturday - Thursday
Banks: 0730-1130 Saturday - Wednesday
             0700-1100 Thursday
Businesses: 0730-1200
             1600-1830 Saturday - Thursday
             Friday is the official rest day

Public Holidays

February 22   Accession of Shaikh Khalifa
September 3   Independence Day

Muslim Holidays

Variable Islamic festivals are based on the sighting of the moon, i.e.,
these holidays depend on the lunar calendar which advances ten or twelve
days each year. For 1980, these holidays were:

January 30   Birthday of the Prophet
June 11   Ascension of the Prophet[1]
July 14   First day of Ramadan
August 13   Eid Al-Fitr — End of Ramadan
October 20   Eid Al-Adha — End of the Pilgrimage
November 9   Al-Hijra — the Muslim New Year
November 18   Ashura — Day of Mourning for Shi'ites

Tourism

The business visitor should visit the Qatar National Museum. Various
types of traditional Gulf sailing craft are of particular interest. Taxis are the
principal means of local transportation.

Visa Requirements

For an entry visa for a period of longer than three days, a no-objection
certificate is needed and must be obtained from the immigration
department. Application should be made at least a month before departure. Permission to enter for a stay of less than 72 hours may be obtained on
arrival at Doha airport.

Hotels

Gulf Hotel: P.O.B. 1911, Doha Tel. 25251, Telex: 4250
Oasis Hotel: P.O.B. 717, Doha Tel. 328221, Telex: 4214
Doha Palace: P.O.B. 710, Doha Tel. 26131, Telex: 263
Ramada Hotel: P.O.B. 1768, Doha Tel. 321321

Press

Al-Ahad: P.O.B. 2531, Doha, daily, Arabic
Al-Doha Magazine: P.O.B. 1836, Doha, monthly, Arabic
Al-Mash'al: P.O.B. 70, Doha, monthly, English and Arabic
Daily New Bulletin: P.O.B. 3299, Doha, daily, English
Gulf Times: P.O.B. 2888, Doha, weekly, English

Selected Embassies

Canada: Teheran, Iran
France: P.O.B. 2669, Doha
Germany, Federal Republic: P.O.B. 3084, Doha
India: P.O.B. 2788, Doha
Japan: P.O.B. 2208, Doha
U.K.: P.O.B. 3, Doha
U.S.A.: P.O.B. 2399, Doha

'For the meaning of religious holidays, see the section on Algeria.

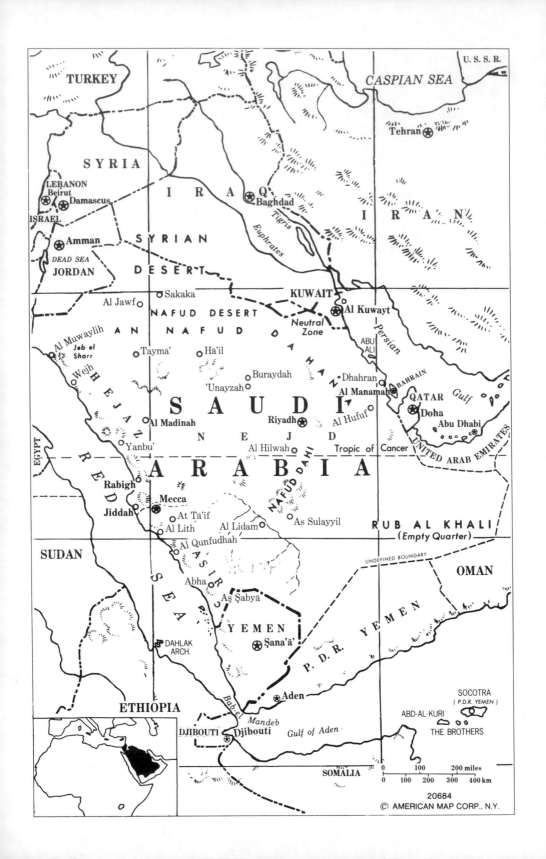

TURKEY

CASPIAN SEA

U.S.S.R.

Tehran ⊛

SYRIA

LEBANON
Beirut
Damascus
ISRAEL

Amman

DEAD SEA
JORDAN

I R A Q

Baghdad ⊛

I R A N

Tigris
Euphrates

S Y R I A N

D E S E R T

KUWAIT

Al Kuwayt

Neutral
Zone

ABU
ALI

Persian

Sakaka

Al Jawf ○

NAFUD DESERT

A N   N A F U D

Al Muwaylih
Jeb el
Sharr

Wejh

H E J A Z

Tayma' ○

Ha'il ○

Buraydah ○

'Unayzah ○

Dhahran ●
Al Manamah ⊛

BAHRAIN

QATAR

Doha ⊛

Abu Dhabi

Gulf

EGYPT

S A U D I

Al Madinah ○

N E J D

Riyadh ⊛

Al Hufuf ○

UNITED ARAB EMIRATES

Yanbu' ○

Al Hilwah ○

Tropic of Cancer

A R A B I A

Rabigh ○
Mecca
Jiddah ○

R E D

At Ta'if ○
Al Lith ○

Al Qunfudhah ○

NAFUD DAHI

Al Lidam ○

As Sulayyil ○

RUB AL KHALI
(Empty Quarter)

SUDAN

S E A

A S I R

Abha ○

As Ṣabyā

DAHLAK
ARCH.

YEMEN

Sana'ā' ⊛

UNDEFINED BOUNDARY

P. D. R.   Y E M E N

OMAN

ETHIOPIA

Bab el

Mandeb

Aden ⊛

SOCOTRA
(P.D.R. YEMEN)

ABD-AL-KURI

THE BROTHERS

DJIBOUTI Djibouti ⊛

Gulf of Aden

SOMALIA

0   100   200 miles

0   100   200   300   400 km

20684

© AMERICAN MAP CORP., N.Y.

Saudi Arabia
(Kingdom of Saudi Arabia)

Size and Location

The total area of Saudi Arabia is 2,150,000 sq. km. (830,000 sq. miles), about the size of the United States east of the Mississippi River. The coast along the Arabian Gulf is flat and low-lying, and from there slopes gently upwards across the country toward the Red Sea.

Saudi Arabia occupies most of a geographical unit called the Arabian Peninsula. The Arabian Peninsula is bordered on three sides by the Arabian Gulf, the Indian Ocean, and the Red Sea. Only about 20% of the land is habitable, and the rest is covered by sand dunes. The southeast is dominated by the Rub-al-Khali (Empty Quarter) which is the world's largest sand region. The boundaries are not precisely delimited. Saudi Arabia shares its boundaries with eight neighbors. Starting with Jordan to the north and moving clockwise, the neighbors are Iraq, Kuwait, Qatar, United Arab Emirates, Oman, People's Republic of Yemen, and Yemen Arab Republic. Saudi Arabia is bounded on the west by the Red Sea.

Climate

The climate is generally dry, and almost all the area is arid. The average rainfall is less than five inches. The country suffers from severe duststorms. The coastal areas have high humidity. Summer temperature averages 44.4°C (112°F), and in the interior, temperatures often rise to 54.4°C (130°F). January and February are the coolest months. Frosts and freezing weather occur in winter.

Population

Saudi Arabia has not had an elaborate and accurate census. With the statistics in some doubt, estimates for the following years should be accepted with caution.

Mid-Year UN Estimates (thousands)

1975	7,180
1976	7,400
1977	7,629
1978	7,866
1979	8,110

Religion

The national religion of Saudi Arabia is Islam. It was here that Islam originated. Saudi Arabia is the site of Islam's two holiest cities, Mecca and Medina. The law of Islam (Sharia) is the law of the land. The appropriateness of all public and private acts are judged in light of the Islamic precepts. Declaration of oneself as a Muslim is a prerequisite for citizenship. Islam exercises a pervasive influence on the lives of all Saudis. Almost all Saudis adhere to the Sunni branch of Islam. The second main sect of Islam, Shia, is also represented in the country — mostly in the east.

Language

Arabic is the only language of the entire indigenous population. Unlike many other Middle Eastern countries, European languages are not widely used. English is the principal foreign language taught in the secondary schools.

Provinces

Administratively, the country is divided into four provinces:

1. The Hijaz, or the western province, contains the religious holy cities of Mecca and Medina and the commercial center of Jeddah.
2. The Najd, or the central province, is the seat of the royal family. Riyadh, originally the capital of Najd, is now the capital of the country.
3. Asir province, in the southwest, offers the best agricultural prospects.
4. Al Hasa, or the eastern province, contains the oilfields and the cities of Dharan and Dammam.

Principal Towns (Population at 1974 Census)

Riyadh (royal capital)	666,840
Jeddah (administrative capital)	561,104
Mecca (birthplace of the Prophet)	366,801
Ta'if (resort town)	204,857
Medina (burial place of the Prophet)	198,186
Damman	127,844

Education

The educational institutions are run by the government. Public education is free at all levels, and grants are provided to study abroad. The estimated literacy rate is 10%. An important domestic priority is given to education under the current (third) five-year plan (1980-85). The school year runs from September to May. The language of instruction is Arabic. There are six universities, in addition to the colleges of education for girls at Riyadh, Jeddah, and Dammam, and the Higher Islamic Judicial Institute.

The Economy

Saudi Arabia is considered one of the richest countries of the world. The national economy is overwhelmingly dominated by oil. The country holds about a quarter of the proven oil reserves in the world, and is the third biggest producer in the world after the United States and the Soviet Union. Saudi Arabia is the biggest oil producer within OPEC, with almost one-third of the organization's oil. Since 1970, and particularly after the dramatic rise in oil revenues in 1973-74, there have been substantial increases in all sectors of the Saudi Arabian economy: government expenditures, gross national product, national income, industrial production, money supply, deposits, exports (consisting almost entirely of oil), and imports. Under the influence of the oil price rises, the country's current account surplus and foreign holdings have dramatically increased.

Development Plans. Saudi Arabia has a free-market economy. However, since 1970, the economy has been guided by a number of five-year plans. Planning is under the Central Planning Organization. The first plan, covering the period 1970-1975, was relatively modest in its goals. After the large rise in oil prices at the beginning of 1974, the second development plan (1975-80) was formulated.

The second plan provided for the expenditure of U.S. $142 billion. It was described as an "experiment in social transformation." The largest single investment in the plan was defense, 16%; followed by education, 15%; urban development, 11%; and industrial and mineral production, 9%. At the heart of the plan was the development of hydrocarbon-based industries. A major feature of the development plan was to create two completely new industrial centers: one at Yambu, and the other at Jubail. Yambu was to have two oil refineries, a natural gas processing plant, a petrochemical complex and other lighter industries. Jubail was planned on a larger scale: three oil refineries, seven petrochemical plants, an aluminum smelter and a steel mill, and other supporting industries. The results of the second plan were, on the whole, successful.

The progress of the actual projects was slower than planned, largely because of deficiencies in the infrastructure and the shortage of manpower.

Although the main projects fell behind schedule, infrastructure did grow apace, endowing the country with the basic transportation and communications facilities.

The third five-year plan (1980-85) is more scientifically based. Most of the important projects of the third plan are those carried forward from the second. However, the emphasis is put on the production sectors, with particular importance accorded to agriculture. The plan stresses the need for manpower training to reduce reliance on foreign labor and encourages Saudi private investors to play a more prominent role in the economy. Planned investment for the five-year period of the plan is set at U.S. $235 billion. Actual expenditure is expected to rise above the planned figure.

Agriculture. Agriculture takes place on less than 1% of the total area of the country. The agricultural sector contributes about 1% to gross domestic product, although it employs 30% of the population. Cultivation is confined to the oases, and only the coastal Asir Province receives appreciable rainfall to permit cultivation without irrigation. The remaining agricultural land is used for low-grade grazing. The problem is essentially one of water supply. The main crops cultivated on irrigated or cultivated soil are wheat, sorghum, maize, millet, barley, and dates. Sheep, goats, and camels are bred extensively, both for meat and for wool.

Attention is being focused on increasing water resources as a means of achieving a measure of self-sufficiency in agricultural products, and hence reducing the dependence on imported food. Other aims are to diversify the economy and to raise rural living standards.

Industry. Oil is the most important industry in Saudi Arabia. Excluding oil, manufacturing's contribution to GNP is about 10%. Most of the manufacturing is geared to the local market, especially construction. Some consumer industries are cotton textiles, carpet mills, shoe factories, and food processing.

Besides oil, deposits of iron ore, copper, gold, lead, zinc, silver, and some uranium are known to exist in Saudi Arabia. However, the only minerals being produced, apart from petroleum, are limestone, gypsum, marble, and salt.

Saudi Arabia is in the middle of major industrial development financed by increasing oil revenues. The cornerstone of the industrial development program is the establishment of refineries and processing industries to utilize the country's oil and natural gas reserves. The principal agent of the industrialization program has been PETROMIN, the state-owned General Petroleum and Mineral Organization. Major projects are usually carried out as joint ventures by the state and foreign firms.

The government is also encouraging the Saudi private sector to develop small-scale industries. Private industrial enterprises are offered basic services at minimal charge with credit available on easy terms. Furthermore, selected industries are protected through the imposition of duties on imports.

Principal Economic Indicators — Millions of Riyals (Years Ending June 30)

	1977	1978	1979
Gross National Product	207,723	225,527	249,988
Per Capita GNP	27,225	28,671	30,825
Per Capita GNP in U.S. $	7,767	9,145	9,160
Gross Domestic Product	205,056	223,747	248,412
Government Consumption	41,033	47,034	56,615
Private Consumption	34,372	54,607	63,506
Gross Fixed Capital Formation	51,191	66,891	78,012
Consumer Price Index (1975 = 100)	146.5	144.2	146.2

Foreign Trade — Millions of U.S. Dollars

	1977	1978	1979
Merchandise			
Exports fob	40,229	36,962	57,847
Imports fob	14,355	20,638	24,973
Services			
Exports	6,136	6,462	7,736
Imports	13,927	17,907	23,746

Finance

Currency — Saudi Riyal (or Rial)
1 Saudi Riyal = 100 halalah = 20 qursh
Coins: 1, 5, 10, 25, and 50 halalah; 1, 2, and 4 qursh
Notes: 1, 5, 10, 50, and 100 Riyals
Exchange rate: U.S. $1 = 3.325 Saudi Riyals as of June 1980

Weights and Measures

The metric system is in force.

Money Supply — Billions of Riyals: End of Period

	1977	1978	1979
Currency outside banks	16.25	19.18	23.71
Demand deposits at banks	22.16	30.03	31.00
Total	38.41	49.21	54.71

Foreign Investment

The Saudi government has adopted a liberal policy toward foreign firms. This includes giving a five-year tax holiday for industrial projects, lifting restrictions on repatriation of profits, exempting important machinery and raw materials from custom duties, loosening the entry restrictions on expatriate employees, and liberalizing eligibility for loans from the appropriate government fund, provided that at least 25% of the total capital of a firm is Saudi.

Some of the regulations governing foreign investments are:

1. Companies must be at least 51% Saudi-owned.
2. Not less than 75% of the employees must be Saudis.
3. The accounts must be in Arabic.
4. The headquarters must be in Saudi Arabia.
5. Muslim laws must be honored.

Banks and Other Commercial Organizations

Saudi Arabian Monetary Agency (SAMA): P.O.B. 2992, Airport Rd., Riyadh

National Commercial Bank: P.O.B. 3555, King Abdul Aziz St., Jeddah.

Riyadh Bank Ltd.: P.O.B. 1047, King Abdul Aziz St., Jeddah.

Al-Bank al-Saudi al-Fransi (Saudi French Bank): P.O.B. 1, Palestine Square, Al-Harithy Center, Jeddah.

Al-Bank al-Saudi al-Hollandi (Saudi Netherlands Bank): P.O.B. 6677, Medina Rd., Jeddah.

Arab National Bank Ltd. (Jordan): P.O.B. 344, Jeddah.

Bank Melli Iran: Ferdausi Ave., Jeddah.

Saudi American Bank (Citibank, N.Y.): P.O.B. 833, Al-Batha St., Riyadh.

Saudi British Bank: P.O.B. 9084, Riyadh.

Saudi Industrial Development Fund: P.O.B. 4143, Riyadh.

Chamber of Commerce and Industries: P.O.B. 1264, Jeddah.

Mecca Chamber of Commerce and Industry: P.O.B. 1086, Al-Ghazza St., Mecca.

Medina Chamber of Commerce: P.O.B. 443, Medina.

Riyadh Chamber of Commerce and Industry: P.O.B. 596, Riyadh.

General Petroleum and Mineral Organization (PETROMIN): P.O.B. 757, Riyadh.

Saudi Basic Industries Corporation (SABIC): P.O.B. 5101, Riyadh.

Government

Saudi Arabia is a monarchy and has no formal constitution. Law is the expression of the will of the monarch. The monarch, however, is limited by tribal customs and religious laws or Sharia (Islamic laws based on the Quran and the teachings of the Prophet). The king combines religious powers as imam (title of the person who leads the faithful in daily prayers) and tribal and military powers. Legislation is by royal decree.

The kingdom's founder was Abdul Aziz ibn Abdul Rahman Al-Faisal Al-Saud (1880-1953) known as ibn Saud. The kingdom has had a fairly stable government, and transitions of power are normally smooth. The present ruler is King Khalid ibn Abdul Aziz.

Assisting the king as head of state and prime minister is the cabinet of ministers, composed mainly of the royal family. The cabinet is empowered to approve the budget, ratify international agreements and commercial concessions, and supervise local governments. In March 1980, an eight-man committee was formed to draw up a basic "system of rule" based entirely on Islamic principles. Plans are also being made for the establishment of a Consultative Council.

Office Hours

Government: Summer: 0700-1200 Saturday - Wednesday
1300-1500

Winter: 0800-1200 Saturday - Wednesday
1300-1600

Note: Visitors are only received during the morning sessions.

Banks: 0830-1200 Saturday - Thursday throughout the year.

Private Jeddah: 0900-1300 Saturday - Thursday
Business: 1630-2000

Riyadh: 0830-1200 Saturday - Thursday
1630-1930

Muslim Holidays

There are mainly religious holidays. The weekly holiday is Friday. The holidays are determined by the sightings of the moon. For example, for 1980 these holidays were:

January 30	Birthday of the Prophet
June 11	Ascension of the Prophet[1]
August 13	Eid al-Fitr — End of Ramadan
October 20	Eid al-Adha — End of the Pilgrimage
November 9	Al-Hijra — The Muslim New Year
November 18	Ashura — Day of mourning for Shi'ites

Tourism

Saudi Arabia is the center of the Islamic faith and includes the holy cities of Mecca and Medina. Every year, thousands of Muslims from all over the world come for five days of ceremonies of the Hajj — the pilgrimate season. Business visitors should try to avoid making business trips to Saudi Arabia during the pilgrimage period.

Visa Requirements

The entry visa should be obtained well in advance. Applications for a visa must be made to a Saudi embassy, accompanied by four passport photographs and a certificate of religion. The holder of a passport showing any evidence of a visit to Israel should consult his own national authorities before applying for a Saudi visa. In no circumstances should visitors carry any alcohol, narcotics, contraceptives, and pork products.

Hotels

Jeddah: Al-Attas: P.O.B. 1299, Tel. 20211/20400, Telex. 401168.
        International: P.O.B. 1700, Tel. 29022/29814, Telex 401116
        Airport Hotel: P.O.B. 2012, Tel. 33489, Telex 401115
        Kaki: Tel. 48071, Telex. 401503
        Kandara Palace: P.O.B. 473, Tel. 23155/25700, Telex. 401095
        Meridien: Tel. 45011, Telex. 401276
        Red Sea Palace: P.O.B. 824, Tel. 28555/28950, Telex 401014.
Riyadh: Al-Khereji: Tel. 35600/39913, Telex. 201162
        Al-Khozama: Tel. 465465, Telex. 200100
        Al-Yamama: Airport Road, Tel. 28200/27927, Telex. 201056
        Intercontinental: P.O.B. 3636, Tel. 34500, Telex. 201076
        Airport Hotel: Airport Road, Tel. 61500, Telex. 201027
        Zahrat al-sharq: Airport Road, Tel. 28216/23978, Telex 201017

Press

Main Arabic Dailies: *Al-Bilad:* King Abdul Azia St., Jeddah.
                    Al-Jazirah: P.O.B. 354, Apt. 88, Municipality Blvd.,
                       Riyadh
                    Al-Medina al-Munawara: P.O.B. 807, Jeddah.
                    Al-Yaum: P.O.B. 565, Dammam
English Dailies: *Arab News*: P.O.B. 4556, Jeddah.
                    Saudi Gazette: P.O.B. 5576, Mina Rd., Jeddah.
                    Saudi Review: P.O.B. 4288, Jeddah.

Selected Embassies

Canada: P.O.B. 5050
France: Jeddah
Germany, Federal Republic: Jeddah
India: Jeddah
Japan: P.O.B. 1260, Jeddah
U.K.: P.O.B. 393, Jeddah
U.S.A.: Jeddah

[1]An explanation of the meaning of religious holidays is provided in the section on Algeria.

Syria
(Syrian Arab Republic)

Size and Location

The total area of Syria is approximately 185,000 sq. km. (71,500 sq. mi.). Syria is located in southwest Asia on the east coast of the Mediterranean Sea. The country is bounded by Turkey on the north, Iraq on the east, Jordan on the south, and Lebanon on the southwest.

Climate

Generally, Syria's climate is pleasant. The presence of mountain ranges and coastline has climatic effects. On the coastal strip, winters are mild, but summers are humid. The temperature ranges from 0.5°C (33°F) in the winter months (November to March) to 35°C (95°F) in the summer months. The mountain regions on the western coast have moderate summers. The interior plateaus have very hot summers, with temperatures often above 43°C (110°F), and cold winters with frost on many nights. The average annual rainfall is 30.5 cm. (10 in.), with great variations between regions. Rainfall is abundant in the west and north, but the amount decreases considerably in the southeastern desert.

Population

The estimates of the population of Syria are based on the last official census held in 1970 when the population was 6,304,685. Syria is one of the most densely populated countries in the Middle East.

Population — Millions: Mid-Year Estimates

1977	7.84
1978	8.09
1979	8.35

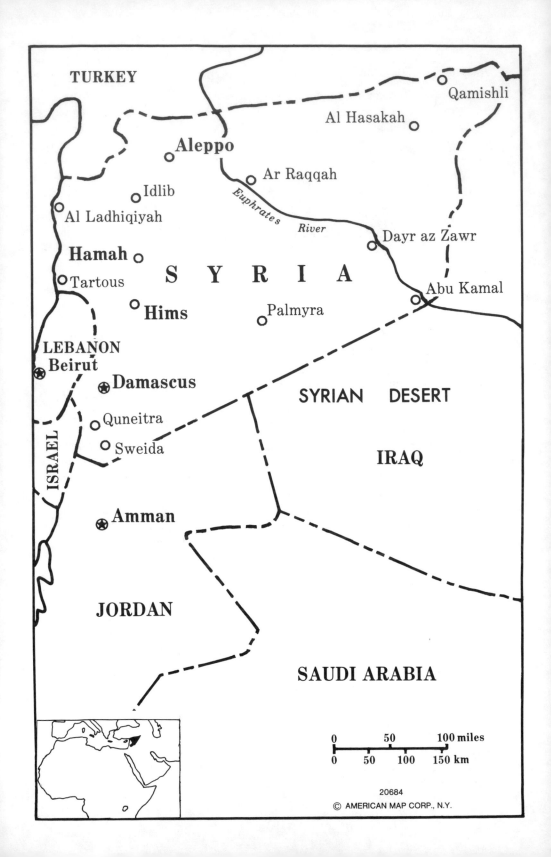

TURKEY

Qamishli

Al Hasakah

Aleppo

Ar Raqqah

Idlib

Euphrates *River*

Al Ladhiqiyah

Dayr az Zawr

Hamah

S   Y   R   I   A

Tartous

Abu Kamal

Hims

Palmyra

LEBANON
Beirut

⊛ **Damascus**

SYRIAN   DESERT

Quneitra

IRAQ

Sweida

ISRAEL

⊛ **Amman**

JORDAN

SAUDI ARABIA

0		50		100 miles
0	50	100		150 km

20684

© AMERICAN MAP CORP., N.Y.

Religion

Unlike most Arab countries, Syria has no official religion, though the constitution prescribes Islamic law as the source of jurisprudence. Most Syrians are Muslims who follow a form of Sunni orthodoxy. There are a number of religious minorities: Shi'ite (split into Alwaites, Druzes, and Ismailis); Christians (divided into a number of denominations); and two tiny communities, Yazidi (Yazidis are known as devil worshippers) and Jews.

Language

The official language of Syria is Arabic. Arabic is spoken over most of the country, but Kurdish, Armenian, and Assyrian are also used in many parts of Syria. French is taught as a compulsory second language in all schools. Most educated Syrians are as fluent in French as in Arabic. English is coming into increasing use and is now being used in business and government circles.

Principal Towns

More than 60% of the population is classified as urban. Migration from the rural communities is steadily swelling the urban areas.

Syrian cities are among the oldest in the world. Damascus, the administrative capital, has streets that date back to biblical times. Aleppo is dominated by a medieval citadel. Homs is central Syria's chief market and houses most of the new industries. Latakia is the main port of Syria.

Population

Damascus (capital)	1,456,000
Aleppo	646,000
Homs	710,000
Hama	583,000
Idleb	490,000
Latakia	467,000
Deir ez-Zor	337,000

Education

Syria has universal, compulsory, and free schooling. Textbooks are free in primary schools. The literacy rate is 50%. Education is expanding rapidly, and in 1979 there were over 2 million students enrolled in schools and institutes. The medium of instruction is Arabic, but French and English are taught as second languages. Higher education is provided by three universities—The University of Damascus, the University of Aleppo, and the University of Latakia. In addition, there are agricultural schools, technical schools, and the Homs Institute of Petroleum.

The Economy

Syria is one of the lower middle-income countries with a centralized and regulated socialist economy in which the public sector is dominant. Almost all large businesses, industrial firms, banks, and insurance companies came under public control.

Syria has embarked on a number of development plans. The first five-year plan was launched in 1961 under the guidance of international agencies. In spite of serious disruptions as a result of the wars of 1967 and 1973, the second and third five-year plans achieved reasonable success. The fourth development plan (1976-1980) called for an 11.9% annual increase in national income with emphasis on infrastructure including transportation, ports, communications, power, and tourism. Tourism is expected to become the country's third main source of foreign currency after oil and cotton.

Gross Domestic Product by Economic Activity—1974

	% of GDP
Agriculture	18
Industry	12
Mining	11
Construction	6
Trade	24
Transport	7
Others	22

Agriculture. Agriculture has for centuries been a mainstay of the Syrian economy. Syria remains primarily an agricultural country in spite of the existence of a strong commercial sector and relatively successful attempts to industrialize.

Agriculture contributes roughly 18% GDP and employs about half the labor force. The main areas of cultivation are the narrow coastal strip along the Mediterranean, the valley of the Orontes River, the steppe-plain running from the Jordanian borders to the Euphrates valley, and the Jezirah region which lies between the Euphrates in Syria and the Tigris in Iraq.

One of the main characteristics of Syrian agriculture is the wide annual fluctuation in output resulting from variations in rainfall. Therefore, irrigation has assumed a special importance as a means of increasing and stabilizing the output. Several irrigation and land development projects are planned, under construction, or completed. The most ambitious irrigation project is located in the Euphrates basin. At the heart of the project (completed in 1975) is a Russian-built dam designed to quadruple the irrigated land available for cultivation and to produce 2 billion kw of electricity annually. In addition to a number of smaller irrigation projects, Syria is expanding and improving her agriculture infrastructure-transportation, port facilities, storage capacity, and food processing plants.

The main food crops are wheat and barley. Cotton is the main cash crop. Sugar beet and tobacco are the most important cash crops after cotton, and they are receiving much attention. Fruits are abundant and some, such as apricots and nuts, are export crops.

Petroleum. Syria is relatively poor in mineral resources. At one time Syria was thought to have no oil. After years of exploration, oil of low quality was discovered in 1956 in the northeast corner of the country.

Syria was the first Arab country to nationalize its oil industry in 1964. For the next 10 years, oil explorations and exploitations were conducted solely by the state-owned General Petroleum Authority and the Syrian Petroleum Company with Soviet assistance. However, in 1975 Syria granted its first concessions for international bidding. As a result, two new oil fields were opened, producing better-quality oil.

Syria's only oil refinery is at Homs with a capacity of three million tons. Work on a second oil refinery at Banias, with a capacity of six million tons, is to be completed in 1981 with Rumanian collaboration.

Royalties. Royalties for the transit of foreign crude oil through Syrian territory have been an important source of revenue. Two pipelines run through Syria, one from Iraq and the second from Saudi Arabia, with a total carrying capacity of 80 tons annually. Transit royalties are roughly equivalent to 35 U.S. cents per barrel.

Industry. Since the early 1970's, Syria has had a steady industrial expansion. The industrial sector has replaced agriculture as the main contributor to the gross domestic product. The industrial boom is mainly based on textiles and food processing. Syria has a long tradition of producing fine textiles. Other areas of industrial development include chemicals, fertilizers, iron, steel, cement, rubber, glass, paper, assembly of tractors, refrigerators, and television sets.

One of the main mineral resources, apart from oil and gas, is phosphates with estimated reserves of 500 million tons. Chemical fertilizer industry in Syria is partly based on the country's phosphate reserves. The production of phosphates increased from 20,000 tons in 1971 to two million tons in 1980.

Syria's principal industrial centers are around the towns of Damascus, Homs, Aleppo, and Latakia.

Principal Economic Indicators — Millions of Pounds

	1977	1978	1979
Gross Domestic Product	27,265	32,696	35,887
Per Capita GDP	3,452	4,042	4,222
Per Capita GDP in U.S. $	880	1,030	1,076
Government Consumption	5,300	6,499	6,824
Private Consumption	18,769	21,627	25,379
Gross Capital Formation	9,272	9,876	--
Gross Domestic Production in 1975 prices	21,832	23,734	24,526

Foreign Trade — Millions of U.S. Dollars

	1977	1978	1979
Merchandise			
Exports fob	1,069	1,062	1,647
Imports fob	2,386	2,194	3,056
Services			
Exports	383	357	470
Imports	452	553	714

Finance

Currency — Syrian pound
1 Syrian pound = 100 piastres
Coins: 2½, 5, 10, 25, and 50 piastres; 1 pound
Notes: 1, 5, 10, 25, 50, 100, and 500 pounds
Exchange rate: U.S. $ = 3.925 Syrian pounds as of June 1980.

Weights and Measures

The metric system is in force.

Money Supply — Millions of Pounds — End of Period

	1977	1978	1979
Currency outside banks	6,797	8,456	9,903
Demand deposits at banks	3,676	4,883	5,552
Total	10,473	13,339	15,455

Banks and Other Commercial Organization

Central Bank of Syria: 29 Ayar Square, Damascus
Commercial Bank of Syria: P.O.B. 933, Muawia St., Damascus
Industrial Bank: Damascus
Popular Credit Bank: P.O.B. 2841, Darwishieh, Damascus
Damascus Chamber of Commerce: P.O.B. 1040, Muawia St., Damascus
Damascus Chamber of Industry: P.O.B. 1305, Muawia St., Damascus
Aleppo Chamber of Commerce: Al-Mutanabi St., Aleppo
Aleppo Chamber of Industry: Al-Mutanabi St., Aleppo
Hama Chamber of Commerce and Industry: Sh. Bachoura, Hama
Homs Chamber of Commerce and Industry: Aboul-Of St., Homs
Latakia Chamber of Commerce: St. Al-Hurriyah, Latakia
Cotton Marketing Organization: P.O.B. 729, Aleppo
Syria Petroleum Company: P.O.B. 2849, Al-Mutanabi St., Damascus

Government

Syria attained her independence in 1946. From 1920 to 1946, Syria was under French rule. After the attainment of independence, Syria has passed through a chain of events and a varying succession of coups and counter-coups. However, since 1970 when General Hafez Al-Assad seized power, the country has enjoyed an unprecedented period of political stability and economic prosperity.

Syria has a republican form of government. The present constitution was approved by a referendum in 1973. The constitution declares that the Syrian Arab Republic is a democratic, socialist, and sovereign state. The President, who must be a Muslim, is elected for a seven-year term by a universal suffrage. The constitution also provides for a council of Ministers and a People's Council. The Council of Ministers is nominated by the President.

The legislative body is the People's Council. The Constitution provides for popular and direct elections of the People's Council. Its members are elected to a four-year term on the basis of universal adult suffrage. The first general election to the Council was held in May 1973.

The judicial power is independent. A High Constitutional Court is the highest court in the judicial system and is charged with the task of considering the constitutionality of laws.

Office Hours

Government and banks: 0800-1400 Saturday - Thursday
Business: May - October 0830-1330
                       1700-2000 Saturday - Thursday
         October - May 0900-1400
                       1600-1900 Saturday - Thursday

Public Holidays

January 1	New Year's Day
February 22	Union Day
March 8	Revolution Day
March 22	Arab League Day
April 17	Independence Day
May 1	Labour Day

Muslim Holidays

Islamic festivals are based on the sighting of the moon and may vary from year to year by a day or two. For 1980, these holidays were:

January 30	Birthday of the Prophet
August 13	Eid al-Fitr — End of Ramadan[1]
October	Eid al-Adha— End of the Pilgrimage
November 9	Al-Hijra — the Muslim New Year
November 18	Ashura — Day of Mourning for Shi'ites

Tourism

Syria is a varied and beautiful country. Historically, Syria has existed in various forms since pre-Biblical times. The geographical location has made Syria a bridge between Europe, Asia, and Africa. The great empires of Egypt, Persia, Rome, and Byzantium have each left its traces. Palmyra, in the desert, is a remarkable example of Greco-Roman architecture. There are many fine examples of Islamic culture. There is also the famous Ommayad Mosque in Damascus.

Visa Requirements

Entry visas can be obtained from Syrian consular offices and Syrian embassies in Arab capitals. Visas are valid for one entry and for up to two weeks. For a longer stay, one has to report to the Department of Security and Police. If the visitor's passport shows evidence of a visit to Israel, it becomes necessary to have a new passport before traveling to Syria.

Airline Services

The Syrian Arab Airlines has domestic services and routes to all major cities in the Middle East—Abu Dhabi, Algiers, Bahrain, Benghazi, and Cairo. It also provides services to Athens, Copenhagen, London, Moscow, Munich, and Paris.

Syria is also served by Aeroflot, Air France, Alitalia, British Airways, Egypt Air, KLM, Lufthansa, Pan Am, Qantas, SAB, and Swiss Air.

Hotels

Damascus: Meridien: Route de Beyrouth, P.O.B. 5531 Tel. 229220, Telex. 11379

Sheraton: Ommayad Square, P.O.B. 4795 Tel. 333547 or 224220, Telex. 11069

Semiramis: Gumhuria Street, Tel. 113813, Cable: SEMIRAMIS

New Ommayad Hotel: Brazil Street, Tel. 117700, Telex. Omatel 11206

Catlan's Hotel: Gumhuria Street, Tel. 112513, International City Center: Tel. 112400

Aleppo: Barou Hotel: Baron Avenue, Tel. 10880

Tourist Hotel

Ramsis: Baron Avenue, Tel. 16701

New Ommayad: Central Bank Street, Tel. 14101

Heliopolis: Bab Al-Faraj Square, Tel. 17456

Semiramis: Kuwatly Avenue, Tel. 19991

Press

Al-Baath: Rue el Barazil, Damascus, daily, Arabic
Barq al-Shimal: Rue Aziziyah, Aleppo, daily, Arabic

Al-Fida: Rue Kuwatly, Hama, daily, Arabic
Al-Thawrah: Damascus, daily, Arabic

Selected Embassies (in Damascus unless otherwise stated)

Canada: Beirut, Lebanon
China, People's Republic: 83 Rue Ata Ayoubi
France: Rue Ata Ayoubi
Germany, Federal Republic: 53 Rue Ibrahim Hanano
India: 40146 Ave. Al-Malki
Japan: 15 Ave. Al-Jabaa
U.S.S.R.: Boustan Al-Kouzbari, Rue d'Alep
United Kingdom: Malki, Rue Muhammad Kurd Ali
U.S.A.: Rue Al Mansour 2

[1]The meaning of religious holidays can be found in the section on Algeria.

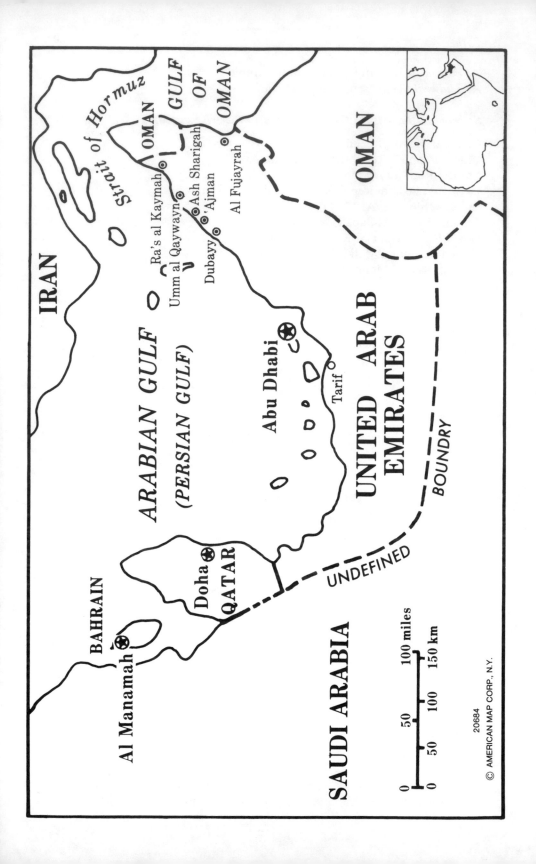

United Arab Emirates
(UAE)

Size and Location

The United Arab Emirates, formerly known as the Trucial States, is a federation of seven emirates: Abu Dhabi, Dubai, Sharjah, Ras al-Khaimah, Umm al-Quwain, Ajman, and Fujairah. The most common estimate of total area is 83,000 sq. km. (32,000 sq. miles). Abu Dhabi is the largest of the emirates with an area of 67,000 sq. km. (26,000 sq. miles). The area is one of extremely shallow seas, with offshore islands and coral reefs, and often an intricate pattern of sandbanks, and small gulfs as a coastline. In the interior, the plain is covered with sand dunes up to 60 meters high.

The UAE is located on the southeastern end of the Arabian Peninsula along both the Arabian gulf and the Gulf of Oman. It is bordered by Saudi Arabia and Qatar on the west and by Oman on the northeast. Disputed boundaries make the geographical extent of this region difficult to define precisely.

Climate

The UAE has an arid, sub-tropical climate. The summer months are very hot and humid with temperatures in July and August exceeding 48°C (118°F) and humidity of more than 85%. The winter months of January and February are pleasant with average minimum temperatures of 10°C (50°F). Rainfall is erratic with an annual average of 8 mm (3 inches). More than 90 percent of total precipitation comes in January and February. Rain tends to fall in short, torrential outbursts. Droughts are frequent.

Population

There are various population estimates for the emirates ranging between 350,000 and 890,000. Two-thirds of the federation's population live in Abu Dhabi and Dubai. Ethnic groups—Indians, Pakistanis, and Iranians—constitute 75% of the total population. There are also other Arab nationals: Palestinians, Egyptians, as well as several thousand Europeans.

Population — Millions: Mid-Year Estimates

1976   .670
1977   .710
1978   .750

Religion

Islam is the state religion. Most of the inhabitants are Muslims of the Sunni sect. About 20% of the Muslims are Shi'ites. An increasing emphasis is being placed on religious education and on the observance of Muslim practices. Religious toleration is extended to Christians of all denominations; and some churches, missions, and schools are permitted to function openly.

Language

The official language is Arabic. The Gulf Arabic is akin to the Arabic spoken in Saudi Arabia and Iraq, which is different from the Arabic of Egypt. English is widely understood and is used in government and business. It is taught as a second language in secondary schools. Urdu (Pakistani) and Farsi (Persian) are also spoken in some cities.

Principal Towns

Many inhabitants are still nomads. The population of each emirate is concentrated largely in its capital. With their seafaring traditions, these towns have attracted large numbers of external migrants from all around the Indian Ocean. Based on 1975 census, the population of each emirate is:

Abu Dhabi (Capital) 235,662
Dubai   206,861
Sharjah   88,188
Ras al-Khaimah   57,282
Fujairah   26,498
Ajman   21,566
Umm al-Quwain   16,879

Education

Education is free, universal, and compulsory for six years between the ages 6 and 12. School uniforms, books, equipment, and transport are also free. The literacy rate is 20%. The medium of instruction is Arabic. The majority of teachers are Egyptians and Palestinians. The Ministry of Education is engaged in an expansion of the educational programs and facilities to cover the whole country. The UAE's first university opened in Abu Dhabi in 1977. Many students receive higher education abroad — U.S.A., U.K., France, Iraq, and Kuwait.

The Economy

Before the discovery of oil, the sea was the mainstay of the emirates. Economic activity was limited to oasis agriculture, fishing, and trade; and the country was without paved roads, running water, electricity, telephones, schools, hospitals, or hotels.

Now the immense oil wealth has boosted income to make the United Arab Emirates one of the highest per capital income in the world. The economy of the UAE is completely dominated by oil. The UAE is the 12th largest oil producer in the world and 5th largest in the Middle East. Today, roads link all major towns, schools, hospitals, and hotels. The communication network is being continually expanded and welfare services and education are freely available to all citizens.

Agriculture. Agriculture is a minor economic activity, and its potential is negligible. Only 10% of land is considered cultivable, and the actual cultivated area is much less than that. The contribution of agriculture to the GNP is less than 1%.

In spite of harsh natural conditions, the government's policy is to achieve self-sufficiency in food. On the island of Sadiyat, the Arid Lands Research Center produces vegetables in an artificial environment based on hydroponics. The project is supervised by the University of Arizona. A similar project was established in the desert at Mazaid. There are also experimental farm complexes at Rawaya and Al-Ain. There is a dairy farm at Al-Ain to provide milk, dairy products, and meat as part of the goal of self-sufficiency in food.

Industry. With the paucity of natural resources and the small size of the local market, the UAE faces immense difficulty in realizing industrial diversification ambitions. The government intends to develop and use indigenous resources to the full. Industrial development is concentrated on hydrocarbon based projects. A major industrial plant is the new gas liquefaction unit on Das Island in Abu Dhabi. Planned projects include a dry dock in Dubai; a petrochemical plant based on ethylene; an iron and steel project, and a fertilizer plant at Mafraq in Abu Dhabi; and an oil equipment factory at Rams in Ras al-Khaimah. A contract for building a chemical plant producing salt, caustic soda, and hydorchloric acid has been awarded. Another major industrial plant is the cement works at Al-Ain which was completed in 1976 with a capacity of 250,000 metric tons a year and is now being enlarged to 750,000 metric tons.

Principal Economic Indicators (Billions of Dirhams)

	1976	1977	1978
Gross Domestic Product	43.6	54.5	53.4
Per Capita GDP	65,075	76,761	71,200
Per Capita GDP in U.S. $	16,363	19,692	18,551
Government Consumption	4.8	6.4	7.2
Private Consumption	5.1	10.4	11.6
Gross Fixed Capital Formation	12.5	18.4	18.4

Foreign Trade

	1976	1977	1978
Exports	35.3	40.2	38.3
Imports	15.0	21.7	22.2

Finance

Currency — UAE Dirham
1 Dirham = 100 fils
Coins: 1, 5, 10, 25, and 50 fils; 1 Dirham
Notes: 1, 5, 10, 50, and 100 Dirhams
Exchange rate: U.S. $1 = 3.70 Dirhams as of June 1980

Weights and Measures

Metric and imperial systems are used. Full conversion to the metric system is planned in stages.

Money Supply — Millions of Dirhams — End of Period

	1977	1978	1979
Currency outside banks	1,392	1,704	1,965
Demand deposits at banks	3,822	4,072	4,303
Total	5,214	5,776	6,268

Banks and Other Commercial Organizations

United Arab Emirates Currency Board: P.O.B. 854, Abu Dhabi
United Arab Emirates Bankers' Association: P.O.B. 2734, Abu Dhabi
Amsterdam-Rotterdam Bank N.V. (Netherlands): P.O.B. 2941, Dubai
Arab Bank (Jordan): P.O.B. 875, Abu Dhabi
Bank Melli Iran: P.O.B. 2656, Abu Dhabi
Banque de Paris et des Pays-Bas (France): P.O.B. 2742, Abu Dhabi
Barclays Bank International (U.K.): P.O.B. 2734, Abu Dhabi
Chartered Bank (U.K.): P.O.B. 240, Abu Dhabi
Citibank (U.S.A.): P.O.B. 749, Dubai

First National Bank of Chicago (U.S.A.): P.O.B. 1655, Dubai
Grindlays Bank Ltd. (U.K.): P.O.B. 241, Abu Dhabi
Lloyds Bank International (U.K.): P.O.B. 3766, Dubai
Royal Bank of Canada: P.O.B. 3614, Dubai
Abu Dhabi Chamber of Commerce and Industries: P.O.B. 662, Abu Dhabi
Dubai Chamber of Commerce and Industry: Ben Yass St., P.O.B. 1457, Dubai
Federal Ministry of Planning: P.O.B. 2847, Abu Dhabi
Abu Dhabi Fund for Arab Economic Development (ADFAED): P.O.B. 814, Abu Dhabi
Abu Dhabi Development Finance Corp.: P.O.B. 30, Abu Dhabi

Government

The UAE is a young national entity, with membership in the United Nations, the International Monetary Fund, and the Organization of Petroleum Exporting Countries.

The British announcement in 1968 that Great Britain would withdraw entirely from the Gulf in 1971, precipitated the formation of the United Arab Emirates. By December 1971, full independence was announced, and a provisional constitution for the UAE was set up. Abu Dhabi was designated as the seat of the federal government. Under the constitution, the highest federal authority is the Supreme Federal Council (composed of the rulers of the seven Emirates). The Council elects a president and a vice-president from among its seven members. The president appoints a prime minister and a cabinet. The Supreme Federal Council is charged with the formulation and supervision of general policies, ratification of federal laws, and preparation of the union budget. Major decisions require the support of at least five members, including the rulers of Abu Dhabi and Dubai.

The legislature is the Union National Council, a consultative assembly of 40 members appointed for a two-year term by the emirates. Each emirate appoints its own representatives separately. In addition, the provisional constitution of 1971 provides for the setting up of a Union Supreme Court and several lower courts. All judges have to take a constitutional oath that the courts must apply the rules of Sharia (Islamic religious laws).

Under the constitution, considerable power is enjoyed by each individual emirate, including control over mineral rights, taxation, and police force. However, there has been a steady growth in federal powers. A large portion of the oil revenues goes to the federal budget. There has also been growing integration of armed forces, communications facilities, and all matters of internal security. The Council of Ministers passed a number of measures to strengthen the federal government and the office of the president.

There are no constitutional provisions for elections in the United Arab Emirates. Consequently, there is no suffrage. As of 1981, the President is Sheikh Zayed bin Al-Nahayan (Emir of Abu Dhabi) and the Vice-President is Sheikh Rashid bin Said Al-Maktoum (Emir of Dubai).

Office Hours

Friday is the official weekly holiday.
Government: Summer: 0700-1300 Saturday - Wednesday
                         0700-1100 Thursday
               Winter: 0800-1400 Saturday - Wednesday
                         0800-1200 Thursday
Banks: 0800-1200 Saturday - Wednesday
                         0800-1100 Thursday (Abu Dhabi)
                         0800-1100 Thursday (Northern Emirates)
Business and Shops: 0800-1300 Saturday - Thursday
    (with variations):   1530-1900

Public Holidays

January 1   New Year's Day
August 6   Accession of the Ruler of Abu Dhabi
December 2   National Day

Muslim Holidays

Variable Islamic festivals are based on the sighting of the moon. The holidays depend on the lunar calendar which advances ten or eleven days each year. For 1980 Muslim holidays were:

January 30   Birthday of the Prophet
June 11   Ascension of the Prophet[1]
July 14   First day of Ramadan
August 13   Eid al-Fitr — End of Ramadan
October 20   Eid al-Adha — End of the Pilgrimage
November 9   Al-Hijra — the Muslim New Year
November 18   Ashura — Day of mourning for Shi'ites

Tourism

Various places of impressive scenery might be visited. There are plans to develop tourism throughout the United Arab Emirates. For information write to:

Ministry of Information and Culture: P.O.B. 17, Abu Dhabi

Visa Requirements

Visa regulations change at short notice. A check should be made with the nearest UAE embassy before traveling. Application should be made to an embassy accompanied by three passport photographs and a company letter giving the status of the visitor and the proposed reason for the trip. Holders of passports showing any evidence of a visit to Israel are refused entry.

Hotels

Abu Dhabi:	Hilton Hotel: P.O.B. 877, Tel. 61900, Telex. 2212
	Al-Ain Palace: P.O.B. 33, Tel. 22377, Telex. 2227
	Khalidiya Palace: P.O.B 4010, Tel. 67470, Telex. 2506
	Meridien: Tel. 356269, Telex 68204
	Ramada: Tel. 77260, Telex. 2567
Al-Ain:	Hilton Hotel: P.O.B. 1333, Tel. 41410, Telex. 0893-2417
Dubai:	Sheraton: Tel. 281111, Telex. 46710
	Inter-Continental: P.O.B. 476, Tel. 227171, Telex. 45779
	Hilton Hotel: Tel. 470000, Telex. 46679
	Carlton Tower: Tel. 227111, Telex. 46328
Sharjah:	Holiday Inn, Tel. 357357, Telex. 68305
	Novotel Sharjah Beach, Tel. 356566, Telex. 68213
	Meridien, Tel. 56557, Telex. 68204
	Carlton, Tel. 23811, Telex. 68012

Press

Abu Dhabi Chamber of Commerce Review: P.O.B. 662, monthly, Arabic
with some articles in English
Al-Bayan: Abu Dhabi, daily, Arabic
Emirates News: Abu Dhabi, daily, English
Gulf News: Dubai, daily, English
Recorder: Abu Dhabi, daily news bulletin, English
Al-Khaleej Times: Dubai, daily, English
Dubai External Trade Statistics: Dubai, monthly, English

Selected Embassies (In Abu Dhabi unless otherwise stated)

Canada: Kuwait City, Kuwait
France: P.O.B. 4014
Germany, Federal Republic: P.O.B. 2591
Indian: P.O.B. 4090
Japan: P.O.B. 2430
U.K.: P.O.B. 248
U.S.A.: P.O.B. 4009

[1]For the meaning of these holidays, see the section on Algeria.

Part III

Doing Business with the Arabs

Chapter 9

Doing Business with the Arabs

Examples abound of American businessmen who headed to the Arab world in the hope of striking a lucrative business deal only to return home empty-handed. Such businessmen were generally guided by the faulty premise that doing business with the Arabs was no different from doing business in the U.S. All one had to do, so the reasoning went, was to offer the Arabs quality products and services at competitive prices. Consequently, the businessmen's standard method was to fly into an Arab capital, call up a local company or government official, and ask to discuss a possible project.

Dealing with the Arabs involves the customary problems of trying to do business with a different cultural group. These include differences in language, customs, perception, food, working habits, and the like. But, more than any other cultural group, the Arabs have a tendency to base their business dealings on personal relationships. It is this basic difference between the Arabic and the Western cultures that often trips up the American businessmen. It is whom you know in the Arab world which, more than any other factor, can make or break a deal.

The purpose of this section is to offer the businessman some tips on how to deal with the Arabs and some guidelines concerning the negotiation of contracts.

Helpful Tips

1. Familiarize yourself thoroughly with the religion, customs, politics, and attitudes of the people in the area. Review the chapters in this book as frequently as necessary.
2. Equip yourself with some basic Arabic words and expressions, particularly those pertaining to saying "hello" and "goodbye." (Consult the sections titled "Meeting People" and "Social Calls" in Part IV.) Familiarity with such a vocabulary can serve as a useful public relations tool. It will leave a favorable impression on the Arabs, thereby providing you with a psychological advantage over the competition.

213

3. Build up your contacts. To cultivate personal relationships, the key to business dealings, you will have to visit the area, perhaps several times. Talk to as many distributors, businessmen, and government officials as possible.

4. Take advantage of the frequent visits made to the U.S. by Arab officials or businessmen. Sell yourself and your company to them.

5. Have the officials or businessmen, whose relationships you have cultivated in the U.S., sponsor your visit to their countries. Some countries, such as Saudi Arabia, grant visas only to those requested by a local sponsor. The sponsor can be helpful in other ways also. He can, for example, arrange meetings for you with the proper government officials.

6. Select an agent or distributor. One of the common and most effective ways of dealing with the free-market countries in the area is to select a local businessman as your agent. Because of his personal connections, the agent can be invaluable to you. In many cases, the agent also becomes a participant in the venture. It is advisable that you check with the U.S. Embassy officials in the country of interest for their recommendations as to the type of agent best suited to your needs.

7. Enhance your chances of success by offering a comprehensive business package. This may include such things as product design, construction, maintenance, and the provision of training and housing of employees.

8. Be patient, and do not pin your hopes on wrapping up a quick deal. Otherwise, you will be in for a rude awakening. The Arabic culture, typical of an agrarian or non-industrialized society, is slow-paced. And business transactions, heavily laced with complex social amenities, normally take a longer time to complete than an American is accustomed to. Actually, it is highly unusual for a deal to be consummated in two meetings.

9. Exercise utmost caution before offering a bribe to a government official. Do not assume that bribery is a common practice in all Arab countries. In Iraq, for examples, all parties involved in a bribery case can be subject to a harsh punishment.

10. Keep abreast of the American law regarding the Arab boycott of Israel. This law is designed to prevent American firms from complying with the Arabs' stipulation that they will not do business with any firm that maintains trade relations with Israel.

11. Be forthright in your dealings and live up to your obligations. The Arabs are known for their prompt-paying habits and readiness to measure up to their word. In return, they expect the foreign businessman to be above board in his dealings with them and to deliver on his promises. As we pointed out earlier, the key to continued success in dealing with the Arabs rests in the cultivation of long-term personal relationships. But such relationships cannot flourish unless an atmosphere of mutual trust and respect is solidly established.

12. Strictly observe the local social customs. Be sensitive to the natives' expectations concerning such matters as alcohol consumption, pork eating, womens' attire, restrictions on visits to Islamic shrines, and so on.

13. Keep abreast of business developments in the area. A good source of such information is the Athens' office of the U.S. Commerce Department, which is set up to provide assistance to businessmen with interest in the Middle East. Another source of information is the American-Arab Chamber of Commerce which has branches in major U.S. cities.

14. You will also do well to keep the following points in mind:

    a. The Arab countries exhibit mixed economies with a varying proportion of emphasis on a private-enterprise market and a planned public sector.

    b. With a few exceptions, fixed-price contracts are used — no escalation clauses.

    c. In almost all Arab countries, bid bonds and performance bonds are required.

    d. Bonded areas have not been commonly provided.

    e. Foreign individuals and firms are taxed on income generated in the Arab countries unless provisions in their contracts are incorporated to exempt them from income taxes.

    f. Outside capital investment regulations require foreign firms to co-operate in ventures (e.g. partnership) with a local or public company having at least 51 percent ownership.

    g. Skilled labor force is in short supply in all Arab countries. Contract formalities give preference to local nationals, but in most cases this requirement is waived.

The information in the following sections has been excerpted from *An Introduction to Contract Procedures in the Near East & North Africa, Second Edition* compiled by the United States Department of Commerce, International Trade Administration, Washington, D.C. 20230.

Contract Negotiations

Algeria

There are three things the U.S. businessman should keep in mind when he sits down to negotiate a contract in Algeria. First, he will be dealing with an Algerian Government organization which is part of a complex bureaucratic system staffed by a thin cadre of highly competent but overworked individuals. Secondly, the utmost patience is required to wait out the often extended delays that meet the potential contractor from the time he decides to seek the contract to the time the project is completed. Finally, the Algerians are tough negotiators and will press hard to get the most favorable financing and performance terms. It is of utmost importance that all terms agreed upon be written into the contract.

The Algerian Government generally requires what it terms "product-in-hand" contracts for major industrial facilities. This formula usually requires the contractor not only to guarantee to turn over the plant to the client in a functioning state, but also to remain on the job until the plant is producing at capacity for a specified period of time. This often involves the contractor in extensive technical assistance and training programs after construction of the facility has been completed.

Performance Requirements

Algerian contracts typically have many performance requirements, interior deadline dates, and other obligations. Many of these clauses carry penalties and all apply effectively only to the foreign contracting party. The contract will state the obligations of the Algerian party, but may include no enforcement clause. Furthermore, any inability of the Algerians to meet their obligations does not legally mitigate the foreign party's obligations. For example, if the foreign firm agrees to erect a building within a given time, subject to penalty, and the Algerian party agrees to provide the necessary cement, the penalty is imposed if the structure is not erected on time even though the cause of delay was lack of adequate and timely deliveries of cement.

Though the Algerian party often has little or not control over the performance of other Algerian organizations, after strenuous negotiations, it will agree to clauses granting some protection to the foreign firm in the event of failure on the Algerian side to live up to its obligations. The U.S. firm can also protect itself from default for failure to complete a project on time due to unforeseen delays by agreeing to a project completion date which allows at least twice as much time as it would take to finish the project.

Bid bonds are not normally required. Performance bonds may not be demanded if a company has had previous experience in Algeria. Small contracts may require a cash guarantee of 10 to 15 percent of the contract value to be repaid over the life of the contract. On larger contracts, an unconditional bank guarantee may be required (again of 10 to 15 percent). The guarantee is considered satisfied when an agreed-upon level of production is reached and the Algerian party formally accepts the project. Imported machinery and equipment will not be accepted as an offset against bonds because the machinery used on a project is owned by the Algerian agency on arrival in the country. A request for unconditional bank guarantees can be tied to an arbitration clause in which the bank will honor the judgment of the arbitrator.

The contract should contain an arbitration clause specifying the mode of arbitration. Arbitration in a third country has been possible, performed in accordance with the rules of arbitration of the International Chamber of Commerce. However, Algerians increasingly are insisting upon arbitration in Algeria.

The definition of force majeure is negotiable, though once it is agreed upon it cannot be altered. The clause might typically include wars, natural catastrophes, and other disrupting occurrences, including new legislation foreclosing the possibility of further work. Strikes may also be included. Onerous factors such as port congestion are not considered force majeure, though they sometimes can be alluded to in arguing for more time.

The Algerians will provide advance payments at the start of the contract. The amount is usually negotiable, but will not be more than 15 percent of the total contract price. Contractors often find that they must continue to import working capital for projects, which necessitates establishing a convertible dinar account. Payments by the Algerian clients are often slow.

Contractors should pay meticulous attention to the details of Algeria's currency laws. Convertible dinar accounts are necessary to move foreign exchange in and out of Algeria legally. Contractors often experience lengthy delays in getting paid, and receiving payment on time often requires a systematic follow-up effort with banks. American construction firms should insist upon being paid by irrevocable letters of credit, rather than by bank drafts or cash against presentation of documents. From time to time, particularly towards the end of the year, the Algerian Ministry of Finance will freeze the foreign exchange or dinar accounts of a particular Algerian national company, which can present considerable cash flow problems for the foreign contractor.

Under Algerian Foreign Exchange Laws, a valid contract with a foreign firm must not only be approved by the contracting entity, but also by the

State Planning Secretariat and the Minisry of Finance. Without these approvals, no foreign exchange can be transferred.

The bid, the contract, and all correspondence must. be in French. The units of measurement must be metric.

Price

The Algerian national companies usually demand fixed price contracts, although a few cost-plus-fee contracts have been signed for very large projects. The cost of equipment is agreed upon by both parties; the insurance and freight costs are reimbursable to the supplier, demurrage is not. There are no escalation clauses. Changes in Algerian legislation which increase costs, and other local cost increases, can be used as a basis for negotiating the project price upward. The Algerians will not guarantee the price of the commodities they supply.

Equipment and Materials

Port and customs clearance delays are serious problems, and the Algerian client rarely assists the foreign contractor in overcoming the difficulties. Import duty must usually be paid on the machinery imported for a project. Re-export of the machinery is generally allowed, but duties paid upon importation are not rebated. However, the guarantee payment paid by the contractor when the machinery is imported may be rebated when the machinery is re-exported. Algerian customs allow a system of temporary admission of project equipment without paying duty, but such equipment must be re-exported within an exact time frame or the equipment will be seized and heavy penalties imposed.

Spare parts must be imported for heavy equipment, but the quantity and period of time for which they must be supplied are negotiable. The contractor must commit himself in his bid to use the maximum amount of local materials and supplies, subject only to availability.

The foreign contractor should ensure that his Algerian client has either an import license (A.G.I.—Authorisations Globales d'Importation) or other written authorization to import project equipment. The slightest discrepancy in documentation can create considerable customs and payments delays, and large warehousing costs paid by the contractor.

Bonded areas can be arranged. However, they are of questionable value in helping to eliminate delays due to customs clearances, unless they can be located on the job site with customs agents on site as well. The cost of maintaining guards, customs escorts, inspectors, and other personnel make bonded areas very expensive.

Labor

Highly skilled and skilled local labor is hard to find and keep. The contractor therefore will need to include a percentage of expatriate labor in his workforce. Though it varies with the nature of the project, the ratio most agree to be required for construction projects is one skilled expatriate for every ten local laborers. The ratio is determined by the contractor and is written into the contract. The Algerian Government is more concerned with performance than with the employment of Algerian laborers. However, the foreign company has to clear plans to bring in expatriate labor with the national labor union (UGTA). This clearance can be torturous. Third country laborers are usually French, Italian, Spanish, and Portuguese, but U.S. firms are starting to make extensive use of Filipinos and other East Asians, particularly for work in remote sites.

Contracts should make the Algerian host company or ministry responsible for all labor union and labor inspector problems. Otherwise, the contract should provide, if possible, that the foreign contractor may close down the project without penalty if labor disputes cannot be resolved within a reasonable period of time.

The Algerian Labor Code (Code du Travail) regulates the conditions under which all workers are employed. This code requires that each employee have a work permit; application for and delivery of the work permit is often a lengthy process. Contractors should ensure that their Algerian client guarantees the requisite number of work permits to avoid serious delays due to unfilled positions of key personnel.

All foreigners working in Algeria must normally obtain a residence permit, and all residents must acquire exit visas to leave the country. Employees of companies with short-term contracts, who will be in Algeria for less than 3 months, do not need a residence permit.

Training is usually an essential part of a major project. The cost is negotiable; a flat fee is normally settled on for the cost per person.

The approximate minimum wage rates in Algerian dinars (DA) per month are as follows (one dinar equals approximately $.25): unskilled workers, DA 1,000; semi-skilled workers, DA 1,000 to DA 1,100; skilled workers, DA 1,100 to DA 1,300; foremen and technicians, DA 1,600. These rates should only be used as general guides.

Employee's personal effects are not subject to import duties if a list of the effects is certified by an Algerian Embassy before the employee's arrival in Algeria.

Recent tightening of Algerian foreign exchange controls expressly prohibits expatriates working for a foreign firm on an Algerian contract from obtaining foreign currency allocations upon leaving Algeria. This new legislation presents additional difficulties for expatriate technicians and managers of foreign firms. Foreigners entering Algeria are required to declare all foreign exchange, including traveler's checks, in their possession; Algerian customs may require conversion as well as declaration of all convertible currency instruments by foreigners with resident visas. Only foreigners with temporary visas (valid up to 90-days) may take convertible currency out of Algeria up to the amount they declared upon entry. Businessmen are advised to carry credit cards which are immediately usable in neighboring countries, or set up alternate arrangements to insure that foreign currency will be available in their countries of destination after their stay in Algeria.

Local Agents, Representatives, and Corporations

The Algerian Government has recently put into force very stringent rules which prohibit the use of intermediaries of any kind. As a result, contracts signed with any state organization must be accompanied by an affidavit attesting to the fact that an intermediary was not used to gain the contract. The Algerian authorities insist that the affidavit be signed before a consular officer of the contracting party's Embassy in Algiers.

Wholly-owned foreign corporations are not allowed. There are some joint-ventures between American firms and Algerian companies in which the Algerian company has at least 51 percent of the ownership.

Taxation

Companies operating in Algeria are subject to taxes on profits, sales, property, salary payments, dividends and interest, and registration. The company must also pay a value-added tax on locally produced and imported goods at each stage of production or transformation and a service tax on all services (such as research, studies, transport) rendered.

In principle, all salary or wage earners in Algeria, whether of foreign or Algerian nationality, must pay Algerian income taxes, which have been substantially lowered in recent years. Algerian law stipulates a monthly withholding tax on income from Algerian sources for non-residents, and a tax on worldwide wages, income, and other emoluments for individuals who are resident in Algeria. Algerian income taxes on expatriate employees are almost never paid by the individuals themselves, but are either shouldered by the foreign contractor or reimbursed by the Algerian client. The contractor can get, and should insist on, a clause in the contract which specifies that Government-imposed taxes will be paid by the Algerian party to the contract.

Bahrain

In Bahrain, the Government participates in most of the major engineering and construction projects. The Ministry of Public Works, Power, and Water administers all of the Government's major projects with the exception of those undertaken by the Ministry of Housing. Both agencies follow similar and flexible criteria in negotiating and executing contracts. Theoretically, the practices of the Bahrain private sector follow those of the Government.

The Government of Bahrain tends to avoid turnkey projects. While a project consultant is often chosen to help propose suitable contractors, the Government is increasingly acting as its own consultant. For projects over 200,000 Bahraini dinars (approximately $526,000), a ministerial project committee will determine the short list and eventual contract winner. For large projects involving design and construction supervision, a consultant is chosen from five or six companies that are invited to bid on rather detailed terms of reference. The companies must be registered with the Director of Projects and Research of the Ministry of Public Works, Power, and Water.

Performance Requirements

Bid and performance bond requirements, licensing formalities, and visa requirements are not negotiable. Almost everything else can be negotiated. Bid bonds are required from all international contractors. They are flat fees rather than a percentage of the total bid because it is felt that the amount of the bid-bond deposits may be leaked and thereby provide competitors with information on each others' bid prices. The fees are stated in Bahraini dinars and vary from a nominal amount to approximately five percent of the bid.

Performance bonds are usually 10 percent of the total contract. Requirements do not vary with the experience of the firm in Bahrain nor do they change when the contractor is in a joint venture with a Bahraini company. Up to this point, the Government of Bahrain has required unconditional bank guarantees for performance bonds. It has indicated a willingness to consider accepting surety bonds, however, because of the importance of this arrangement to U.S. companies. It is also prepared to discuss the possibility of offsetting the performance bond total with imported machinery and equipment.

Force majeure is defined in the tender conditions and the language and definition closely follow the American Institute of Architects (AIA) standare requirements. There is room for negotiating the language of force majeure clauses, but it will not go far beyond the AIA guidelines. Strikes are prohibited in Bahrain, so work stoppages are not a problem. If they were to occur, the Government is likely to be reasonable in judging the effect on a contractor's progress. Delivery delays due to port congestion are considered force majeure conditions.

All contracts stipulate that Bahraini law should be used for the settlement of disputes. If a company insists, the Government will agree or recourse to the International Chamber of Commerce in Brussels. In the one major case of default on the part of an international construction firm, the Government of Bahrain took the firm to a local court to sue in default of contract. Preliminary inspection of the firm's books led to a rapid renegotiation of the contract, i.e., the Bahrainis eventually agreed with the firm's contentions.

All bids must be in English and the specifications in metric measurements.

Price

The Government of Bahrain greatly prefers fixed price bids. It does, however, sometimes agree to escalation clauses to cover inflationary increases in costs when those increases can be easily determined. For example, the Government distinguishes between capital- and labor-intensive projects. Generally speaking, it insists on a one-year, fixed price agreement on equipment and materials and expects the contractor to be in a position to order and import all or most of his requirements within the one year period. The Government is agreeable to a discussion of escalation clauses on labor.

At the present time, the Government will not accept cost-plus-fee contracts, though there are Bahraini technocrats working to institute the system. Provision is made in the contract for price escalation due to demurrage charges. The Government also plans in the future to make provision for declines in demurrage charges, the benefits of which now go to the contractor.

Equipment and Materials

It is possible to negotiate a waiver of customs duties on imported machinery, but the machinery must then be re-exported at the conclusion of the project. The original customs assessment must be paid if the machinery is sold on the local market. There are no bonded areas available to eliminate the delays in port and customs clearances.

Preference is given to bidders who will use local materials, goods, and equipment, when practical, and who will employ local subcontractors.

Labor

The Government of Bahrain favors projects and bidders that will employ local labor. Native Bahrainis, however, constitute only 27 percent of the local non-governmental work force. If Bahraini workers possessing required skills are unavailable, foreign workers may be hired. Contractors may be required to give the Ministry of Labor and Social Affairs 1 month's notice of all job openings prior to being allowed to fill these vacancies with expatriate employees. It is difficult to hire foreign labor locally.

Most of the foreign labor in Bahrain is from Pakistan, India, Korea, the Philippines, and Thailand. The contractor is responsible for the transportation of foreign workers to and from their country of origin, and for their accommodations in Bahrain.

There is a financial incentive to the contractor, in the form of the social insurance law, to avoid the importation of a large number of laborers piecemeal after a project has begun. Foreign manpower contracted as individuals is subject to the law's provisions whereas labor brought in as a group is not. The law applies to companies employing a large number of people in Bahrain and requires that employers pay 14 percent and employees 7 percent of each worker's monthly wage into national insurance funds.

Wages in Bahrain vary with the nationality of the worker. The average wage for a Bahraini worker is BD 217 ($572) per month, and for a non-Bahraini worker BD 152 ($400) per month.

Suppliers of machinery and equipment to the Government as well as foreign contractors undertaking Government project work are required, if needed, to provide on-site and other training. For each contract or project, details of the required training by foreign firms will be negotiated and spelled out in the contract agreement. Training abroad at the company's facilities also is subject to negotiation and agreement. Training equipment may be imported and re-exported on a duty-free basis.

Local Agents, Representatives, and Corporations

A Bahraini local agent is recommended, but not legally required, in all business transactions in Bahrain, except those related to national security. Government technocrats are attempting to limit the agent's role, but at the present time, he is both useful and necessary. Commissions and fees are subject to private negotiation and vary significantly with the agent and the project.

The Government encourages contractors to establish permanent representation in Bahrain, preferably in the form of a joint venture, once they have been awarded a contract. Consultants also find it useful to have a Bahraini partner.

Firms engaging in industrial activity in Bahrain must be 51 percent Bahraini owned. However, foreign firms wishing to use Bahrain as a base for non-Bahraini operations are exempted from this ownership requirement under the Offshore Companies Law of 1977. Firms taking advantage of this legislation are termed "exempted companies" by the Government. Companies registering with the Ministry of Commerce as "exempted" must post an insurance fund of not less than BD 5,000 ($13,044) if their capital is not in excess of BD 500,000 ($1,304,450). Firms with more capital are obliged to deposit 1 percent of their capital or BD 20,000 ($52,178), whichever is lower. An annual registration fee of BD 2,500 ($6,522) must be paid by all such companies, unless the firm offers shares for public subscription, in which case the annual fee is BD 10,000 ($26,089). Under the provisions of the law, offshore companies are able to operate regional assembly, maintenance, and warehousing centers in Bahrain, as well as using the free port area.

Taxation

There are no corporate or income taxes in Bahrain. There are some newly introduced "fees" for operation in the country and these may be included in the tender. The contract can contain clauses which allow for renegotiation if the Government introduces taxes during the life of the contract.

Egypt

State organizations play a major role in the Egyptian economy. Most large industrial firms, transport companies, and even some retail outlets, as well as most financial institutions and many foreign trade and wholesale firms, are in the public sector. Hence, the major projects are generally in the public sector. The Government usually requests separate contracts for the consulting, design and engineering, and construction phases of its projects. Foreign firms are invited to bid for consulting

International calls for tender may be issued through announcements in local newspapers and dissemination by Egyptian Embassies abroad. Sometimes, however, the call for tender is issued to a limited number of companies who have prequalified by making their capabilities known to the Egyptian organization undertaking the project. The bids are reviewed by a technical committee which usually chooses the two or three lowest price proposals meeting the specifications and begins negotiating with these firms. In the course of these bargaining procedures, the Egyptians may show the bids to the competing firms in an attempt to get better terms and prices. Even the firm submitting the lowest bid can expect demands for significant concessions before the contract is signed.

It is of primary importance that companies submit bids which respond accurately and fully to the specifications stated in the invitation to bid. The technical committees reviewing bids are usually quite proficient and can quickly dismiss those which display careless preparation or fail to adhere to the specifications.

Performance Requirements

The Egyptian Government normally requires foreign contractors to put up both bid and performance bonds. In some cases, the performance bond must be in the form of a bank guarantee. The amount of the bond varies between 1 and 5 percent of the contract price for bid bonds and between 5 and 10 percent for performance bonds.

Letters of guarantee from a non-Egyptian bank directly to the Egyptian client that do not involve a local bank are not normally acceptable. An American bank can issue the letter of guarantee to the client, but must ask an Egyptian bank to confirm the guarantee. This may be accomplished by adding a phrase directed at the local bank in the letter of guarantee, which states the following: "Under our full responsibility, please add your confirmation to this letter of guarantee # (insert number), dated (insert date), issued in favor of (name of party)".

The definition of force majeure and the mechanism for settling contract disputes are negotiable and are specified in the contract. Egyptian law regulates arbitration. The arbitration agreement must be in writing. There may be one or more arbitrators (an odd number is required) and the arbitrator's decision may be appealed to the courts. The Egyptian Government will accept international arbitration by the International Chamber of Commerce.

An advance payment is provided and is normally 10 percent of the total contract price. Graduated payments may be provided for in the contract. However, 10 percent of the total price for civil works contracts will be retained as a performance bond for one year after the construction is completed, in accordance with the Egyptian liability law for civil construction.

Articles 651-654 of the Egyptian Civil Code state that contractors and consultants are to be held strictly liable, jointly and severally, for any defects in the constructed project, regardless of fault, for a period of 10 years after project completion. Ongoing negotiations between the U.S. and Egyptian Governments have resulted in the exemption of the AID-financed Cairo sewer project from this requirement, and are attempting to limit a contractor's exposure for other AID-funded projects.

Law 106 of 1976 requires that insurance be procured to meet the decennial liability of the civil code. However, insurance protection is normally subject to an upper limit which, particularly in the case of large projects, may not be nearly sufficient to cover liability, for which there is no maximum limit. Firms undertaking project work in Egypt are strongly advised to consult legal counsel well-versed in the enforcement and ramifications of these laws.

There are no strict language requirements. English is preferred to all languages except Arabic. The Egyptians use the metric system of measurement but bids will not necessarily be rejected for the use of another system unless the tender asks for metric specifications.

Price

The government generally requires fixed price bids for contracts of 2 years duration or less. On long-term contracts, a fixed price is required only for the first year. The bid can include an escalation clause with a percentage increase specified for each year of the remaining term of the contract. The clause ordinarily is not permitted to apply to the cost of building supplies since the price of building materials is to some extent officially controlled. Not all projects, however, will have access to materials at the controlled price. Bidders may specify that their offer is contingent on the availability of those supplies at the particular established price.

Tender conditions which include the purchase of equipment normally require the bidder to provide a separate quotation on a 5-year supply of spare parts. The price must remain fixed for one year and can be increased for the remaining 4 years.

Equipment and Materials

It is possible to negotiate a waiver of customs duties on necessary imported machinery, equipment, and supplies if the Government places a high priority on the project. Used machinery and equipment can be re-exported. There is a market in Egypt for used construction equipment, but if the equipment is sold locally, customs duties must be paid on the value of the equipment at the time of entry. Machinery and equipment brought in duty free cannot be abandoned. Bonded areas are available. Companies using them must provide a $5,000 guarantee.

Labor

Egypt has a large and diversified labor force. Though high wages in some of its Arab neighbors have caused a shortage of skilled workers such as electricians, plumbers, and carpenters, there is an adequate supply of workers with other skills and plenty of unskilled and semiskilled labor.

Employees brought into Egypt can obtain an exemption from the payment on duties on their personal effects. They can repatriate a maximum of 50 percent of their salary to their home country. The contract usually stipulates that part of the salary of expatriate personnel must be paid in local currency.

The wages of senior mechanics, bricklayers, and carpenters are about 5 to 10 Egyptian pounds (£E) per working day ($7.15 to $14.30); unskilled laborers are usually paid £E 2 to £E 3 per day ($2.86 to $4.29). Contracts for projects which require complicated equipment generally provide for training of local personnel in the supplier's plant. Training equipment which is brought into Egypt can be imported and re-exported duty free.

Local Agents, Representatives, and Corporations

Though some exceptions are made, Egyptian law generally requires that a foreign firm doing business in Egypt have an Egyptian agent.

However, this requirement does not apply in the case of transactions or projects involving U.S. AID financing. Both private and public companies act as agents. However, the appropriate public sector firm may represent several companies with conflicting interests. In this case, a private firm may be more aggressive in looking after the U.S. company's interests.

Responses to Government and public sector tenders normally must be submitted through an Egyptian agent. Nevertheless, the presence of a representative from the home office, with a power of attorney to negotiate contract terms, is highly desirable, and sometimes required, when a firm is submitting a proposal on a large project.

A foreign firm may establish a branch office in Egypt. However, most foreign contractors and engineers prefer to form a joint venture with an Egyptian company to take advantage of the local firm's knowledge of the market and, in the case of the contractor, access to local labor and material supplies.

Taxation

Normally, agreements with foreign firms working on Egyptian Government or internationally-financed contracts provide for an income tax exemption for the firm and its employees. In the absence of some special provision of laws, firms working on private jobs would be subject to Egyptian taxes.

The wages and salaries of expatriate employees of ventures formed under Egypt's investment law are exempt from the general income tax but would normally be subject to an earnings tax. Companies formed under the investment law are exempt from the corporate profits tax for a period ranging from 5 to as much as 15 years, in the case of certain types of projects.

Projects in the free zones are exempt from normal Egyptian tax laws. With some exceptions, however, they are subject to an annual duty not to exceed one percent of the value of the goods entering or leaving the free zone on the account of the project. Projects not requiring the ingress or egress of goods are subject to an annual duty not to exceed 3 percent of the annual value added.

Egyptian tax laws are quite complex and a revision of the tax code is currently being considered by the Egyptian People's Assembly. A tax treaty between Egypt and the United States is also pending. Firms should therefore seek the advice of competent counsel on matters relating to taxation.

Iraq

American contractors wishing to do business in Iraq invariably find that they must deal directly with the Iraqi Government. The private sector accounts for less than 10 percent of total Iraqi imports, and is involved in few large infrastructure or industrial projects. This minimal role for the private sector offers little competition to foreign consultants and contactors, and provides few business opportunities.

Government agencies do not adhere to a universal contract format. Flexibility and willingness to negotiate on exceptions varies from agency to agency. The one universally non-negotiable condition is that the contract have a fixed price.

Most projects are contracted on a turnkey basis. While some projects continue to be awarded through international tender, the Government has moved increasingly toward invitational bidding. It is therefore important for contractors to register with the Ministry of Planning and appropriate client agencies to be eligible to receive invitations to bid as they come up. Requests for the "Form for Registration of Foreign Companies" should be addressed to:

Iraqi Interests Section
Indian Embassy
1801 P Street, N.W.
Washington, D.C. 20008

In both international and invitational tenders, the companies submitting the two or three most attractive bids are normally invited in for negotiations. Iraq has a good reputation for meeting its financial obligations, and expects the firms it deals with to meet their contractual obligations to the letter.

Performance Requirements

Almost all Iraqi Government tenders require bid and performance guarantees. These must be unconditional bank guarantees to the Rafidain Bank, Baghdad, through one of its correspondents. The Bank then issues a guarantee to the Government agency. Surety bonds are not acceptable. The guarantee is released immediately if the bid is not accepted and must be forfeited if the firm submits the winning bid but declines to accept the award.

Two weeks to one month after signing the contract, the contractor must convert his bid guarantee into a performance guarantee equivalent to between 2 and 7 percent of the value of the contract. The performance guarantee may be refunded in stages—agreed on in the contract—as the work on the project progresses. However, the final part is released only after a specified period following the completion of the project to ensure that it meets contractual stipulations. There is no reduction for joint ventures with a local partner. Requests to lower the amount required are seldom accepted and are viewed as an indication of lack of financial strength. The Government can draw on the guarantee on demand, and has frequently demanded renewal of the bank guarantee beyond its due date.

The Minister of Finance is authorized to advance foreign contractors up to 20 percent of the contract value after it is signed. The advance payment must be made against a confirmed bank guarantee. However, the contractor may subsequently decrease the value of the guarantee by offering imported machinery and equipment as collateral. The advance can be deducted on a regular monthly schedule or on a pro rata basis from the monthly progress payments.

The Iraqi Government has no standard force majeure clauses. Some agencies will accept clauses used by the International Chamber of Commerce if they are stipulated in the bid offer and subsequently written into the contract before it is signed. Labor disputes and delivery delays due to congestion in ports of origin or transit are not usually considered force majeure, though compensation has been made in some instances for extended delays in Iraqi ports.

All contract disputes must be resolved in Iraqi courts unless the contract states otherwise. The contract may contain a clause providing for arbitration of disputes by an independent body composed of members of the Iraqi client agency, the contracting company, and an international organization such as the International Chamber of Commerce.

Arabic is the official language of Iraq. Though commercial correspondence is still normally in English, legislation requires the increased use of Arabic. Iraq uses the metric system of measurement.

Price

The Government of Iraq insists on fixed price bids, expecting inflation and other risks to be calculated into the contractor's selling price. Cost-plus-fee contracts are unacceptable even for consultants.

Price escalation clauses may be used for cement, steel, timber, and wages paid to Iraqi labor. In fact, however, the clauses are of no practical benefit to international contractors. The escalation clause on cement applies only to Iraqi production, which is virtually never available to foreign contractors, since supply is not sufficient to meet demand. Escalation clauses also apply only to steel and timber purchased from the state-owned General Company for Trade in Steel and Timber (GECIST), and GECIST standard prices are normally far above world market prices, making it advisable to purchase supplies from other sources. Higher labor costs can be reimbursed if the minimum wage stipulated by the government is increased, but the prevailing wage rates are much higher than the minimum wage.

Many U.S. engineering and construction firms have been able to bid on large projects in Iraq by joint venturing with third-country companies. The Governments of third-country firms will sometimes provide insurance and other incentives which make it possible for the companies to accommodate the risks involved in submitting a fixed price and competitive bid.

Equipment and Materials

There is a shortage on all materials in Iraq, so the contractor seldom asked or expected to use local sources of supply. All imported machinery, equipment, and materials, including training equipment if any, are admitted on a temporary basis. Final payment on the contract may not be forthcoming until a "no objection" certificate from the customs authorities is furnished to the Iraqi client declaring that the goods have been re-exported or disposed of according to the regulations.

There is a market for used construction machinery and equipment and it may be sold locally, on completion of the project, if the contract includes a clause to this effect. The client normally reserves the option to purchase the equipment duty free. Other buyers must pay the customs duty. Passenger cars may be sold only to other foreign contractors working in Iraq or to an Iraqi Government agency.

Contracts normally guarantee a supply of spare parts for one to three years. Bonded areas can be arranged.

Labor

Iraqi regulations require that the ratio of expatriate staff and labor to local labor on a project be maintained at one to ten. The requirement can be waived, however, if the contractor can demonstrate that local labor is not available. The use of third-country workers, primarily from other Arab countries, India and Pakistan, has been increasing. To ease the labor shortage, the Government encourages citizens from other Arab countries to work in Iraq. Entry visas and work and residence permits are not required for Arab citizens. Obtaining entry documentation for non-Arabs has not been a problem, but the requirement imposes an additional workload which is not necessary when Arab workers are used.

To meet demands for technical expertise, the Government is insisting that the contractor employ the full number of non-Iraqi engineers and technicians stipulated in the contract. Furthermore, the foreign conractor cannot pay Iraqi personnel more than twice the amount they would receive in comparable jobs in the Iraqi Government agencies. These regulations have been enforced in an attempt to prevent the drain of scarce, highly trained personnel from the public sector.

Due to the shortage of trained personnel, the Government places heavy emphasis on the training component of contracts. One company attributes its success in obtaining a huge contract in Iraq to its reputation for training local workers in other parts of the world to operate sophisticated plant and equipment. Contracts usually include training in the supplier's plant, if appropriate.

Due to the acute housing shortage in Iraq, contractors must provide prefabricated housing for their expatriate employees if the project employs more than 15 expatriates and work at any one site is valued at more than ID5 million ($17 million). For most major projects, particularly those located away from a large city, the contractor usually must provide on-site medical, food, and recreational facilities for expatriate staff. At construction sites near towns, the contractor is expected to arrange transportation to and from work for the local laborers, and to build canteen facilities where a catering contractor, paid by the workers, can serve food. Routine ailments can be treated by several good doctors and dentists in Baghdad.

Personal effects are not subject to import duties, but they must have been consumed or be re-exported when leaving the country. Expatriates are paid by the contractor and they may repatriate up to 50 percent of their gross cash income paid in Iraq.

Local Agents, Representatives, and Corporations

Though the use of agents in Iraq is not prohibited ,the Government has advised its purchasing organizations to deal directly with foreign companies wherever possible and has imposed strict controls on the activities of commission agents. An agent must be registered and licensed. The terms of all agency agreements, including the commission and other remuneration, must be registered within 7 days after the agreement has been authenticated, and the party on whose behalf the agent acts must accept responsibility for any failure of the agent to fulfill his obligations under the contract.

Given the severity and complexity of the regulations governing agents, firms contemplating an agency agreement should consult an Iraqi attorney. A list of attorneys specializing in commercial law can be obtained from the U.S. Interest Section, Embassy of Belgium, MASBAH 52/5/35, P.O. Box 2447, Alwiyah, Baghdad, Iraq.

Consultants and consulting engineers are legally required to form a partnership with an Iraqi consultant as a precondition to obtaining contracts. In practice, however, this requirement is waived with increasing frequency. Foreign construction firms are not officially encouraged, nor is it particularly helpful, to form joint ventures with private Iraqi firms. However, the Government-owned State Contracting and Construction Company has recently formed joint ventures with several foreign companies that provide specialized construction techniques.

Firms wishing to establish a branch office in Iraq should register with the Register of Commerce at the Directorate General of Registration and Control of Companies in Baghdad. An application for registration is likely to be denied unless the firm has actually been awarded a contract or been invited by a Government ministry to establish a presence in Iraq. Branch office activities are likely to be restricted to the fulfillment of contract terms, thereby precluding the use of the office for sales and marketing purposes.

Taxation

Iraq's tax laws require that foreign individuals and companies in Iraq be taxed on the income and remuneration received from their business in Iraq. However, most foreign contractors incorporate in their contracts provisions exempting them and their employees from corporate and individual income taxes.

Jordan

Business in Jordan tends to be conducted in a straight-forward manner that is more familiar to U.S. businessmen than the business methods in some of the other countries of the Near East and North Africa. Jordan essentially has a free enterprise system and a relatively efficient bureaucracy. Most economic activity is carried out in the private sector although the Government is a shareholder in 29 large industrial companies. The Government's general policy is to finance such companies when private capital is insufficient, and gradually to sell the Government's interest to private investors once the companies are firmly established. Projects undertaken solely by the Government are limited to infrastructure and social welfare facilities.

The Jordanians do not request consortium-type bids. Contracts for the design and engineering, construction, and material and equipment supply are awarded separately. Bids are requested either through international tender or by inviting firms to negotiate a contract. Very often a request for prequalification is announced and those successfully responding are asked to submit a propsal.

Contract conditions vary according to whether the project is being undertaken by the government or the private sector and according to the source of financing. Some of the conditions are not negotiable, including delivery periods, payment terms, guarantees, and document certifiication. However, most requirements can be negotiated within certain limits.

Performance Requirements

The Government of Jordan and the private sector require bid and performance guarantees from all potential contractors, including both local and foreign firms and joint-ventures. A guarantee of 5 to 10 percent of the contract price (the amount is determined by the Jordanian client) must be made when the bid is submitted; it is refunded to the unsuccessful bidders. A 10 percent performance guarantee is required of the successful contractor at the time the award is made. The guarantees cannot be waived nor can the amount be reduced. They must be in the form of unconditional bank guarantees. These guarantees for non-Jordanian contractors should be issued by local Jordanian banks and bonding companies and backed by counter-guarantees procured from sources located outside Jordan.

The conditions which constitute a force majeure can be written into the contract and are negotiable. They are not normally defined in the tender documents.

All contract disputes known to U.S. Government agencies in Jordan have been handled locally. Contracts may be written to include a provision defining procedures for settling disputes. If a dispute occurs and the applicable contract does not contain a provision for settling it, the parties to the dispute usually choose one or two arbitrators to examine the problem. The decision of the arbitrators can be appealed, but is usually upheld by the Jordanian courts.

Advance payments will be made against a bank guarantee. The amount is negotiable, and in most cases ranges between 10 and 20 percent. Regular monthly payments can also be arranged and will be paid on presentation of appropriate documentation certifying progress on the project.

Jordanian Temporary Law 43, known as the Decennial Liability Law, imposes strict liability on engineers and/or contractors under certain circumstances for 10 years. The ten-year liability period begins once the finished project is handed over to the Jordanian client. The engineer designing the project and the contractor carrying out the construction may be held jointly liable for the partial or total collapse of the structure, or any defect threatening its safety or strength, if the contractor executed the project under the supervision of the engineer. An engineer who worked on the design phases of a project without supervising its construction is liable only for design defects; similarly, a contractor who worked under the supervision of the client or an engineer not responsible for project design is liable only for flaws in the execution of the project. While Article 790 of the law states that a contractor or engineer may not be exempted from this liability, it is advisable to explore the full ramifications of the laws, as well as possible exceptions and other conditions, with the Jordanian client before signing the contract.

Arabic is the official language of Jordan, but English is widely used as a commercial language. Both languages are acceptable for commercial documentation. The metric system of measurement is used.

Price

Both the public and private sectors normally insist on fixed price bids. Cost-plus-fee contracts for services are rare but have been negotiated. Escalation clauses may be included for specific contingencies, such as an increase in the price of cement which is set by the Government. The Government will not guarantee the price of any commodity.

At the beginning of 1978, the Government began quoting all its contracts in Jordanian dinars (JD). Despite the recent liberalization of currency control laws, foreign firms undertaking work in Jordan may wish to protect themselves against losses due to exchange rate fluctuations by purchasing foreign exchange in the recently-established forward exchange market. The foreign firm which wins a contract priced in dinars buys dollars or other foreign currencies at a fixed rate from a local bank; this foreign exchange is deliverable on the date the contract expires.

Equipment and Materials

Duty-free entry may be negotiated for both new and used machinery and equipment. Import duties are levied on spare parts and supplies; rates range from 4 to 23 percent. Used machinery can be re-exported when the project is completed; however, there is a demand for used machinery in Jordan. If machinery which entered Jordan duty free is sold locally, the import duties must be paid at the time of sale.

When the contract includes the supply of machinery and equipment, the value of the spare parts provided should be a minimum of 15 percent of the total value of the equipment. The Jordanians consider it essential to have an adequate supply of spare parts to prevent a shutdown in operations.

The only construction materials available in Jordan are cement and reinforcing bars. Therefore, contractors are not required to use local materials on their projects. However, cement may only be imported through the Jordan Cement Company unless the Government authorizes otherwise.

Bonded areas can be arranged.

Labor

Jordan has a highly regarded labor force which is employed to a large extent outside of Jordan. Many of the technical and clerical personnel and semi-skilled laborers are in the oil-producing states of the Arabian Peninsula, and there are even occasional shortages in Jordan of unskilled labor. Consequently, expatriate labor can be imported, where it has been established that local labor is not available. Egyptians, Koreans, and Pakistanis comprise the bulk of the foreign labor force. At least 50 percent of the professional employees on a project must be Jordanian. Work and residence permits are not difficult to obtain. Jordan's labor laws apply equally to Jordanian and expatriate employees.

Present wages in Jordan for mechanics, carpenters, and other skilled workers range from $20 to $30 per day and are being bid up constantly by the attractive salaries offered in neighboring countries as well as in Jordan. Workers are normally paid weekly.

Adequate housing, food, clothing, and medical and dental care are available. Expatriates' household effects are normally subject to import duties. However, exemptions may be negotiated on Government contracts.

It is to the bidder's advantage to offer training of Jordanian personnel and indicate its cost as a separate item in the bid. Contractors are usually requested to provide training. The location, i.e., on the site or in the supplier's facility, and the sharing of costs are subject to negotiation.

Local Agents, Representatives, and Corporations

If a foreign firm operating in Jordan does not establish an office or branch, it is required by law to have an agent, except in some cases when it is doing business directly with the Government. The agency agreement must be written and submitted to the Registrar of Companies. Commissions vary according to project size, but general practice entitles local agents on Government tenders to 3 to 5 percent for small projects (JD 25,000 to JD 50,000), 1 to 2.5 percent on large projects (JD 50,000 to JD 500,000), and 0.5 to 1 percent on the largest projects (over JD 500,000).

All engineers practicing in Jordan must be accepted as a member of the Jordan Engineering Association. Foreign engineers must also have a local representative who is in the same field of engineering and is a legal resident of Jordan. The representation agreement must be submitted to the Registrar of Companies. In some instances, U.S. firms have established a partnership with a Jordanian company. These arrangements have worked well.

Taxation

Both local and foreign employees and companies are subject to Jordanian taxes on income and profits earned in Jordan. The personal income tax increases progressively from 4 percent on the lowest bracket to 40 percent on the highest. The corporate tax on company profits in the most recent tax year was a flat 45 percent. However, the personal and corporate taxes can be negotiated on Government contracts and under certain other circumstances. They can be eliminated entirely in some cases.

Kuwait

According to officials of U.S. companies operating in Kuwait, the Kuwaitis tend to be more flexible in administering contracts though the Kuwait Government's contracting regulations are both more detailed and more inflexible than those of neighboring countries. This is a reflection of the relative sophistication of the Government in handling huge sums of money and of a large and experienced merchant class, which includes engineers and contractors. Recently, the country's construction boom has outstripped the capacity of local firms to cope with the tremendous needs for technical expertise or construction management skills as well as with the sheer size of some projects. The Government therefore has begun to modify some of its procedures to encourage more foreign and local firms to bid on contracts and increase the competition.

The Kuwaitis do not request bids from consortia nor do they ask for turnkey bids. Consultants and engineers on Government and public sector projects are chosen by a Consulting Firms Selection Committee, which is under the aegis of the Kuwait Ministry of Planning. The Committee invites offers from firms which have been prequalified by the Registrar of Consultants. Contracts may be negotiated or concluded by price bidding among five or six firms.

The basic piece of legislation covering contracting procedures in Kuwait is the Public Tenders Ordinance (PTO), Law No. 37/1964, amended by Law No. 18/1970 and Law No. 81/1977. It established a Central Tenders Committee (CTC) which consists of representatives of the Ministry of Finance, the Ministry of Commerce and Industry, the Ministry of Public Works (MPW), the client ministry for which the project is being built, and six representatives appointed by the Council of Ministers.

Invitations to tender usually are issued by the CTC and published in Kuwait's Official Gazette, *Kuwait Al Youm*. However, the law permits the client government agency to restrict the invitation to tender to companies that are listed with it.

In order to be eligible to receive tender documents, a contractor must be registered with the Kuwait Commercial Registry in the Ministry of Commerce and Industry, as well as with the Kuwait Chamber of Commerce and Industry. These registrations must be filed with the CTC. Tenderers must be Kuwaiti citizens or companies, or foreign firms represented by a Kuwaiti agent or joint-venture partner. Contractors for public works projects must be prequalified by the CTC to undertake a project of the kind being tendered. Kuwaiti firms are capable of undertaking many of the projects, so foreign firms are not asked to bid unless the project involves large management or technical problems or the Government wants it completed quickly. The award of the contract must be made to the bidder with the lowest price unless his bid is determined to be unreasonable or the Council of Ministers decides to make the award to a higher bidder at the request of the CTC.

The PTO and subsequent implementing regulations and procedures apply to projects undertaken by the MPW (responsible for the construction of roads, ports, and all public buildings), the Ministry of Electricity and Water, and the Ministry of Communications. The following clients are not bound by the PTO, though in practice they adhere to it fairly closely: the Shuaiba Area Authority, which controls the Shuaiba Industrial Area where most of Kuwait's petroleum and petrochemical industries are located; the National Housing Authority, responsible for the Government's $1 billion a year lower- and middle-income housing program; the Ministry of Defense; the oil sector which is under the supervision of the Ministry of Oil; and the private sector, including the National Real Estate Company and the Kuwait International Investment Company.

Performance Requirements

Regulations for bid and performance guarantees apply by law only to the civilian ministries. However, they also are widely used by the Ministry of Defense and the National Housing Authority. Kuwaiti practice normally calls for a bid bond ranging from 2 to 5 percent, depending on the government ministry, and for a 10 percent performance bond. Bonds are in the form of bank guarantees issued by a local bank and must usually be backed by a letter of credit from a correspondent bank in the contractor's country.

In general, Kuwait's performance guarantee requirements have been less onerous than those applied elsewhere in the region for a number of reasons. In at least one very large project, the contract was split into three parts—foreign services, local services including labor, and capital equipment—and the guarantee was required only on the foreign services which were 10 percent of the several hundred million dollar project. Kuwaiti banks have also issued guarantees to well-known companies without any counter guarantee or with the acceptance of the guarantee by the contractor's parent firm. Also, foreign contractors in joint-ventures with Kuwaiti firms are only liable for a portion of the guarantee determined by their share in the partnership.

The Major Projects Department at the Ministry of Public Works has been known to require foreign contractors to subcontract about 30 percent of the value of the project to local firms in contracts valued at over KD 1 million ($3.6 million). It is doubtful that this clause can be negotiated out of the contract if it is specified in the tender documents. However, the requirement has not been burdensome, particularly for firms that joint venture with Kuwaiti companies to bid on tenders; all foreign contractors working on large projects in Kuwait use local contractors for some portion of the project.

Force majeure clauses in contracts in Kuwait only spell out conditions such as war, civil disturbances, and similar unforeseen circumstances. However, the Government accepts arguments which include other force majeure in settling contract disputes.

Contracts can contain provisions for international arbitration in accordance with the procedures of the International Arbitration Board. In all known cases, Kuwaiti procedures have been used and they call for the appointment of three arbitrators: one chosen by the client, one chosen by the contractor, and one who is mutually acceptable to both parties. If agreement cannot be reached, the arbitrators refer the dispute to the courts. Court processes are slow, however, and most contractors and their Kuwaiti clients have preferred to settle out of court.

Kuwait practice with regard to advance payments varies widely. Some contracts allow an advance payment for mobilization, plus an advance for the purchase of necessary equipment up to 10 percent of its value. The advance can be deducted from subsequent payments to the contractor, or may be in the form of a loan which the contractor repays separately.

The metric system of measurement is always specified. Arabic is the dominant language, but English is the second language and is generally acceptable in commercial and government circles. Most contracts are prepared in both Arabic and English; the Arabic version is used for all legal interpretations.

Price

Some government agencies have begun to move away from the practice of requiring fixed price bids. Contractors have traditionally been required to bid on a per-unit basis. Their bids are compared with estimates of the quantities of material required for the project and of the cost per unit provided by MPW engineers. In the course of the project, increases in the price of the contract have been allowed only when it could be shown that additional materials were necessary.

Recently, however, the MPW and the Shuaiba Area Authority have allowed price escalation both on labor and on materials such as cement, reinforcing bars, and asphalt. For MPW contracts, the Ministry of Planning supplies base price information on wage rates and the cost of materials. The contractor is entitled to additional payment for escalation in costs above the base rate and must rebate any payments made at the base price if actual costs are lower. The amount of the price escalation is determined by the Ministry of Planning. Other Kuwait Government agencies and the private sector continue to require fixed price bids because they lack access to adequate cost indices.

Equipment and Materials

There is a 4 percent ad valorem tax on all goods imported into Kuwait, including machinery, equipment, and construction materials. Machinery and equipment does not have to be re-exported at the conclusion of the project; it can be sold in the local market.

In the past, the Government has required contractors to purchase certain building materials from local companies such as the Kuwait Cement Company. However, material requirements have outpaced the capacity of local firms to meet the demand. In most recent contracts, therefore, local suppliers only have to be used to the degree possible, and in at least one instance there was no local supply requirement at all. Provisions for the supply of materials and equipment are usually included with the bid.

There are no bonded areas which would allow special customs treatment for the goods imported for a project. Materials and equipment for high priority Government projects can be landed at the Ahmadi South Pier; this bypasses congested port areas but not customs clearances. Also, materials for petrochemical and petroleum related construction projects can be brought in on site or through KOC facilities at Shuaiba or Ahmadi Ports. High KOC charges and a shortage of trucking capacity limits the expediency of landing at the two ports to goods to be used on projects in the immediate vicinity.

Labor

The Government of Kuwait prefers that contractors hire the largest possible number of Kuwaitis or other Arabs. However, the manpower shortage in Kuwait generally necessitates importing construction labor for new projects. The National Housing Authority usually specifies that only 20 percent of the labor needed for a project can be obtained on the local market, but administrative difficulties have limited the enforcement of this requirement.

Iran, Iraq, India, and Pakistan are traditional sources of labor. More recently workers have been imported from Turkey, Thailand, the Philippines, and South Korea. Egyptians, Palestinians, and Indians are used in many mid-level engineering positions.

Most foreign contractors have built camps for their workers, with housing, a cafeteria, and recreational facilities near the project. This is not required by the Government but by the situation in Kuwait, where housing is at a premium and recreational facilities are scarce. Permits may be obtained to import household goods and personal effects duty-free. Work and residence permits are required but are not difficult to obtain.

Skilled workers, such as plumbers and electricians, are generally paid between $45 and $55 per day. Unskilled laborers are normally paid $20 to $25 per day. Contract laborers earn between $4,000 and $5,000 yearly.

A recently passed social security law, which covers only Kuwaiti citizens, requires employees to contribute 5 percent of their salary and the employer to contribute 10 percent. The law provides benefits for old age, disability, disease, death, and retirement. The impact of this legislation on foreign contractors is minimal, however, since few Kuwaiti workers are used by foreign firms in construction and engineering projects.

Kuwait's labor laws allows the formation of unions and regulate age limits, hours and conditions of work, overtime, compensation for injury, and termination benefits for private sector employees, except domestic servants and workers in establishments with less than five employees. There is also legislation covering the payment of Government workers. The two laws have the effect of maintaining fairly high pay scales in Kuwait. While Kuwait allows trade unions, only employees in Government and in the petroleum and banking sectors are organized. Non-Kuwaitis may only join unions after completion of 5 years residence in Kuwait, and are not permitted to hold union office.

Training of workers at the supplier's plant is usually included in Government contracts. The Government pays all costs.

Local Agents, Representatives, and Corporations

Kuwait's commercial laws require the use of a Kuwaiti agent for all commercial transactions undertaken by foreign firms in Kuwait. As noted above, construction firms must also be represented by a Kuwaiti agent or joint-venture partner in order to bid on tenders. Foreign consultants and engineers are not allowed to have a local agent when performing consultancy services. If their services extend to project management, they must obtain a local agent, but the Government has generally been reluctant to deal with consultants who also bid to provide management services.

A well-chosen agent or joint-venture partner can be helpful in fulfilling registration requirements and is a good source of information on upcoming projects. In addition, local construction firms can offer their own experience in Kuwait and other Gulf States and may be instrumental in securing labor and materials. Agents' fees vary from flat rates to a percentage of the value of the contract. Five percent is typical. All forms of business organization in Kuwait require at least 51 percent Kuwaiti ownership. Most U.S. companies have formed partnerships or joint-ventures.

A joint-stock company or corporation can only have non-Kuwaiti ownership if foreign capital or technical expertise is needed.

Taxation

Kuwait has no personal income tax. Corporate bodies are required
to pay a tax on income earned in Kuwait. The tax is progressive, ranging from 5 to 50 percent. In practice, only foreign companies (and the
foreign share of local firms) established under the commercial laws have
been required to pay the tax. For more detailed information on Kuwait's
tax rates and the definition of corporate bodies see: "Marketing in Kuwait," *Overseas Business Report,* OBR 79-18 U.S. Department of Commerce, Washington, D.C., 1979.

Libya

It takes considerable initiative and perseverance to negotiate and implement a contract in Libya.* The Libyan Government is most often the client and undertakes the major infrastructure and industrial projects. The government attempts to impose contract terms that are heavily weighted in its favor but will modify many of them with persistent negotiations. It is to the contractor's advantage to insist that the contract language be as unambiguous as possible to avoid disputes. The contractor should also insert protective clauses when the Government stipulates, as it often does, that the contract is subject to new laws which come into force during the life of the contract as well as to those in force at the time the contract is signed. The regulations discussed below are those of the Government; the small private sector is more flexible and negotia tions with private firms are easier.

Foreign engineering and consulting firms are allowed to work only on projects listed in the Libyan Development Plan, and only when their expertise is not available from local companies. Each Government agency maintains a register of companies from which a committee of the Council of Ministers picks firms to negotiate or bid for contracts. The contract may be for preliminary studies, preparation of the tender documents, or supervision of project implementation. The contract for actual implementation is usually turnkey and let by international tender. All contractors bidding on public works projects must be registered with the Ministry of Housing.

Performance Requirements

The Libyan Government requires both bid and performance bonds. Bids must be accompanied by a bid bond or provisional guarantee of between 1 and 5 percent of the value of the bid. For U.S. firms, the bond is usually in the form of a certified check backed by a standby letter of credit. The bond is returned to the unsuccessful bidders within 30 to 60 days after the bid opening.

The performance bond ranges from 10 percent on small projects to 20 percent on large ones. It must be an unconditional bank guarantee issued by the contractor's bank to the Libyan bank which issues a counter-

* The official name of the country is now The Socialist People's Libyan Arab Jamahiriyah.

guarantee for the amount in dinars to the Libyan organization responsible for the project. The guarantees must be payable on demand to the Libyan client. It must normally be valid for one year after the project is completed. The contract can and should stipulate the time period for maintaining the performance guarantee and the conditions under which claims can be made against it.

The force majeure clause usually follows the guidelines of the International Chamber of Commerce. It can be negotiated to some extent. Labor disputes and port congestion have been included in contracts as force majeure.

The Libyan Government prefers to have disputes settled in Libyan courts, though contracts can contain provisions for arbitrating disputes by international arbitration, usually by the International Chamber of Commerce in Paris. Some contracts provide only for arbitration by a judge or board mutually agreed upon by the arbitrating parties.

Advance payments are usually made only against a letter of guarantee for the same amount, which must be valid until the delivery or work conditions of the contract are fulfilled. The amount of the advance payment varies from 10 to 20 percent for supply contracts and is generally 10 percent for service contracts. Monthly payments are made against vouchers submitted by the contractor. Ten percent of each monthly payment is withheld until the completed project is accepted.

Though it is not difficult to find business and Government officials in Libya who speak and understand English, the Government has imposed a total ban on the use of any language but Arabic in public display signs in Libya. English may be allowed in the initial correspondence and the technical aspects of the contract, but the official contract will be in Arabic and the bid is usually required in Arabic. The Libyans use the metric system of weights and measures.

Price

The Libyan Government almost always insists on fixed price bids quoted c.i.f. in Libyan dinars. Bids should contain a clause which states that the prices are subject to escalation at the time the contract is signed or that they are good only for a specified period of time. The contract should also specify the time for which the prices are valid and the dollar/dinar exchange rate to be used. Parts supply contracts do not have to be fixed price; they can stipulate that the price will be based on the current list price at the time the goods are shipped. Additional charges cannot be made for the cost of demurrage; the contractor is advised to quote c.&f. or c.i.f. anchorage in the Libyan port. The Government, on occasion, has fixed the price it will pay for commodities purchased from local manufacturers in order to encourage production, but is not known to have guaranteed the cost to the contractor.

Equipment and Materials

It is possible to obtain a waiver of customs duties on some materials and equipment. The contract should specify which goods are subject to customs duties and which are to be re-exported. Machinery and equipment does not have to be re-exported when the project is completed. The law requires penalties for abandoning machinery, but it is not always enforced. Bonded areas can be arranged but it is rarely done and is not advisable since storage space is limited.

Locally produced building materials are in short supply.

Labor

The law requires that a certain percentage of the employees on the project be Libyan nationals. However, there are severe shortages of all categories of labor and, in practice, contractors are only expected to hire as many Libyans as possible. Egypt, Tunisia, Turkey, and the East European countries are the major sources of labor. Foreign technicians may be hired if a qualified Libyan cannot be found. Contractors have found Libyan employees reluctant to learn clerical or administrative jobs.

The contractor is required to make all the arrangements for bringing expatriate workers into Libya, including obtaining work permits and the visas for entry, residence, and exit. The contract should make clear the terms of employment of Libyans and expatriates. Housing is scarce in the cities, but there is adequate food and medical care available. Where construction camps are necessary, the contractor is expected to supply all of the needs of the camp's personnel. In addition to food and accommodations, mechanics receive about 150 Libyan dinars (LD) per month (approximately US$500) and bricklayers about LD95 (US$320) per month. month.

The contractor is expected to train Libyans. Training is always provided for in the contract and is considered part of the cost of the contract to the buyer. Training equipment can be imported on a temporary basis and re-exported if it has the proper documentation.

Local Agents, Representatives, and Corporations

All agents must be Libyan nationals or a Libyan-controlled company. Private agents and representatives are very necessary to advise on business practices, arrange meetings, and assist in the administration of the contract. However, their legal status is not clear because the laws defining their role have not been fully implemented. A foreign firm can choose whether or not to use an agent in dealing with the private sector, but must often work with the Government and other public agencies only through a public sector company. See "Marketing in the Libyan Arab Republic," *Overseas Business Report,* OBR 76-45, U.S. Department of Commerce, Washington, D.C., 1976, for a description of the laws applying to agents. Commissions are usually 5 to 10 percent of the price of the contract.

Only consulting engineers and firms providing technical services to the petroleum industry can operate wholly foreign-owned branches in Libya. All other companies must have at least 51 percent Libyan ownership and the foreign firm must be able to offer technical or marketing expertise not otherwise available in Libya. Some types of businesses are the exclusive preserve of Libyans. Tax and other liabilities make it inadvisable to operate in Libya as a wholly foreign-owned company.

Taxation

The foreign firm and all its employees are subject to Libya's individual income and corporate profits taxes. The tax rates are progressive, ranging from 15 to 90 percent on income and from 20 to 60 percent on profits. See "Marketing in the Libyan Arab Republic" (cited above) for more detail on Libya's complex tax structure.

Oman

Though the complete informality which traditionally has characterized business transactions in Oman is falling prey to increasing regulation, Omanis attach a high degree of importance to personal relationships. Business, therefore, is conducted almost entirely with companies which have a local presence; and frequent visits by the foreign firm's home representatives are virtually a prerequisite for market penetration even after local representation is established. Furthermore, opportunities for consultants, architects, engineers, or contractors are not always published; information on upcoming projects can best be obtained by a competent local representative.

The Oman Government undertakes all the major infrastructure projects and is a joint-venture partner in the large industrial projects. Oman's active private sector is composed primarily of traders or merchants who spend much of their time representing foreign companies seeking Government contracts.

The Ministry of Communications with its project consultants, has the primary responsibility for the evaluation of bids and selection of contractors for civil construction, highways, electric power, and desalting projects. The Ministry of Petroleum and Minerals has a similar role in contracts for natural gas and oil pipelines, refineries, mining activities, and other projects related to natural resources. The Ministry of Commerce and Industry is primarily involved in non-petroleum-related industrial projects, while agricultural and fisheries projects are the responsibility of the Ministry of Agriculture and Fisheries.

The Government does not generally award turnkey contracts. The design/engineering and construction contracts are awarded separately. Contracts for the design/engineering phase of small projects are awarded on a negotiated basis to Oman-based firms. On the large projects, the executing or client agency generally will invite a few firms to submit proposals. Normally, other firms who become aware of the project may submit prequalification information and ask to be included on the list of those presenting proposals.

The Oman Government has established a Tender Board, composed of officials from various Government agencies, to make information on projects available to foreign contractors. In order to actually bid, contractors must have obtained a local sponsor or Omani partner and be registered with both the Tender Board and the Ministry of Commerce and Industry. Bids are evaluated by the project consultant and reviewed by the Tender Board. The contract will not necessarily be awarded to the lowest bidder. A period of negotiation often follows the award of the contract before it is signed.

Performance Requirements

The Oman Government requires both a bid bond and performance bond, in the form of bank guarantees, of 5 percent and 10 percent, respectively, of the value of the bid. The bid bond is submitted with the bid and the performance bond must be submitted within 15 days after the company is notified of the award of the contract.

Force majeure clauses are defined in the tender conditions and include unforeseen circumstances such as wars and natural disasters. Labor disputes and delays due to port congestion are not considered force majeure, but they do not occur in Oman.

Omani law requires that private business controversies be submitted to the Committee for the Settlement of Commercial Disputes. The Committee is composed of the Chairman of the Chamber of Commerce, three officials in the Ministry of Commerce, and five local merchants. It seeks a settlement which is mutually agreeable to the parties concerned. Its decisions are binding and cannot be appealed. Most controversies between the Government and foreign firms are handled by direct negotiation. Provisions for international arbitration, usually under the auspices of the International Chamber of Commerce, are routinely written into most contracts. However, few, if any, disputes have to be referred to international arbitration.

Advance payments of 10 to 20 percent of the value of the contract can be obtained. However, the Omanis prefer contractors who can finance the project themselves or can line up commercial bank financing.

Arabic is the official language in Oman, but English is used in Government and commercial circles and is generally acceptable for bids and contracts. The metric system of weights and measures is used.

Price

There are no Government regulations for pricing contracts. Contracts with a negotiated fixed price, contracts with escalation clauses, and cost-plus-fee contracts are used. For most large projects, prices are fixed during the negotiations after the contract has been awarded and before it is signed.

The Government does not guarantee the prices of commodities. Generally, there are no provisions made for escalation of the contract price for demurrage charges nor for escalation in the price of parts.

Equipment and Materials

A customs duty of 2 percent of the c.i.f. value of the goods is applied to most imports. However, a waiver may be negotiated for machinery, equipment, and materials for Government projects. Used machinery and equipment need not be re-exported. There are no bonded areas.

Oman does not produce the commodities needed for construction projects, so there are no requirements to use local supplies. However, contracts often stipulate that goods be purchased through local importers rather than directly from the overseas manufacturer.

Labor

Contractors are expected to hire Omanis whenever possible, particularly for administrative and middle management positions. However, there is a shortage of Omani labor, both skilled and unskilled, which becomes acute during the harvest and holidays when many workers return to their homes. Contractors, therefore, must import most of their workers. Europeans (primarily British) are employed as managers in many private establishments and in the Government, and Indians and Pakistanis fill lower administrative staff positions and are employed as laborers. The expatriate work force is concentrated in the construction, petroleum, and transportation industries, and in banking.

The Department of Labor, in the Ministry of Labor and Social Welfare, and the Immigration Department of the Royal Oman Police control the importation of foreign workers. The Immigration Department has initiated increasingly tough controls on labor from the Indian subcontinent. Work permits are required and are difficult to obtain for unskilled workers.

Contractors are required to bear responsibility for the well-being and discipline of their employees and are expected to pay for medical services, transportation, and accommodations. Food for expatriates also is provided by the contractor. No customs duties are assessed on imported personal effects.

Expatriates are paid in Omani currency, which is freely convertible. Mechanics, carpenters, bricklayers, and other skilled laborers receive around $310 per month and unskilled workers receive $10 to $15 per day. The salaries of clerical employees generally start at about $360 per month. Firms are usually generous in paying fringe benefits to local employees, and the housing and utilities allowance can be as much as 50 percent of the basic salary.

Oman does not have an organized labor movement, and strikes are forbidden. The Department of Labor adjudicates disputes between all employees and their employers, but its main concern is assisting Omani workers.

Firms with 50 or more employees are required to pay a 5 percent payroll tax, which is used to finance vocational training. This tax is waived if a company has its own training program for its Omani workers.

Local Agents, Representatives, and Corporations

Foreign firms, with the exception of engineers and consultants working solely for the Oman Government and branches of international banks, are required to have an Omani agent in order to do business in Oman. The agent must be a citizen of Oman and registered with the Ministry of Commerce and Industry. Agents are also helpful in identifying opportunities, smoothing administrative problems, arranging local financing, and achieving influence for the foreign firm in the appropriate Government circles. Normal commissions are about 3 to 5 percent on contracts for projects but can run up to 20 percent on imports.

Only international banks and consulting and accounting firms can establish a wholly-owned subsidiary in Oman. Other foreign firms must joint-venture with an Omani company which must have a minimum of 35 percent of the equity. Again, Omani joint-venture partners are crucial to developing fruitful relationships with the Government.

Taxation

There are no personal income taxes in Oman. Firms incorporated in the country are required to pay taxes on income over 20,000 rials ($69,000). For foreign firms with less than 35 percent Omani ownership, the rates are progressive, beginning at 5 percent of net income over about $15,000 and going up to 50 percent of net income over approximately $1.5 million. Firms with 51 percent or more Omani ownership pay only 15 percent income tax, while firms with 35 to 50 percent Omani ownership pay 20 percent tax. The Oman Government allows a tax holiday of up to 5 years for income earned on investment in priority sectors of the economy. Also, though wholly foreign-owned banks, accounting, and consulting firms working in the private sector are subject to the local tax, consulting and accounting firms working directly for the Government are exempt.

Qatar

The Government of Qatar is by far the largest purchaser of goods and services in the country. It is responsible for all of the country's infrastructure and social welfare facilities and is a joint-venture partner in all of the major industrial projects, including the exploitation and processing of oil and gas resources, steel-making, and production of cement, fertilizers, and petrochemicals. Though there is an increasing tendency for private Qatari firms to take part in joint ventures with foreign firms to execute a project, particularly in the construction phase, most local companies are engaged in pursuing Government contracts for the foreign companies they represent.

All foreign firms operating in Qatar are required by law to have a local agent or representative who is a Qatari citizen. Personal relationships are more important than the organizational chart in the decision-making process of the Qatari Government agencies. The Qatari representative, therefore, is important not only to fulfill the legal requirement; he is essential to the foreign firm in making the appropriate contacts in the Government and in dealing with those contacts from the time a project is first conceived, through negotiating and signing the contract, to final completion of the project.

American firms have generally found it difficult to compete successfully in Qatar. Much of the architectural and design work done for Qatari projects is carried out by two or three local architectural firms, which are staffed largely by resident British architects. Nevertheless, persistent and aggressive efforts on the part of some American firms have enabled them to win major project contracts in Qatar.

The Qatari Government does not request turnkey bids. The procedures for seeking bids are regulated by Law No. 8 of 1976, "Bidding and Tender Regulations," which applies to all Government agencies except the security forces and the Qatar General Petroleum Corporation (QGPC). Contracts for small projects are awarded to locally-based firms. On large projects, a Central Tenders Committee announces the tender, using local media and, in some cases, Qatar's embassies abroad. Though Law No. 8 does not limit bidding to prequalified firms, the Government continues to announce the opportunity to prequalify and to invite bids only from those companies that have prequalified. Law No. 8 also provides for the classification of contractors, by a committee, based on the firms' financial strength and areas of experience. Presumably, contractors must be appropriately classified for the type of work sought in the tender in order to bid.

The Ministry of Public Works has the responsibility for most of the civil construction and highway projects, and the Industrial Development Technical Center is responsible for the heavy and light industrial projects and for agriculture. The QGPC undertakes all petroleum-related projects, including the production and processing of oil and gas.

Performance Requirements

Bid and performance bonds in the form of unconditional bank guarantees with the Qatar National Bank are required. The standard bid bond is 5 percent; it can be negotiated down on large contracts. It is returned to all bidders after the contract is signed. The performance bond is set at 10 percent of the value of the contract. Imported equipment can be used to offset the performance bond to some extent; again, the amount depends on the negotiating capability of the Qatari partner.

The force majeure clause is fairly standard and includes war, floods, fire, and acts of God. It can include labor strikes, though they are illegal in Qatar. Delay due to port congestion is not considered a force majeure condition.

Though Qatar has no specific regulations governing arbitration, Government contracts normally contain an arbitration clause. The typical clause states that arbitration will take place in Qatar; no provision is made for international arbitration.

Contractors generally receive an advance payment of 20 percent against an unconditional bank guarantee, and progress payments are made as the project moves along. There have been cases where the progress payments have been delayed. This is a problem that can be alleviated by the influence and contacts of the Qatari agent.

The official language in Qatar is Arabic, though English is widely used. Bids should be in both English and Arabic. However, all official documents must be authenticated in Arabic. The translator's signature must appear on the authenticated document. Specifications are usually written to British standards. Qatar uses the metric system of measurement.

Price

The Government requires fixed price bids without exception. Escalation clauses are not used under any circumstances and there are no cost-plus-fee contracts.

Equipment and Materials

The Government of Qatar assesses a 2.5 percent ad valorem tariff on all imported items, except for steel bars, which are assessed at 20 percent.

However, during the contract negotiations, a waiver can be obtained for machinery and equipment imported for the project if the goods are to be re-exported. Customs duty must be paid on the value of the machinery at the time of import if it is to be sold in the local market on the project's completion.

The Government encourages contractors to use local supplies. However, cement is the only construction material produced in Qatar in any appreciable quantity. The local supply portion of the bid can be contracted separately or included in the main contract. In either case, the bid and performance bonds apply as they do to the overall contract. If a local supplier reneges on his contract, for reasons other than force majeure, he is banned from Government contracts for a period of 6 months. If a foreign supplier reneges on his contract, other than for force majeure, he is permanently blacklisted.

Labor

Qatar has a severe shortage of all types of skilled, semi-skilled, and unskilled labor. Foreign labor, therefore, makes up almost the entire workforce on all projects. The workers come principally from other Arab countries, Iran, and the Indian subcontinent, though there are small numbers of workers from the Philippines, Thailand, and Korea.

Visas and work permits are required for all workers. To obtain a visa, one must have a local sponsor and, if employed, work for the sponsor. To change sponsorship, it is necessary to leave the country and apply for reentry under the new sponsor. Work permits are issued by the Department of Labor and Social Welfare. All job vacancies must be registered with the Department, and must be filled by a Qatari if a qualified candidate is available. There are no labor unions; the Department of Labor handles all disputes.

The severe lack of housing that characterized the local economy until 1978 has been alleviated by a rapid building program; rents are slowly declining. There is even a small surplus of prefabricated houses. Food and clothing are available but at prices about three times as high as those in the United States. Medical and dental care is available for common ailments; serious disease or traumatic illnesses must be treated outside Qatar. There are minimal recreational facilities. It is to the contractor's advantage to supply some of these facilities to his workforce to get the project underway and keep it running smoothly.

Labor is usually paid in cash on a monthly or semi-monthly basis. The labor contractors which supply the workers usually set the wages. Individual unskilled construction workers generally receive $15 to $20 per day, and trained clerical personnel start at about $600 per month. Fringe benefits normally given to skilled workers can amount to more than 100 percent of the basic salary. Personal effects are subject to the 2.5 percent ad valorem customs duty. There are no general requirements to provide training.

Local Agents, Representatives, and Corporations

As mentioned above, all foreign firms operating in Qatar must have local representation. Agency agreements are the most commonly used method of fulfilling this requirement. A well respected agent with good contacts is useful in setting up appointments, making hotel reservations, and obtaining information on upcoming opportunities. However, since he often represents several, sometimes competing, firms, the degree of his usefulness depends on the profit to be made from the sale of a company's goods or services and on the amount of personal contact in the form of visits to Qatar by the foreign company's home office personnel. Commissions and fees are negotiated between the parties concerned. The agency agreement must be registered with the Ministry of Economy and Commerce.

Foreign firms with a major interest in the Qatari market have found it advantageous to establish a partnership with a local private or public sector company. The joint venture must have at least 51 percent Qatari ownership.

Taxation

Qatar has no individual income taxes and no municipal or sales taxes. All firms operating in Qatar are subject to a corporate profit tax on income earned in Qatar that exceeds QR 70,000 (US$18,600). The tax is progressive, with rates ranging from 5 percent on the first bracket to 50 percent on income exceeding QR5 million (US$1.33 million). Companies working for the Government may be exempted from the tax by Emiri decree for the initial 5 years of the contract. In some cases, the exemption has been extended beyond the 5 years.

Saudi Arabia

The consultant, architect, engineer, and contractor have two very large customers in Saudi Arabia—the Arabian American Oil Company (ARAMCO) and the Saudi Government. The Government of Saudi Arabia has a rather complex system for bidding and contracting which is set out in laws and decrees, supplemented by interpretations or rulings on individual cases issued by the Ministry of Finance and National Economy (MFE).

For all contracts for consulting, architectural design, or engineering work worth more than one million Saudi riyals (SR) or about $300,000, the Government must invite at least three firms to submit bids. No less than five contractors must be invited to submit offers for construction contracts. Bids are opened in public and a committee composed of three or more persons from the MFE, or from the Government agency concerned with the project, reviews the bids and awards the contract by majority vote. The award will normally go to the company with the lowest bid which meets the specifications.

Firms wishing to submit proposals for projects in Saudi Arabia are required to make themselves known to each of the ministries undertaking the work on which they want to bid. The Saudi Government is beginning to compile a central list of foreign firms from which all government agencies can choose companies to bid on projects. Registration requires completion of a questionnaire (in both Arabic and English), a copy of the firm's latest annual report, two references, two copies of a list of completed projects, and a copy of two recently signed contracts. These documents are submitted to:

> Contractor's Classification Committee
> Non-Saudi Contractors Division
> Ministry of Public Works and Housing
> Al-Washem Street
> Riyadh, Saudi Arabia
> Attention: Director
> (telephone nos.: 404-3889; 404-3990)

In normal practice, a ministry undertaking a project will have a consultant draw up tender documents with the specifications against which the invited firms must bid. On small projects, turnkey proposals may be requested which will require an offer for the complete facility, including

the training of personnel to operate it. On the large industrial and infrastructure projects, the contracts for the master plan, detailed engineering,
and management of construction may all be awarded to separate firms.
The companies which have performed the consulting and design phases
of the project are usually not allowed to participate in its construction.

The Saudi Government is required by law to give preference in award-
ing contracts to Saudi companies, or to joint-ventures with more than
50 percent Saudi participation. Saudi Arabia is increasingly attempting
to "fractionalize" its projects into their various component phases, which
would be more manageable for Saudi contractors, and guarantee greater
competition between Saudi and foreign firms. Foreign firms are awarded
contracts only when a qualified Saudi company cannot be found. All
bidders are required to have a local address to which notices can be sent.
This requirement can be met by establishing an office in Saudi Arabia
or by using the address of the foreign firm's local agent or representative.

Local representation is required of foreign companies engaged in work
with the Saudi Government. A Saudi representative or joint venture
partner is essential to maintain the contact with Government officials
that is necessary to receive advance notice of upcoming projects and to
ensure that the foreign firm is placed on the bidders' lists. The good local
representative can also explain the highly technical goods or services a
firm might be offering that are unfamiliar to the Saudi client, as well as
ascertain and communicate to the firm how it might prepare a proposal
to fit Saudi requirements. Since the bid specifications can be very general,
too many U.S. companies have submitted proposals using state-of-the-art
technology only to find themselves underbid by third country firms offering
less complex and less expensive facilities that are better suited to Saudi
requirements.

In general, all companies working in the Kingdom are required to register
with the Ministry of Commerce. Consultants should attempt to fill out prequalification forms in order to be in an advantageous position in bidding.

Performance Requirements

The Saudi Government requires bid and performance bonds from most
foreign firms of 1 percent and 5 percent, respectively, of the value of
the contract. The bonds must be cash, a certified check drawn on a local
bank, or a bank guarantee payable on demand. About 100 foreign banks,
including major U.S. banks, are authorized to act as direct guarantors,
though each guarantee must be approved by a bank in Saudi Arabia
acting as the agent of the foreign bank. Unconditional surety bonds will
be accepted as guarantees if they are payable on demand, issued by an
approved U.S. surety company, and cover at least 25 percent of the value
of the contract. The Saudi Government has published a list of acceptable
insurance firms.

The performance bond is not required for consulting work, service contracts, the supply of spare parts, nor for contracts which the Government awards by direct purchase—contracts which are less than SR 1 million in value and do not have to be tendered. In some joint ventures, the Saudi firm has been persuaded to put up the whole guarantee. The performance bond is reduced on operation and maintenance contracts as work progresses on the project. However, it cannot go below 5 percent of the value of the uncompleted work.

The bid bond is always required, except in the case of a purely negotiated contract where there are no competitors. It is returned automatically to the bidders when the period specified in the tender announcement for the bids to remain open expires. The performance bond is generally due from the winning bidder within 10 days after he has been notified of the award. It is returned to the contractor on final completion of the project, though the contractor remains liable for the collapse of the structure and for defects for a period of 10 years.

The Saudi client may make an advance payment of 20 percent of the cost of the project at the signing of construction contracts, although this is now subject to negotiation. The advance must be backed by the contractor with a bank guarantee of an equal amount. Though this is sometimes referred to as a suicide bond, most contractors accept the payment and earn interest on it during the time between the contract signing and the start-up of work. The Government will also pay up to 75 percent of the value of construction materials when they are imported, if they are stored in a way that will avoid damage and deterioration. The Government will make progress payments of up to 90 percent of the work completed. The remaining 10 percent is held pending final delivery of the project. However, Saudi companies and joint ventures in which the Saudi partner holds at least 60 percent of the capital can be paid in full for work completed without the requirement of submitting a bank guarantee.

The Saudi Tender Regulations allow for delays or default in completion of work due to force majeure, and clauses can be put in the contract which specify force majeure conditions. However, the Saudi regulations do not define force majeure. Labor strikes are not considered force majeure nor are delays due to port congestion, if these delays can be anticipated. A Saudi lawyer versed in the Shari'a law should be employed to negotiate the force majeure clause.

Contracts always include a provision for settling disputes. However, Saudis are extremely reluctant to accept international arbitration. Some Government non-ministerial agencies have reportedly agreed to it, but such a departure from customary procedure presumably requires the approval of the Council of Ministers. The decision of an arbitration panel located outside of Saudia Arabia probably would not be enforceable in the Kingdom anyway. Both public and private sector organizations strongly prefer to resolve commercial disputes through personal contacts and negotiations or through the Saudi arbitration system. Arbitration or Grievance Boards have been established for settling some forms of commercial disputes, particularly with Government agencies. The decision of the boards can be appealed to the Shariah court. The Saudi Council of Ministers has been known to get involved in major disputes.

Arabic is the official language in Saudi Arabia. English is widely spoken and understood. Firms resident or working in Saudia Arabia must conduct all of their official business with the Government in Arabic. However, the Tender Regulations say that bids may be in any language, and in practice, the tender announcement for each project generally specifies the language of the bid. English is used in most of the major contracts. Any document concerning the formation of a joint venture and the representation and agency agreements must be in Arabic to be legally binding. In any dispute, the Arabic text will prevail.

The Saudis use the metric system of measurement.

Price

The Saudi Government has required fixed price, lump sum bids for almost all contracts, even those for services extending over a period of many years. New regulations allow for cost-plus-fee contracts only for project management. The Saudi Government resists any notion of an escalation clause, but such clauses are known to have been negotiated in at least two contracts. The Tender Regulations allow price increases for changes in transportation charges, insurance rates, or in raw material prices. However, there must be a limit to the increase and it must be approved by the Council of Ministers. The Regulations also allow the contractor to claim compensation for factors beyond his control, including costs incurred due to the Government's failure to make decisions on time, though actually getting the supplementary payments can be a difficult process.

Foreign companies have sought to insure themselves against losses by making worst-case bids. In an effort to stop this practice, several Government agencies have recently cancelled all bids when the prices have greatly exceeded the cost estimated by Government consultants. The Government is expected to continue to insist that the bid prices come reasonably close to its own estimates.

Payment for contracts over SR 300 million ($90 million) is made in dollars, while contracts for lesser amounts are paid in riyals, which are freely convertible into dollars and other foreign currencies. Since January 1979, all contracts over SR 100 million ($30 million) require the personal approval of Crown Prince Fahd.

Equipment and Materials

Saudia Arabia's tariff rates generally range from zero to 3 percent. Imports of certain items produced in Saudi Arabia, such as aluminum or wooden window frames, are assessed a tariff of 20 percent ad valorem. Most contracts provide for the importation of supplies, machinery, and equipment duty free. However, the Government may recommend that equipment and material be purchased from Saudi dealers where possible. In these instances, the Government will not reimburse the dealer for duties already paid on stocked goods.

Used machinery does not have to be re-exported, and re-exportation of trucks and other vehicles in working order generally is forbidden. Because of the high attrition rate of construction machinery due to the climate and the inexperience of many of those who use it, most contractors write off the costs of the equipment imported for construction projects.

The Tender Regulations require the Government to purchase Saudi manufactures if they serve the purpose intended even if they are of a higher price and lower quality than similar imports. The regulation is moot, however, since the shortage of materials and equipment makes it necessary to import most of the requirements of a project.

There are bonded areas at Saudi ports, but they do not need to be used because Saudi authorities do everything possible to get off-loaded goods cleared through customs as quickly as possible. Goods not cleared within 15 days are subject to confiscation and public auction. To facilitate customs clearance, original export documents should be legalized by Saudi consular authorities in the country from which the good is exported.

Labor

There is an extreme shortage of labor of all skills in Saudi Arabia and a shortage of accommodations for a workforce. Consequently, labor must be imported, housed, and fed. Much of the labor is imported as a group through arrangements with labor contractors in South Korea, Pakistan, the Philippines, or Thailand. This facilitates obtaining visas and residence and work permits and generally cuts down on turnover which is very high, particularly in the construction industry. Other Arab countries (primarily Egypt and the Yemens) and India are also sources of labor.

Unskilled workers (mainly Yemeni) are fairly easy to recruit, although labor costs are rising rapidly. Semi-skilled and skilled labor is more difficult to come by and obtaining managers who will agree to go to, and stay in Saudi Arabia once they get here, can be a large problem. Incentives to get and keep managers include the costs of medical care, insurance, airfare, generous rest and recreation allowances, and housing (a decent 3-bedroom apartment costs $20,000-40,000 per year). Managers require a hefty salary; unskilled labor is paid as much as $30 per day; and mechanics, carpenters, and bricklayers command $40 to $80 per day.

Work and residence permits are required and are issued by the Ministry of Interior. The worker, or the labor contractor of groups of workers, must present a labor contract to the Ministry in order to obtain a work permit. Foreign workers entering the Kingdom must be sponsored by native Saudis or Saudi-based companies which agree to be responsible for them. Personal effects may be imported duty-free; duty-free entry for household effects can be arranged and written into the contract.

Training is required for all projects which include the operation of complicated machinery or equipment. The cost of training is included in the bid.

Local Agents, Representatives, and Corporations

The form of a foreign company's representation in Saudi Arabia will vary with the type and size of the company and project. A Saudi agent is recommended for firms seeking supply contracts. Fees and commissions are negotiable and are usually agreed to only after hard bargaining over the amount of compensation and the extent of the services to be rendered. An agent's commission on Government contracts is now limited by law to 5 percent, and a company may not be represented by more than one agent for government bidding. A company should include a clause in the agency agreement to the effect that the agent who has been given the power to bid in its name does not add to the price for his own profit.

Saudi agents regulations prohibit an agent from representing both the consulting engineer and the implementing contractor in a single project, in order to prevent a conflict of interest. Furthermore, a foreign contractor in Saudia Arabia may have more than one Saudi agent performing service as opposed to commercial functions, but no more than one service agent is allowed for each Saudi project in which a firm may be interested. No service agent is permitted to represent more than ten foreign firms.

According to Ministry of Commerce Resolution 680, foreign firms that do not use a Saudi agent and wish to subcontract for service or supply tenders must register for a license with that Ministry and establish an office in Saudi Arabia. Foreign firms which are invited to bid on a tender by the Saudi Government need apply for a license and establish an office in the Kingdom only if they are awarded the contract.

Partnerships with Saudi firms are advisable for foreign companies seeking to manufacture in the Kingdom or to provide services. Manufacturing facilities and specific service firms with at least 25 percent Saudi ownership qualify for the same concessions (e.g., loans, tax allowances, etc.) as wholly-Saudi-owned firms.

U.S. firms should be particularly careful in selecting an agent or partner in Saudi Arabia. Dissolving a partnership or changing an agency agreement with a Saudi can be a long, drawn-out affair, and unless done on mutually agreed terms it can mean the end of business in the country for the foreign firm.

Taxation

Income taxes on the salaries of expatriate employees were abolished by Royal Decree, June 1, 1975.

According to Saudi law, all foreign and Saudi companies are subject to a company profits tax on profits earned in Saudi Arabia. However, foreign companies with contracts for large projects have managed to negotiate a clause in their contracts which exempts them from the tax.

Joint ventures with at least 25 percent Saudi ownership enjoy a 5 year or 10 year tax holiday, depending on the nature of the firm. All companies are required to report their existence and activities in the Kingdom to the tax department of the Ministry of Finance. A copy of the contract must be included to determine the company's tax status. The records of the company's activities in Saudi Arabia must be in Arabic and kept within the country. Company books should be audited in accordance with established U.S. and Saudi accounting procedures.

For companies which must pay the tax, the rates on net profits are 25 percent on the first SR100,000; 35 percent on SR100,000 to SR500,000; 40 percent on SR500,000 to SR1 million; and 45 percent on profits exceeding SR1 million. The Zakat, a religious tax, is levied on all Saudi companies; the rate is 1.25 percent of profits. The final payment on a contract is withheld until the client receives a certificate from the Ministry of Finance which states that the contractor is either exempt from payment of taxes and the Zakat or has satisfactorily paid all taxes due. The Zakat is not paid by the foreign partner in a joint venture.

Syria

Syria's role in the uncertain political situation in the region and, until the recent start of the U.S. AID program, the lack of availability of financing from U.S. Government sources have militated against U.S. participation in engineering and construction projects in the country. However, U.S. commodity sales are growing rapidly and the Syrian Government has repeatedly expressed interest in the participation of U.S. firms in its development program. The Government is the largest customer in Syria, particularly for engineering and construction services, although the country's peculiar brand of socialism tolerates a small and flourishing private sector which engages in trading, tourism, and light industry.

In Syria, almost everything commercial is negotiable. The Government is bound by contracting regulations but they allow ministers and other responsible officials to waive certain rules and procedures if it is deemed to be in the public interest. Consequently, special administrative and legislative decrees granting exemptions for individual contracts have been added to the regulations, some of which have been in force since 1946, creating a thicket of complex and sometimes contradictory rules governing the public sector's contracts. Firms are strongly advised to make sure that the contract terms negotiated govern every possible detail, no matter how unimportant they may seem.

The Syrian Government may request turnkey or consortium bids for the construction, supply and installation of equipment, and start-up phase of the project. The study and design/engineering phases are usually contracted separately. Bids are invited by international tender in most cases, but may also be requested only from firms who have prequalified for the type of work being sought, or the contracts may be negotiated directly. The Government gives the right of first refusal on the construction phase of public works projects to the seven public sector construction companies. However, these companies can handle only a fraction of the work under way or projected.

Recent amendments relaxing tender limitations for local private construction contractors now allow these firms to tender for public contracts valued in excess of one million Syrian pounds (approximately $250,000) when such projects are financed by foreign governments or organizations. Foreign firms tendering for large projects in Syria can thus expect the possibility of greater competition from the Syrian private sector than existed previously.

Performance Requirements

The Syrian Government requires bid and performance bonds on all contracts. They usually must be in the form of unconditional bank guarantees issued by the Commercial Bank of Syria (CBS). Bid bonds range from one to five percent of the value of the contract and must be valid long enough to cover the contract award. A bid bond will be considered valid only if the conditions of offer are accepted by the Syrian Government.

The performance bond varies up to 10 percent and remains valid until a specified date which ends the life of the contract; this period can be extended. Though not required by law, all Government agencies demand that the CBS guarantee be backed by a guarantee from a correspondent bank in the contractor's home country.

Precise wording for terms and conditions of performance bonds should be included in the contract so as to guarantee that the bond not revert to the beneficiary (Syrian client) upon completion of the contract. The CBS will not accept language requiring it to make a judgment on facts of the case, such as when a project is completed, but will accept language on procedure. An exact date of expiry should be specified along with a clause requiring advance notice (30 days) or encashment to the bank opening the letters of credit. The term "delivery" should be clearly defined; carefully review the Arabic/French/English translations of this term to ensure that the parties to the contract are in complete agreement.

The Syrians sometimes will give advance payments of 5 to 15 percent of the value of the contract if they are backed by a bank guarantee.

A force majeure clause is occasionally spelled out in the tender conditions and is always included in the final contract. The language of the force majeure clause is negotiable; labor disputes are considered force majeure, delivery delays due to port congestion normally are not.

All contracts contain a clause providing for arbitration. The Syrians prefer to have disputes arbitrated in local courts under Syrian law, but international arbitration can be specified if the foreign company insists. The arbitrating body is usually the International Chamber of Commerce in Paris. Syria is a member of the New York Convention of 1958 for Enforcing Arbitration Awards.

Arabic is the official language in Syria; English and French are widely used. The tender announcement will specify the language in which bids must be submitted. The metric system of measurement is preferred.

Price

Fixed price, lump sum bids are almost always required, though escalation clauses have been negotiated in some recent contracts for large projects. The Government has been known to reimburse the foreign contractor for unanticipated increases in the costs of imported commodities if these increases have exceeded 15 percent over the life of the project. Provision should be made for this in the contract. The contract can also include clauses for escalation in the price of parts. Cost-plus-fee contracts are very rare. To avoid demurrage charges, permission to import commodities to implement a project, as well as preferential port unloading privileges, should be written into the contract. The Government controls the prices of all locally-procured commodities.

Equipment and Materials

Machinery, equipment, and materials imported for a project may be exempt from customs duties by a "temporary admission" clause in the contract. The goods may be re-exported at the end of the project or sold in Syria after customs duty has been paid on the value of the used equipment. Passenger cars must be re-exported. There is a good local market for used machinery and equipment. The contract usually includes a provision for the supply of spare parts.

The Syrian Government is most interested in obtaining foreign technology and does not as a rule give special preference to bids which include the use of local materials and services. However, it is often necessary to use Syrian products and subcontractors because the tender will require that part of the contract be paid in Syrian pounds. Where local supply is used, it may be contracted separately or included in the overall contract.

Bonded areas can be arranged but are generally not necessary since customs clearances normally present no serious problems.

Labor

Syria is experiencing occasional shortages of unskilled workers and the lack of skilled and semiskilled personnel is becoming acute. Palestinians, Turks, and Iranians are employed temporarily (and illegally) in some cases on their way to and from the pilgrimage to Mecca. Work and residence permits are difficult to obtain. Foreign employees must pass a security clearance; this requirement is usually satisfied by a letter from the Syrian Government contracting agency.

Foreign employers must provide Syrian workers with social security and workman's compensation and, depending on the location and nature of the project, family allowances, transportation, and food supplements. Food, clothing, medical and dental services, and recreational facilities are available. Adequate housing exists but is quite expensive. Employees' personal effects may be imported duty-free, if it is specified in the contract.

Wages in Syria have risen rapidly with inflation in the last several years. Currently, masons earn about 100 Syrian pounds (SP) per day; heavy equipment operators earn SP3,000 per month; carpenters receive SP

2,000-3,300 per month, auto mechanics, SP2,000 per month; and unskilled laborers, SP30-50 per day. (US$1 = SP3.9.)

Government tenders usually require that the contractor provide training in the equipment supplier's plant or on-the-job (or both). The cost of the training is included in the bid.

Local Agents, Representatives, and Corporations

A foreign firm is not legally required to have a local agent in Syria, and may deal with Government agencies directly. However, an agent is almost essential for providing commercial intelligence, facilitating contacts, arranging translation services, providing long-term follow-up and servicing, and generally looking after the foreign firm's interests.

The agent may be the exclusive representative of the foreign company and he must be a Syrian national, registered with the Ministry of Economy and Foreign Trade. Commissions and fees are negotiated and vary widely with the nature of complexities of the services the agent provides.

Foreign firms may establish a branch office in Syria, which should be registered with the Ministry of Economy and Foreign Trade. Unless registered specifically under foreign joint venture laws, partnerships and corporations must be at least 51 percent Syrian-owned. The Government has recently shown interest in forming partnerships with foreign firms wherein it supplies a major share of the financial equity and the foreign company supplies the technology.

Taxation

The expatriate employees of U.S. firms with contracts in Syria are not subject to Syrian income taxes, provided that this is written into the contract. Companies which are operating in Syria but do not have a local presence are not subject to the corporate taxes. Companies resident in Syria pay tax on income earned in the country at rates ranging from 11 percent on the first SP 10,000 to 66 percent on income over SP 700,000. Companies in partnership with the Syrian Government can negotiate an exemption to the corporate tax.

United Arab Emirates

The United Arab Emirates (UAE) consists of seven states, each of which regulates its own business affairs. The procedures of the two richest Emirates, Abu Dhabi and Dubai, will be discussed here. Both have had longer experience in the execution of large projects and have developed a set of definable procedures which they follow in undertaking new projects.

In Abu Dhabi, business practices are relatively structured. The Government codified its tendering procedures in the 1977 Tenders Law. The Abu Dhabi Government also has a large network of departments and committees with narrowly defined spheres of influence and authority. By contrast, all the major development projects in Dubai are undertaken by the small Department of His Highness the Ruler's Affairs and Petroleum Affairs which is under the direct supervision of the Ruler. The local presence and contacts of foreign firms are important in both Emirates, but particularly so in Dubai.

Foreign contractors seeking to bid on Abu Dhabi Government tenders are required to register their companies with both the Abu Dhabi Municipality and the Abu Dhabi Chamber of Commerce and Industry. Registration requires that the foreign firm obtain the services of a local agent or sponsor.

Projects in Dubai are usually negotiated directly and awarded to firms that have been established in the Emirate for a number of years and have developed a good reputation with their clients.

Performance Requirements

All Government agencies in the UAE require that bids be submitted with a 90-day standby letter of credit from a local bank, equal to 5 percent of the value of the bid. The winning bidder must replace the bid guarantee with a 10 percent performance guarantee, also in the form of a standby letter of credit issued by a local bank. The local bank usually requires that the letter of credit be fully backed by a standby letter of credit from a correspondent bank in the contractor's home country.

The Abu Dhabi Government normally pays a 10 percent advance to the contractor which must be backed by a bank guarantee. Many Abu Dhabi Government departments require that two offers be submitted by firms bidding on projects that are expected to cost more than 50 million dirhams (DH) ($13.4 million) one offer is to be made on the assumption that the contractor will receive the 10 percent advance payment; the other offer is to be on the basis that no advance payment is made.

The Dubai Government usually makes monthly or quarterly progress payments against invoices. In the rare instances when an advance payment is given it must be backed by a bank guarantee.

The language of force majeure clauses can be negotiated but it is usually limited to "acts of God" such as wars and natural disasters. Labor strikes and port congestion are not considered acts of God.

In all known cases, commercial disputes in the UAE have been settled by negotiations between the parties concerned. However, clauses providing for arbitration are written into all contracts. In Dubai, arbitration under the Rules of Conciliation and Arbitration of the International Chamber of Commerce is specified in most major contracts. Abu Dhabi is only allowing arbitration in the Emirate under Abu Dhabi law.

Arabic is the official language of the UAE, but English is used in commercial circles. The Abu Dhabi Government tender documents usually specify that bids must be in English; most foreign firms use English in making their offers in both Abu Dhabi and Dubai. Both the metric and the British imperial systems of measurement are used.

Price

Fixed price bids are required in both Abu Dhabi and Dubai. Bids submitted with escalation clauses in Abu Dhabi have been consistently disqualified. Government officials claim not to have sufficient manpower to administer contracts with escalation clauses or cost-plus-fee contracts.

There have been unpublished exceptions to the fixed price requirement in Dubai in contracts with companies that are very large and well known to the Dubai client. Also, cost-plus-fee contracts can be negotiated for feasibility studies and consulting services.

Neither the Abu Dhabi Government nor the Dubai Government will guarantee the supply of commodities at a fixed price for construction projects. However, they have been known to guarantee the price of a fixed supply of fuel for the operation of industrial facilities.

Equipment and Materials

Imports of construction materials, machinery, and equipment enter Abu Dhabi duty free. The contract specifies whether the used commodities are to be re-exported. If they are to be sold on the local market, the Government contracting agency usually has the right of first refusal.

A recent Abu Dhabi law (Executive Council General Secretariat Circular No. 2 of 1979) requires foreign contractors to procure all goods and materials needed for a project from the local market or, if unavailable there, to import these supplies through local trading companies with majority Abu Dhabi ownership. Because industry in the UAE is in an embryonic stage, contractors will have to import a large part of project materials. The cost of a project is therefore increased because of the need to pay a local importer for his services. If the contractor's agent or sponsor has an import license, goods may be imported through him. The latter's compensation is left to negotiation between contractor and sponsor.

Amendments to this law allow ADNOC to import high technology equipment directly from foreign suppliers. In practice, not only ADNOC, but also the Abu Dhabi Company for Onshore Oil Operations, the Abu Dhabi Marine Operating Company, and ADNOC's numerous joint venture companies have been able to import directly from foreign suppliers.

Dubai assesses a customs duty of from 1 to 3 percent on machinery, equipment, and supplies. The duty is not waived except on very large projects at the discretion of the Ruler. There is no requirement at present for foreign firms working for the Dubai Government to import using local middlemen; import licenses may be obtained directly. Used machinery and equipment does not have to be re-exported; there is a good local market for it.

In both of the Emirates, contractors can expect the local exclusive agent of a foreign manufacturer to insist on a commission for supplies purchased from that manufacturer, even if the contractor concluded the transaction directly. If the principal refuses to pay the commission, the agent can bring pressure to bear on the contractor for payment.

There are no bonded areas in the UAE. Customs delays are not a problem. Delays in the ports are caused principally by the physical limitations of the port facilities.

Labor

Technically, contractors are required to give first preference in hiring to UAE nationals who have registered their availability with the UAE Ministry of Labor, which acts as the national employment agency. In practice, however, native Abu Dhabians will generally only work as drivers or guards, and a laboring class is almost nonexistent in Dubai. The contractor, therefore, must use third country nationals primarily from India, Pakistan, Iran, and other Arab countries for almost his entire workforce. He is responsible for obtaining their work permits and visas, and for providing housing and other necessities.

The Abu Dhabi Labor Law, which governs work hours, overtime, conditions of employment, leave, and labor disputes, requires that contractors responsible for projects more than 10 kilometers from the cities of Abu Dhabi or Al-Ain provide a camp, including room and board, for their workers. The Abu Dhabi Government will provide medical care, but will charge the contractor DH100 ($27) per day if an employee is hospitalized.

Estimates vary on the relative productivity of laborers in the UAE. Some have found them to be comparable to U.S. workers, while others have found them to be only one-third to one-half as productive. Wages for unskilled workers range from DH35 to DH40 ($9-$11) per day; tradesmen get DH70 to DH100 ($19-$27) per day; and skilled labor, when available, commands DH200 to DH225 ($53-$60) per day. Third country nationals are paid in dirhams.

Employees' personal effects may enter Abu Dhabi duty free, but may be subject to import duties (ranging from 1 to 3 percent) when entering Dubai. Work permits are required; they are issued by the Ministry of Labor and must be renewed annually.

The contractor is expected to train local personnel on complicated equipment, either in the supplier's plant or on-the-job after the equipment has been installed. The cost of the training is specified in the bid. Training equipment can be imported and re-exported duty free.

Local Agents, Representatives, and Corporations

Abu Dhabi law requires that foreign firms have a local agent who is an Abu Dhabi national in order to do business in the Emirate. Though in rare instances a Government department has gone directly to a foreign firm to purchase goods and services, most will not release the tender documents to the foreign company until the name of its agent is known. The agency agreement must be registered at the Abu Dhabi Chamber of Commerce. The commission paid to the local agent of a foreign contracting company is limited by law to a maximum of 2 percent on projects less than DH10 million ($2.65 million), 1.5 percent on projects estimated to cost between DH10 million and DH50 million ($13.4 million), and 1 percent on projects which cost over DH50 million.

Companies seeking contracts with Abu Dhabi oil companies must be registered to do business in, and have their main UAE office in, the Emirate of Abu Dhabi. Foreign firms interested in non-petroleum-related projects should consider opening a main office in Abu Dhabi if they intend to do business in that Emirate.

A recent ruling requires all trading and contracting firms operating in the UAE to have at least 51 percent ownership by native UAE citizens. This requirement does not apply to firms offering professional services, such as architects, consultants, and lawyers, nor does it apply to contracting firms working in Government contracts. Though meant to apply to companies in all the Emirates, the requirement is only being enforced in Abu Dhabi for firms registered with the Municipality, i.e., Abu Dhabi firms, and in the Emirate of Umm al-Qaiwain. Most successful foreign firms in Dubai seem to have a local partner, however, with some equity participation in the Dubai operations of the company.

Under Dubai law, a local agent is not required to obtain government contracts; a foreign firm may even set up a wholly foreign owned corporation in the Emirate. However, companies that do not have a UAE citizen or firm as a sponsor must pay a fee of DH100,000 ($26,500) to enroll in the Commercial Register and do business in Dubai. It is advisable for U.S. firms to obtain a Dubai agent or partner. The local representative can provide contacts, influence, and knowledge of the market. He can also simplify the administrative details of setting up operations in the Emirate. The amount of the fees or equity participation is not regulated. A good agent can command a commission of up to 5 percent of the value of the contracts delivered. The amount of equity held by a local partner is negotiable between the parties concerned.

While foreign firms can register in Dubai, Sharjah, and other major UAE port cities (except Abu Dhabi) without a local agent or sponsor, the UAE Government is currently considering regulations extending local agent or sponsor requirements to all of the Emirates.

Taxation

There are no individual income taxes in the UAE. Both Abu Dhabi and Dubai have corporate profits taxes which theoretically apply to all companies operating in the Emirates. However, to date, they have been levied only on the profits of companies producing oil.

Part IV

Conversational Arabic

Chapter 10

Conversational Arabic

A Note on Transliteration

The following list gives the values of some of the symbols and letters used in the transliteration.

Symbol/letter	Description
,	Glottal stop like that before the vowel in "oh."
a	As in "along."
aa	As in "fat" but lengthened.
ay	As in "may."
d	As in "door."
dh	As in "father."
e	As in "bed."
ee	As in "week."
gh	A gargling sound like the Parisian "r."
i	As in "pin."
kh	As in "loch" as pronounced by the Scotch.
oo	As in "shoot."
q	As in "king" but produced farther back in the throat.
u	As in "put."

Meeting People

1. Peace be onto you	Assalaamu alaykum
2. And peace be onto you	Wa alaykum assalaam
3. Greetings	Marhabaa (or marhabaat)
4. Good morning	Sabaah al-khayr
5. Good afternoon (evening)	Masaa' al-khayr
6. How are you?	Kayf al-haal?
7. I am fine	Al-hamdu lillaah (lit. praise be to God)[1]
8. Good	Jayyid
9. Not bad	Laa ba's
10. Thank you	Shukran
11. I would like to	(Anaa)[2] Ahib
12. I would like to introduce myself	Ahib aqaddim nafsee
13. I am Bill Smith	Anaa Bill Smith
14. My name is Bill Smith	Ismee Bill Smith
15. Who are you?	Man anta?
16. What's your name?	Maahuwa ismak (f. ismik)[3]
17. I want to	Areed
18. I want to introduce my wife	Areed aqaddim zawjaty
19. I want to introduce my husband	Areed aqaddim zawjy
20. This is my wife, Susan	Haadhy zawjatee Susan
21. This is my husband, Bill	Haadhaa zawjee Bill
22. This is the president	Haadhaa arra'ees
23. I would like to introduce the president of the company	Ahib aqaddim ra'ees ashsharikah
24. I want you to meet	Areedkum tuqaabiloon
25. My friend, Bill	Sadeeqy Bill
26. My friend, Mary	Sadeeqaty Mary
27. Do you speak English?	Hal titkallam ingileezy?
28. Do you know Arabic?	Hal ta'rif araby?
29. No	Laa
30. Yes	Na'am
31. A little	Qaleel
32. I do not speak Arabic	Laa atkallam araby
33. I speak a little Arabic	Atkallam araby qaleel

[1] Lit. stand for literal translation.
[2] The "anaa," or I, is often omitted when it is followed by a verb.
[3] F. stands for feminine form of the verb.

34.	Where are you from?	Min ayn anta?
35.	I am from America	Anaa min amreekah
36.	I am from the United States	Anaa min al-wilaayaat al-muttahidah
37.	Where do you live?	Ayn taskun?
38.	I live in Chicago	Askun fee sheekaago
39.	Are you an Arab?	Hal anta araby?
40.	Pleased to meet you	Fursah sa'eedah
41.	The pleasure is mine	Anaa as'ad
42.	Goodbye	Ma'a assalaamah
43.	See you	Araakum
44.	God willing	Inshaa allaah

On Arrival

1.	Airplane	Tayyaarah
2.	Airport	Mataar
3.	Passport	Jawaaz
4.	Visit (noun)	Ziyaarah
5.	Visitor	Zaa'ir
6.	Tourism	Siyaahah
7.	Tourist	Saa'ih
8.	Visa	Ta'sheerah
9.	Transit visa	Ta'sheerah murooriyyah
10.	Form	Istimaarah
11.	Bag	Haqeebah
12.	Bags (luggage)	Haqaa'ib
13.	Money	Fuloos
14.	Your passport	Jawaazak (f. jawaazik)
15.	This is my passport	Haadhaa jawaazy
16.	How long do you plan to stay?	Kam satabqaa (f. satabqeen)?
17.	One week	Usboo' waahid
18.	Two weeks	Usbooayn
19.	Three weeks	Thalaathat asaabee'
20.	Do you have anything?	Hal ma'ak (f. ma'ik) shay'?
21.	Do you have anything to declare?	Hal ma'ak shay' yajib an tusarrih (f. tusarriheen) bihi?
22.	No, nothing	Laa, laashay'
23.	How much money do you have with you?	Kam ma'ak (f. ma'ik) fuloos?

24. I have two hundred dollars	Ma'ee (or indee) mi'atayn doolaar
25. What is the purpose of?	Maa gharad?
26. Your visit?	Ziyaartak (f. ziyaartik)?
27. Business	Ashghaal (or aa'maal)
28. Tourist	Saa'ih
29. I need a tourist visa	Ahtaaj ta'sheerah siyaahiyyah
30. I want a transit visa	Areed ta'sheerah murooriyyah
31. What is your profession?	Maa mihnatuk (f. mihnatik)?
32. I am a businessman	Anaa rajul aa'maal
33. Fill out this form	Imla' haadhee al-istimaarah
34. Please	Min fadlak
35. I don't understand	Anaa laa afham
36. Where do I sign?	Ayn awaqqi'?
37. Here	Hunaa
38. Where is the luggage?	Ayn al-haqaa'ib?
39. My bags are not here	Haqaa'iby laysat hunaa
40. How many bags to you have?	Kam haqeebah indak?
41. I have one bag only	Indee haqeebah waahidah faqat
42. This is my bag	Haadhee haqeebaty
43. Are these your bags?	Hal haadhee haqaa'ibak (f. haqaa'ibik)?
44. Is there a porter here?	Hal yoojad hammaal (or shayyaal) hunaa?
45. Can you help me?	Mumkin itsaa'idny?
46. Take this bag	Khudh haadhee al-haqeebah
47. Thank you very much	Shukran jazeelan

Taxi and Bus

1. Taxi (cab)	Taaksy
2. Bus	Baas
3. Car	Sayyaarah
4. Driver	Saa'iq
5. Fare	Ujrah
6. How much?	Kam?
7. Take me	Khudhny
8. Where can I get a taxi?	Ayn mumkin ajid taaksy?
9. Where is the taxi stop?	Ayn mawqif attaksy?
10. Where is the bus stop?	Ayn mawqif al-baas?
11. Does the bus go to the city?	Hal yadhhab al-baas ilaa al-madeenah?

12. I need a taxi	Ahtaaj taaksy
13. Where is the driver?	Ayn assaa'iq?
14. Where do you want to go?	Ayn tareed an tadhhab?
15. I want to go to the Baghdad hotel	Areed adhhab ilaa findiq Baghdad
16. Take me to the American Embassy	Khudhny ilaa assafaarah al-amreekiyyah
17. How far is the hotel?	Kam yab'ud al-findiq?
18. How far is the embassy?	Kam tab'ud assafaarah?
19. About	Hawaaly
20. Ten kilometer (miles)	Ashrat kiloometraat (amyaal)
21. Stop here	Qif hunaa
22. This is the hotel	Haadhaa al-findiq
23. This is the fare	Haadhee al-ujrah
24. Tip	Bakhsheesh

At the Hotel

1. Hotel	Findiq
2. Reservation	Hajiz
3. Room	Ghurfah
4. Rooms	Ghuraf
5. Single	Munfaridah
6. Double	Muzdawajah
7. Bath	Hammaam
8. Key	Miftaah
9. Is there a good hotel?	Hal yoojad findiq jayyid?
10. I want a cheap hotel	Areed findiq rakhees
11. Can I help you?	Mumkin asaa'dak?
12. Yes, do you have vacant rooms?	Na'am, indakum ghuraf faarighah?
13. Do you have a reservation?	Indaq (f. Indik) hajiz?
14. No, I don't	Laa, maa indy
15. Yes, I do	Na'am, indy
16. Yes, we have vacancies	Na'am, indanaa ghuraf faarighah
17. Do you have a single room?	Indakum ghurfah munfaridah?
18. Do you have a double room?	Indakum ghurfah muzdawajah?
19. I want a room with a bath	Areed ghurfah ma'a hammaam
20. How much does the room cost?	Kam tukallif al-ghurfah?
21. Twenty dinars per night	Ishreen dinar fil laylah
22. How many days will you stay?	Kam yawm satabqaa?
23. I will stay for three days	Sa'abqaa thalaathat ayyaam

24. Please, fill out this form	Min fadhlak, imla' haadhee al-istimaarah
25. This is the room key	Haadhaa miftaah al-ghurfah
26. What's the room number?	Maa raqm al-ghurfah?
27. Thirty	Thalaatheen
28. Where is the room?	Ayn al-ghurfah?
29. On the first floor	Alaa attaabaq al-awwal
30. On the second floor	Alaa attaabaq aththaani
31. Please, take my luggage to the room	Min fadhlak, khudh haqaa'iby ilaa al-ghurfah
32. Do you like the room?	Hal tuhib al-ghurfah?
33. Yes, it's a nice room	Na'am, hiya ghurfah lateefah
34. No, I don't like the room	Laa, la ahib al-ghurfah
35. The room is...	Al-ghurfah...
—small	—sagheerah
—dark	—mudlimah
—cold	—baaridah
—hot	—haarrah
36. There is no hot water	Laa yoojad maa' haar
37. I need...	Ahtaaj...
—a towel	—minshafah
—a blanket	—battaaniyyah
—an ashtray	—minfadah
—soap	— saaboon
—clotheshangers	—illaaqaat
—room service	— khidmat al-ghurfah
38. Is there a restaurant in the hotel?	Hal yoojad mat'am fee al-findiq?
39. Where is the bar?	Ayn al-baar?
40. I lost my key	Dayya'tu miftaahy
41. Are there any letters for me?	Hal toojad makaateeb lee?
42. Are there any messages?	Hal toojad rasaa'il?
43. I want to check out	Areed atruk
44. The bill, please	Al-faatoorah, min fadlak
45. Can I have a receipt?	Mumkin ti'teeny wasil?
46. Surely	Bilta'keed
47. Have a nice trip	Safrah sa'eedah

Telephoning

1. The telephone	Attalifoun
2. A call	Mukhaabarah

3.	Number	Raqm
4.	Line	Khat
5.	Phone book	Daleel talifoun
6.	Change	Fakkah
7.	Is there a public phone?	Hal yoojad talifoun umoomy?
8.	There is a phone in the restaurant	Yoojad talifoun fil mat'am
9.	Please, may I use the phone?	Min fadhlak, mumkin asta'mil attalifoun?
10.	Is there a phone book?	Hal yoojad daleel talifoun?
11.	How do I use the phone?	Kayf asta'mil attalifoun?
12.	I need change	Ahtaaj fakkah
13.	Can I dial direct?	Mumkin akhaabir mubaasharatan?
14.	No, call the operator	Laa, khaabir (f. khaabiry) al-aamilah
15.	I would like to call New York	Ahib akhaabir New York
16.	What's the number?	Maahuwa arraqm?
17.	What's the person's name?	Maahuwa ism ashshakhs?
18.	Sorry, the line is busy	Aasif (f. aasifah), al-khat mashghool
19.	There is no answer	Laa yoojad jawaab
20.	Try again	Haawil (f. haawilee) marra thanyah

Eating Out

1.	Restaurant	Mat'am
2.	Food	Ta'aam
3.	Menu	Qaa'imat atta'aam
4.	Chicken	Dajaaj
5.	Rice	Ruzz
6.	Fish	Samak
7.	Steak	Stayk (or steek)
8.	Well done	Mustawy jiddan
9.	Medium	Wasat
10.	Rare	Ghayr mustawy
11.	Water	Maa'
12.	Tea	Shaay
13.	Coffee	Qahwah
14.	Beer	Beerah
15.	Breakfast	Futoor
16.	Lunch	Ghadaa'
17.	Dinner	Ashaa'
18.	Is there a good restaurant?	Hal yoojad mat'am jayyid?

19. I want a native restaurant   Areed mat'am sha'by
20. Come on in   Itfaddal udkhul
21. Welcome   Ahlan wa sahlan
22. How many people?   Kam shakhs?
23. Two   Ithnayn
24. I would like to see the menu   Ahib araa qaa'imat atta'aam
25. I am hungry   Anaa ju'aan
26. I am thirsty   Anaa atshaan
27. Where is the waiter?   Ayn al-garsoon?
28. I want roasted chicken   Areed dajaaj mashwy
29. I want fish and rice   Areed samak wa ruzz
30. I want okra   Areed baamya
31. Okra stew   Marqat baamyah
32. I need...   Ahtaaj...
    —a knife   —sikkeen
    —a fork   —shawkah
    —a spoon   —mil'aqah
    —a cup   —koob (or finjaan)
    —a plate   —sahan
    —a napkin   —footah
    —salt   —milh
    —pepper   —filfil
    —sugar   —sukkar
    —milk   —haleeb
    —orange juice   —aseer purtuqaal
33. I didn't order this   Lam atlub haadhaa
34. There is a mistake   Hunaaka khataa'
35. Did you like the food?   Hal ajabaka atta'aam?
36. Yes, very much   Na'am, jiddan
37. No, this food is cold   Laa, haadhaa, atta'aam baarid
38. The meat is not cooked   Al-laham ghayr mustawy
39. Where is the manager?   Ayn al-mudeer?
40. Would you like anything else?   Hal tuhib shay' aakhar?
41. Would you like tea or coffee?   Hal tuhib shaay aw qahwah?
42. I would like black coffee   Ahib qahwah murrah
43. With a little sugar   Ma'a sukkar qaleel
44. With a lot of sugar   Ma'a sukkar katheer
45. I would like Arabic coffee   Ahib qahwah arabiyyah
46. I am so full   Anaa shab'aan (f. shab'aanah) jiddan

Shopping

1.	To shop	Yatasawwaq
2.	A shop (store)	Dukkaan
3.	Market	Sooq
4.	Price	Thaman (or si'ir)
5.	How much?	Kam?
6.	Clothes	Malaabis
7.	Vegetables	Khudrawaat
8.	Fruits	Fawaakih
9.	Cigarettes	Sagaa'ir
10.	Matches	Kibreet
11.	Toothpaste	Ma'joun asnaan
12.	Razor blade	Shafrat hilaaqah
13.	Shaving cream	Saboon hilaaqah
14.	Post card	Bitaaqah bareediyyah
15.	I want to go shopping	Areed adhhab atasawwaq
16.	Is there a market nearby?	Hal yoojad soooq qareeb?
17.	When does the store open?	Mataa yaftah addukkaan?
18.	Where are the best shops?	Ayn ahsan addakakeen?
19.	Let's go into this shop	Da'naa nadkhul fee haadhaa addukkaan
20.	May I help you?	Mumkin asaa'dak (f. asaa'dik)?
21.	No, I am just looking	Laa, anaa atafarraj
22.	Yes, I would like to buy...	Na'am, ahib ashtary...
	—a shirt	—qamees
	—a jacket	—jaakayt
	—a coat	—mi'taf
	—a dress	—fustaan
	—a tie	—rabtah
	—slacks	—bantaloon
	—socks	—jawaareeb
	—underwear	—malaabis daakhiliyyah
	—shoes	—ahdhiyah
23.	What size?	Ay hajim?
24.	Small size (medium, large)	Hajim sagheer (wasat, kabeer)
25.	Do you have a larger size?	Indakum hajim akbar?
26.	I prefer...	Afaddill...
	—white	—abyad
	—black	—aswad

—red	—ahmar
—blue	—azraq
—yellow	—asfar
—green	—akhdar
27. Is there a jewelry store?	Hal yoojad dukkaan mujawharaat?
28. I want to buy...	Areed ashtary...
—bracelet	—siwaar
—gold bracelet	—siwaar dhahabee
—ring	—mihbas (or khaatam)
—silver ring	—mihbas fiddy
—necklace	—qilaadah
—earrings	—taraaky
29. What's the price?	Kam aththaman
30. Expensive	Ghaaly
31. cheap	Rakhees
32. Can you lower the price?	Mumkin itnazzil aththaman?
33. Not possible	Maa mumkin
34. I like this	Ahib haadhaa
35. I don't like this	Laa ahib haadhaa
36. I want to change this	Areed tabdeel haadhaa
37. Why?	Limaadhaa?
38. Too tight	Dhayyiq jiddan
39. When did you buy it?	Mataa ishtaraytahu?
40. Yesterday	Ams
41. today	Al-Yawm
42. Two days ago	Qabla yawmayn
43. One week ago	Qabla usboo'

At the Post Office

1. The post office	Daa'irat al-bareed
2. The mail	Al-bareed
3. A stamp	Taaba'
4. Stamps	Tawaabi'
5. A letter	Maktoob (or risaalah)
6. An envelope	Darf
7. An address	Unwaan
8. A post card	Bitaaqa bareediyyah
9. A parcel	Ruzmah
10. Fragile	Qaabil lil kasr

11.	Telegram	Barqiyyah
12.	Surface mail	Bareed 'aady
13.	Air mail	Bareed jawwy
14.	Registered	Musajjal
15.	Express	Musta'jal
16.	Where is the post office?	Ayn daa'irat al-bareed?
17.	When does the post office open?	Mataa taftah daa'irat al-bareed?
18.	What are the hours?	Maahiya assaa'aat?
19.	Is there a mail box?	Hal yoojad sundooq bareedy?
20.	I would like some stamps	Ahib tawaabi'
21.	How many stamps?	Kam taaba'?
22.	I want to send this letter	Areed ab'ath haadhee arrisaalah
23.	Where to?	Ilaa ayn?
24.	I would like to send this by air mail	Ahib ab'ath haadhaa bil bareed ajjawwy
25.	How long will it take?	Kam sata'khudh?

At the Bank

1.	The bank	Al-bung
2.	Government bank	Bung hukoomy
3.	Private bank	Bung khusoosy
4.	Cash (to cash)	Naqd (yoosarrif)
5.	Notes	Awraaq naqdiyyah
6.	A check	Chek
7.	Money	Filoos
8.	Money order	Hawaalah maaliyyah
9.	Black market	Sooq sawdaa'
10.	Is there a bank in the hotel?	Hal yoojad bung fee al-findiq?
11.	Is there a bank nearby?	Hal yoojad bung qareeb?
12.	How far is the bank?	Kam yab'ud al-bung?
13.	When does the bank open?	Mataa yaftah al-bung?
14.	Is the bank open now?	Hal al-bung faatih al aan?
15.	The bank opens at 9 o'clock	Al-bung yaftah assaa'ah tis'ah
16.	In the morning	Fee assabaah (or sabaahan)
17.	I want to cash this check	Areed asarrif haadhaa al-chek
18.	I would like to cash these checks	Ahib assarrif haadhee al-chekkaat
19.	I want notes	Areed awraaq naqdiyya
20.	Big notes	Awraaq naqdiyyah kabeerah
21.	Wait a minute	Intadir lahdah

22. I want Kuwaiti dinars	Areed danaaneer kiwaytiyyah
23. I want British pounds	Areed paawanaat ingileeziyyah
24. You must sign here	Yajib an tuwaqi' hunaa
25. Fill out this form	Imla' haadhee al-istimaarah

At the Bookstore

1. Bookstore	Maktabah
2. Book	Kitaab
3. Books	Kutub
4. Newspaper	Jareedah
5. Newspapers	Jaraa'id
6. Magazine	Majallah
7. Magazines	Majallaat
8. Map	Khareetah
9. Dictionary	Qaamoos
10. Do you sell English newspapers?	Hal tabee'oon jaraa'id ingileeziyyah?
11. Do you have American magazines?	Hal indakum majallaat amreekiyyah?
12. I want to buy a map	Areed ashtary khareetah
13. Do you have a map of Libya?	Indakum khareetat leebyah?
14. I need an English-Arabic dictionary	Ahtaaj qaamoos ingileezi araby
15. Do you have...?	Indakum...?
—a notebook	—daftar mulaahadaat
—a writing pad	—waraq kitaabah
—pens	—aqlaam (sing. qalam)
—a pencil	—qalam rasaas

Sightseeing

1. Tour	Jawlah (or siyaahah)
2. Information	Ma'loomaat
3. Museum	Mathaf
4. Art museum	Mathaf al-funoon
5. Historical museum	Mathaf taa'reekhy
6. Pyramids	Ahraam
7. Sphinx	Abul hawl
8. Ruins	Aathaar
9. Old	Qadeem
10. Century	Qarn

11. Mosque	Masjid
12. Church	Kaneesah
13. Castle	Qal'ah
14. Bazaar	Sooq
15. Old part of town	Qism al-madeenah al-qadeem
16. Palace	Qasr
17. Zoo	Hadeeqat al-haywaan
18. University	Jaami'ah
19. Library	Maktabah
20. Picture	Soorah
21. Where is the tourist office?	Ayn maktab assiyaahah?
22. I want information about museums	Areed ma'loomaat an al-mataahif
23. Where can I get information?	Ayn mumkin ahsal alaa ma'loomaat?
24. Go to the ministry of tourism	Idhhab ilaa wizaarat assiyaahah
25. Where is the ministry?	Ayn al-wizaarah?
26. On Republic street	Alaa shari' al-jumhooriyyah
27. What do you recommend I visit?	Maadhaa tansah an azoor?
28. Visit the historical museum	Zur al-mathaf al-taareekhy
29. Is there a bus tour?	Hal toojad jawlah fee al-baas?
30. Where does it begin?	Ayn tabda'?
31. When does it begin?	Mataa tabda'?
32. How long does it take?	Kam ta'khudh?
33. Two hours	Saa'atayn
34. Three hours	Thalaathat saa'aat
35. How much does it cost?	Kam tukallif?
36. Which bus goes to the museum?	Ayy baas yadhhab ilaa al-mathaf?
37. Do you have a guide book?	Indakum kitaab daleel?
38. Is there a map?	Hal toojad khareetah?
39. English map	Khareetah ingileeziyyah
40. Can I take a picture (pictures)?	Mumkin altaqit soorah (suwar)?
41. Pictures are not allowed	Al-suwar (or tasweer) ghayr masmoohah
42. I would like to see the city	Ahib araa al-madeenah
43. What is this?	Maa haadhaa (f. haadhee)?
44. What is this building?	Maa haadhee al-binaayah?
45. What is the name of this church?	Maa ism haadhee al-kaneesah?
46. Is the museum open today?	Hal al-mathaf maftooh al-yawm?
47. How much is the entrance fee?	Kam ujrat addukhool?
48. Is this the kings' palace?	Hal haadhaa qasr al-malik?

49. This is the oldest mosque   Haadhaa aqdam masjid
50. This is the biggest museum   Haadhaa akbar mathaf
51. It was built in the 8th century Buniyah (f. buniyat) fee al-qarn
                                     aththaamin
52. I am tired   Anaa ta'baan
53. Thank you for the tour   Shukran alaa ajjawlah
54. It was enjoyable   Kaanat mumti'ah
55. Very beautiful   Jameelah jiddan

Photography

1. Camera   Kaamerah
2. Film   Filim
3. Black and white   Aswad wa abyad
4. Color film   Filim mulawwan
5. Movie film   Filim seenamaa'ee
6. Exposure (exposures)   Soorah (suwar)
7. Print (prints)   Nuskhah (nusakh)
8. Flash bulbs   Lampaat lil flaash
9. Lens   Adasaat
10. I want a color film   Areed filim mulawwan
11. I need some flash bulbs Ahtaaj lampaat lil flaash
12. I also want   Areed aydan
13. An 8-mm film   filim thamaaniyah millimetraat
14. A 35-mm film   Filim khamsah wa thalaatheen
                            millimetraat
15. With 20 exposures   Bi ishreen soorah
16. I need a lens   Ahtaaj 'adasah
17. I need a movie film   Ahtaaj filim seenamaa'ee
18. How much does it cost? Kam yukallif?
19. Do you print photos?   Hal tatba'oon suwar?
20. I want three prints   Areed thalaathat nusakh
21. When will they be ready? Mataa yakoonoon jaahizeen?
22. My camera is broken   Kaamerty maksoorah
23. Can you repair the camera? Mumkin tusallih al-kaamerah?
24. Excuse me   Ismahly
25. Can you take a picture of me? Mumkin taa'khudh soorah lee?
26. Of course   Tab'an
27. Do you know how to use it? Hal ta'rif kayf tasta'milhah?
28. It is easy   Baseetah (or sahlah)

29. Thank you very much	Shukran jazeelan
30. May I take your picture?	Mumkin 'aakhudh (or altaqit) soortak?
31. Certainly	Bilta'keed
32. Can I take a picture here?	Mumkin altaqit soorah hunaa?
33. Sorry, no	'Aasif (f. 'aasifah), laa
34. Picture-taking is prohibited	Attasweer mamnoo'

Entertainment

1. Movie	Filim
2. Movie house	Seenamah
3. Night club (clubs)	Malhaa (malaahy)
4. Bar (bars)	Baar (baaraat)
5. Club (clubs)	Naady (nawaady)
6. Theater (theaters)	Masrah (masaarih)
7. Play (plays)	Masrahiyyah (masrahiyyaat)
8. Program (programs)	Barnaamaj (baraamij)
9. Ticket (tickets)	Tadhkirah (tadhaakir)
10. Is there a night club nearby?	Hal yoojad malhaa qareeh?
11. Is there a good movie house?	Hal toojad seenamah jayyidah?
12. I want to see an American movie	Areed 'araa filim amreeky
13. What's playing?	Maadhaa yoo'rad?
14. Do you have tickets?	Indakum tadhaakir?
15. How many tickets?	Kam tadhkirah?
16. One ticket, please	Tadhkirah waahidah, min fadlak
17. Two tickets	Tadhkiratayn
18. Is the play any good?	Hal al-masrahiyyah jayyidah?
19. The play is...	Al-masrahiyyah...
—funny	—mudhikah (m. mudhik)
—musical	—mooseeqiyyah (m. mooseeqy)
—sad	—hazeenah (m. hazeen)
—very good	—jayyidah jiddan (m. jayyid jiddan)
—not bad	—laa ba's
20. I want to see belly dancing	Areed ashaahid (or 'araa) riqs sharqy

Social Calls

1. Invitation	Da'wah
2. Visit	Ziyaarah
3. Lunch	Ghadaa'

4. Dinner	Ashaa'
5. Welcome	Ahlan wa sahlan
6. Help yourself (come on in, go on)	Itfaddal
7. Come visit us	Ta'aal zoorna (pl. ta'aaloo zooroonah)
8. Would you like to have dinner with us?	Hal tuhib an tata'ashshah ma'anaa?
9. Sorry, I can't today	Aasif, laa aqdar al-yawm
10. When?	Mataa?
11. Tomorrow	Ghadan
12. Next week	Al-usboo' al-qaadim
13. Come on in	Itfaddal
14. Make yourself at home	Haadhaa baytak
15. Pleased to have you	Fursah sa'eedah
16. It is an honor	Tasharrafnaa
17. Please, sit down	Min fadlak, ijlis
18. Dinner is ready	Al-ashaa' jaahiz
19. Go on and eat	Itfaddal ukul
20. Please, drink	Min fadlak, ishrab
21. Would you like...?	Hal tuhib...?
—coffee	—ghahwah
—tea	—shaay
—water	—maa'
—milk	—haleeb
—dessert	—halwa (or halawiyyaat)
22. I am not hungry	Anaa ghayr ju'aan
23. I am not thirsty	Anaa ghayr atshaan
24. You didn't eat much	Lam ta'kul katheeran
25. I am full	Anaa shab'aan
26. I ate too much	Akaltu katheeran
27. This is delicious	Haadhaa ladheedh
28. Thank you for your hospitality	Shukran alaa diyaafatikum
29. You are very generous	Antum kuramaa'
30. May God reward you	Allaah yukrimkum
31. May God protect you	Allaah yahfadkum

Medical Treatment

1. Sick	Mareed (f. mareedah)
2. Help	Musaa'adah

3.	Doctor	Tabeeb
4.	Nurse	Mumarridah
5.	Dentist	Tabeeb asnaan
6.	Drug store	Saydaliyyah
7.	Hospital	Mustashfaa
8.	Emergency	Haalat tawaari'
9.	Ambulance	Is'aaf
10.	Pain	Alam
11.	Tooth (teeth)	Sin (asnaan)
12.	Stomach	Mi'dah
13.	Temperature	Haraarah
14.	Poisoning	Tasammum
15.	Pregnant	Haamil
16.	Heart condition	Marad qalb
17.	Diabetes	Marad sukkar
18.	Epilepsy	Sara'
19.	I am sick	Anaa mareed
20.	I need help	Ahtaaj musaa'adah
21.	Is there a doctor in the hotel?	Hal yoojad tabeeb fee al-findiq?
22.	Take me to the hospital	Khudhny ilaa al-mustashfaa
23.	There is a pain in my chest	Yoojad alam fee sadry
24.	I have a heart condition	Indy marad qalb
25.	I can't breathe	Laa aqdar atanaffas
26.	I feel dizzy	Ash'ur bidawkhah
27.	I am diabetic	Indy marad sukkar
28.	I am epileptic	Indy sara'
29.	I have food poisoning	Indy tasammum akl
30.	My back hurts	Dahree yu'limny
31.	My head hurts	Ra'see yu'limny
32.	I need a dentist	Ahtaaj tabeeb asnaan
33.	I have a toothache	Indy alam bil sin
34.	I have . . .	Indy . . .
	—a cold	—nashlah
	—a cough	—qahhah
	—a sore throat	—bal'oom multahib
	—indigestion	—'usr hadm
	—a headache	—waja' (or alam) raas

Emergencies

1.	Help me	Saa'idny
2.	Stop	Qiff
3.	Look out	Ihdhar
4.	Fire	Hareeq (or naar)
5.	Police	Shurtah
6.	Thief	Haraamy
7.	Wallet	Jizdaan
8.	Handbag	Haqeebah
9.	Money	Filoos
10.	Leave me alone	Itrukny
11.	Call the police	Naady ashshurtah
12.	This is a thief	Haadhaa haraamy
13.	I'll scream	Sa asrakh
14.	Catch the thief	Imsak al-haraamy
15.	He stole my money	Saraqa filoosy
16.	I have lost...	Dayya'tu..
	—my passport	—jawaazy
	—my ticket	—tadhkiraty
	—my keys	—mafaateehy
	—my wallet	—jizdaany
	—my jewelry	—mujawharaaty
17.	My camera has disappeared	Kaamerty ikhtafat
18.	They stole my handbag	Saraqoo haqeebaty
19.	I have lost my way	Dayya'tu tareeqy
20.	Don't worry	Laa taqlaq
21.	Come with me	Ta'aalaa ma'ee

Numbers

1.	Zero	Sifr
2.	A quarter	Rub'
3.	A third	Thulth
4.	A half	Nisf
5.	One	Waahid
6.	Two	Ithnayn
7.	Three	Thalaathah
8.	Four	Arba'ah
9.	Five	Khamsah
10.	Six	Sittah

11.	Seven	Sab'ah
12.	Eight	Thamaaniyah
13.	Nine	Tis'ah
14.	Ten	Ashrah
15.	Eleven	Ahad ashar
16.	Twelve	Ithnaa ashar
17.	Thirteen	Thalaathat ashar
18.	Fourteen	Arba'at ashar
19.	Fifteen	Khamsat ashar
20.	Sixteen	Sittat ashar
21.	Seventeen	Sab'at ashar
22.	Eighteen	Thamaaniyat ashar
23.	Nineteen	Tis'at ashar
24.	Twenty	Ishreen
25.	Twenty one	Waahid wa ishreen
26.	Twenty two	Ithnayn wa ishreen
27.	Thirty	Thalaatheen
28.	Thirty one	Waahid wa thalaatheen
29.	Thirty two	Ithnayn wa thalaatheen
30.	Forty	Arba'een
31.	Fifty	Khamseen
32.	Sixty	Sitteen
33.	Seventy	Sab'een
34.	Eighty	Thamaaneen
35.	Ninety	Tis'een
36.	One hundred	Mi'ah
37.	One hundred and one	Mi'ah wa waahid
38.	Two hundred	Mi'atayn
39.	Three hundred	Thalaath mi'ah
40.	Four hundred	Araba' mi'ah
41.	One thousand	Alf
42.	Two thousand	Alfayn
43.	Three thousand	Thalaathat 'aalaaf
44.	Four thousand	Arba'at 'aalaaf
45.	One million	Milyoun
46.	First	Awwal
47.	Second	Thaany
48.	Third	Thaalith
49.	Fourth	Raabi'

50. Fifth	Khaamis
51. Sixth	Saadis
52. Seventh	Saabi'
53. Eighth	Thaamin
54. Ninth	Taasi'
55. Tenth	Aashir

Time

1. Time	Saa'ah (lit. waqt)
2. Now	Al'aan
3. Soon	Qareeban
4. As soon as possible	Fee aqrab waqt mumkin
5. Today	Al-yawm
6. Yesterday	Ams (or al-baarihah)
7. Tomorrow	Bukrah (or ghadan)
8. Tonight	Al-laylah
9. At night	Fee al-layl
10. At midnight	Fee nisf al-layl
11. In the morning	Fee assabaah
12. In the afternoon	Ba'd adduhr
13. In the evening	Fee al-masaa'
14. Last week	Al-usboo' al-maady
15. Last month	Ashshahr al-maady
16. Last year	Assanah al-maadiyah
17. See you tomorrow	Araaka bukrah
18. After tomorrow	Ba'd bukrah
19. See you later	Araaka ba'dayn
20. Excuse me	Ismahly
21. What time is it?	Kam assaa'ah?
22. It's one o'clock	Assaa'ah waahidah
23. It's almost two o'clock	Assaa'ah taqreeban ithnayn
24. It's a quarter to four	Assa'ah arba'ah illaa rub'
25. It's a quarter after five	Assa'ah khamsah wa rub'
26. It's eight thirty	Assaa'ah thamaaniyah wa thalaatheen
27. It's half past seven	Assaa'ah sab'ah wa nisf
28. It's ten after six	Assaa'ah sittah wa 'ashrah
29. He is late	Huwa muta'akhkhir
30. She is early	Hiyah mubakkirah

31. Sorry, I am late — Aasif anaa muta'akhkhir
32. Am I early? — Hal anaa mubakkir?
33. When shall we meet? — Mataa sanataqaabal?
34. I'll be here — Sa'akoon hunaa

Days

1. Monday — Al-ithnayn
2. Tuesday — Aththalaathaa'
3. Wednesday — Al-arbi'aa'
4. Thursday — Al-khamees
5. Friday — Ajjum'ah
6. Saturday — Assabt
7. Sunday — Al-ahad

Months

1. January — Kaanoon aththaany
2. February — Shubaat
3. March — Aadhaar
4. April — Neesaan
5. May — Maays (or ayyaar)
6. June — Huzayraan
7. July — Tammooz
8. August — Aab
9. September — Aylool
10. October — Tishreen al-awwal
11. November — Tishreen aththaany
12. December — Kaanoon al-awwal

Seasons

1. Spring — Arrabee'
2. Summer — Assayf
3. Autumn — Al-khareef
4. Winter — Ashshitaa'

Weather

1. Weather — Jaww (or taqs)
2. Rain — Matar
3. Clouds — Ghuyoom
4. Fog — Dabaab

5. Snow	Thalj
6. Storm	Zawba'ah
7. Dust	Turaab (or ajaaj)
8. Hot	Haar
9. Cold	Baarid
10. Temperature	Darajat al-haraarah
11. Sun	Shams
12. What's the temperature?	Maa darajat al-haraarah?
13. What's the weather like?	Kayf ajjaww?
14. The weather is...	Ajjaw...
—mild	
—cold	
—hot	
—changeable	—mutaghayyir
15. It's a cloudy day	Yawm ghaa'im
16. It's a rainy day	Yawm mumtir
17. It's a sunny day	Yawm mushmis
18. It's a beautiful day	Yawm jameel
19. It's a nice night	Laylah lateefah
20. It's too hot	Haarrah jiddan
21. It's too cold	Baaridah jiddan
22. I like cold weather	Ahib jaww baarid

Names of Selected Arab Countries

1. Algeria	Ajjazaa'ir
2. Egypt	Misr
3. Jordan	Al-urdun
4. Lebanon	Lubnaan
5. Morocco	Marraakish
6. Saudi Arabia	Assu'oodiyyah al-arabiyyah
7. Syria	Sooryah
8. Tunisia	Toonis
9. United Arab Emirates	Al-imaaraat al-arabiyyah al-muttahidah